BY AGNES E. MEYER

CHINESE PAINTING AS REFLECTED IN THE THOUGHT AND ART
OF LI LUNG-MIEN 1070–1106

BRITAIN'S HOME FRONT

JOURNEY THROUGH CHAOS

OUT OF THESE ROOTS

Translated By Agnes E. Meyer

THE COMING VICTORY OF DEMOCRACY
by Thomas Mann, translated by Agnes E. Meyer

STANDARDS AND VALUES
by Thomas Mann, translated by Agnes E. Meyer
for the Washington *Post*

OUT OF THESE ROOTS

Agnes E. Meyer

From a portrait bust by Charles Despiau

Out of These Roots

THE AUTOBIOGRAPHY OF
AN AMERICAN WOMAN

by
AGNES E. MEYER

An Atlantic Monthly Press Book

Little, Brown and Company · Boston

ATLANTIC–LITTLE, BROWN BOOKS
ARE PUBLISHED BY
LITTLE, BROWN AND COMPANY
IN ASSOCIATION WITH
THE ATLANTIC MONTHLY PRESS

*Published simultaneously
in Canada by McClelland and Stewart Limited*

PRINTED IN THE UNITED STATES OF AMERICA

TO
OUR CHILDREN
AND
OUR CHILDREN'S CHILDREN

. . . the measure of civilization is the degree
in which the method of co-operative intelligence
replaces the method of brute conflict.

—JOHN DEWEY, *Renascent Liberalism*

Author's Note

IT WOULD NEVER have occurred to me to write an autobiography. Nor would my full share of interest in what Paul Claudel has called "that terrible path toward oneself" have held me to its description for two years. But since I now feel the same satisfaction over the completion of this ordeal which mothers feel after the birth of a lusty infant, it is only just to declare the paternity of this child of my old age.

Edward Weeks, editor of the *Atlantic Monthly*, had the idea of publishing in book form a collection of my speeches and articles. I wrote a short introduction picturing my delightfully democratic childhood in a rural American community typical of our halcyon era which ended with the devastating impact of the First World War. After being swept from this strong mooring, I became, for reasons more fully outlined in this book, a priggish, introverted, and I fear not uncommon type of self-centered American girl. The introduction ended with the brief statement that my eyes had been turned away from myself and outward toward the beneficent world of realities by the slow but irresistible influence of the democratic process to which all Americans are, more or less, exposed.

This theme fascinated Weeks: "We're going to throw out all those old essays," he announced categorically, "and you're going to approach the work you have done in recent years biographically. Then people will understand that it came out of these roots."

Thus he not only lured me with what is every human being's favorite theme but gave me my title. And with the double nature of the born publisher who knows when to hold before the donkey's nose the subtle scent of appreciation and when to hit him with the club of devastating criticism, he kept me going forward amid a multitude of distractions until the task was completed.

AGNES E. MEYER

May 30, 1953
Washington, D.C.

Contents

OUT OF THESE ROOTS

CHAPTER I
Childhood

FORTUNATE ARE THE PEOPLE whose roots are deep. Doubly fortunate those who are born at the right time, in the right place! In my own case, my history was largely determined by the fact that my parents inherited ancient traditions and that my earliest years coincided with a long era of world peace whose tranquillity was reflected in the amiable democracy of a small American village.

My birth took place in 1887 in New York City. When I was less than three years old my family settled in Pelham Heights, then a lovely, hilly woodland in which there were only five or six widely scattered homes. Across the railroad tracks was the village they called Pelhamville, which during the early nineties had a population of some five hundred people. Now the whole area is a suburban community with houses cheek by jowl but with some of its pristine beauty still preserved.

Mine was a typical American childhood of the period, disciplined yet free, and of that singular happiness which was the lot of children thrown for amusement upon their own imaginative resources. The common, lovely things were ours — woods, fields, and wild flowers; the Big Brook, deep enough for fishing, and the Little Brook, for wading and sailing paper boats. Our winters were full of purposeful activity, our summers of delicious idleness.

The book that most perfectly depicts the relationship of childhood to nature as I experienced it is Tolstoi's *Childhood and Youth*. No one else has so piercingly described the first overpowering rapture of children who are radiantly happy within their own vigorous bodies and with their snug little places in an immense yet friendly universe.

Old as I now am, when my nerves are strung to the breaking point by too much work and too many human contacts, Antaeuslike I can always regain that childish security and ecstasy if I am allowed to touch earth again. I have an instinctive feeling for the very different contributions made to our virile democracy by our hardy pioneers, by the independent spirit of woodsmen like Parkman and Thoreau, by the curious Utopians who throughout our history have always tried to reconcile a natural environment with ideal social conditions. The American character was originally formed on New England whalers and trading vessels, on Western farms, prairies and mountains, and by the many climates of our country, the mercurial weather that made us so changeable but so tough and resistant. Like Walt Whitman, "I conceive of no flourishing and heroic elements of Democracy in the United States, or of Democracy maintaining itself at all, without the Nature-element forming a main part — to be its health element and beauty element — to really underlie the whole politics, sanity, religion and art of the New World."

My confidence in life and the beneficence of nature was early put to a supreme test. When I was nine, Bill, my next older brother, and I discovered a strange instrument around the house which aroused our curiosity. It was a .32-caliber pistol. I was about a foot away from the muzzle when he pressed the trigger. At the flash I threw my head aside and avoided being hit in the middle of the forehead. But the bullet plowed through the right temple into the back of the brain. My poor mother beheld a terrible sight as she rushed into the room. I had pressed my hand over the wound, but four great streams of blood gushed between my fingers at every heartbeat.

This was the day before telephones or automobiles. It was hours until the doctor arrived. In the meantime, my mother, in anguish, was holding a huge towel pressed to my head. *"Muss ich jetzt sterben?"* "Do you think I am going to die?" I asked her. "No, no," she murmured without conviction. "Well, I don't think so, either," I reassured her. This inner calm, the doctors told me later, was of importance in my recovery. For three days the country doctors poked around in the gaping wound. Then I was moved to the hospital of a famous German surgeon, Dr. Fritz Lange, in New York City. He opened my skull right behind the right ear, by guesswork in this pre-X-ray era, and extracted most of the bullet but not all of it. In two months I was again running about the countryside with a hunting dachshund which Dr. Lange gave me as a reward for getting well. When my head was X-rayed for sinus trouble some thirty years later, the laboratory assistants were in an uproar, and assured me I ought to be dead. There is very little bone on the right side of my skull, the whole brain is sprinkled with what can only be powder, and resting behind my right ear is the rest of the bullet. After I had recovered, my religious mother conceded that God had performed a miracle on my behalf, but solemnly cautioned me that even God's grace has its limits and that I must never abuse it. The fact that God's grace is never deserved always seems to irritate virtuous people like my good mother.

Fortunately for me, the exhilarating and spontaneous life of nature was balanced by the influences of a puritanical and almost Spartan family atmosphere. My parents were both born in North Germany; my father, Frederick H. Ernst, in the independent Kingdom of Hanover where his father and his father's fathers, probably as far back as the Reformation, were Lutheran clergymen. My mother's family, many of them seafaring men or small merchants, lived in the same little village near Bremen for three hundred years or longer. The family records were destroyed when the local church in Lesum was burned during the Thirty Years' War. My paternal grandfather was clergyman to the last king of Hanover. When Prussia defeated the Hanoverian Army in 1866, he sent his six sons out of the country as he despised the militarism and authoritarianism of the less cultured Prussians and foresaw the vulgarization of life which eventually engulfed the German people. The new government officials demanded that he swear allegiance to the king of Prussia. "But I have already sworn allegiance to the king of Hanover. If I now break that oath and swear allegiance to his enemy and conqueror, how," he asked, "could you trust me to be loyal to this second oath?" As there was no answer to that argument, he was deprived of the right to preach, but his influence among his parishioners was augmented by this fierce independence of spirit. He supported the five daughters who remained at home on a small pension granted him by the royal Hanoverian family and the money which his sons sent him from foreign lands.

My father together with three brothers, two of whom were clergymen, came to America. He studied law, met my mother who was on a visit to New York, and persuaded her to remain here permanently as his wife. Our German traditions, therefore, hark back to a Germany that collapsed even before the organization of the Empire. It was the burgher tradition which Thomas Mann describes in *Buddenbrooks,* sober, ethical, restrained, hard-working, yet full of gaiety, music and romantic idealism. My father combined with this heritage a hatred of tyranny, injustice and brute force natural to a young man who had been driven from his homeland by the authoritarian and militaristic Prussian dynasty. His favorite paper was the *New York Evening Post,* edited before the turn of the century by E. L. Godkin, who represented the best traditions of British and American liberalism on which my father discoursed with enthusiasm at the family dinner table. He became an ardent Democrat in his politics and we children absorbed his love of freedom as the dominant link between the Germany we had never seen and the democratic village atmosphere in which we moved with such joyous abandon.

My clergyman grandfather continued to be a living influence upon the families of his exiled sons to the very end of his ninety-three years. In a clear, firm German script he would send long letters of Christian admonition regarding the sacredness of family life, the education of children, and the need to maintain cultural standards in a new civilization whose traditions seemed to him too young to give the individual adequate and trustworthy support. He insisted that it was the duty of his sons to be loyal American citizens and to uphold at the same time their German Lutheran heritage. These erudite, well-written letters were valued by my parents as something akin to Luther's *Table Talk* and were read to us even when we were very little, in much the same spirit as Moses handed down the Ten Commandments to a weak and erring people. I never saw this grandfather but he became such a real figure and such an ideal of wisdom, virtue and spiritual valor that I still keep a small profile

— the photograph of a drawing — of his handsome, manly face upon my work table.

This European background gave our life in a small American village a curiously cosmopolitan atmosphere, and a stability no less formidable than the continuity of life, thought, and habits characteristic of our ancestors. During my earliest, most formative years we children lived in a daily routine of freedom and authority which we never questioned. The influence of my parents on their children was all the greater because it was exerted by this remote control and by an atmosphere of order, tranquillity and purposefulness which pervaded the whole household. Many people have forgotten today that the daily routine of early life has the most subtle, profound and enduring influence upon the physical, moral and emotional development of children. An orderly existence creates primarily an unconscious relationship to the silent progression of the days, the seasons, and the music of the spheres. Thus it helps the child to feel at home in the universe and conveys an emotional security which the misadventures of life can never utterly destroy. It confers a deeper sense of ethics, duty and responsibility than any dogmatic teaching can possibly convey. Above all, it implants in the human spirit a love of rhythm and beauty, whether in nature or in art, a sense of mysterious affinity with the moment and with eternity that is religious in the highest meaning of the word.

To the budding personality, an orderly home is more important than church or school or society. By the time these institutions begin to exert an influence for good or evil, the child's nature has already developed its more enduring traits, which can be modified but not eradicated. This is why women as mothers are the cultural and moral arbiters of the race, an appalling responsibility which too many

American women try to ignore without being able to forget it. Woman represents the continuity of life. It is she who is the dominant influence on her children during the impressionable early years. She determines the unconscious responses to life, whereas the father grows more effective as the child's conscious strivings gradually come into the foreground.

This, at any rate, was my experience. Until I went to school, at the age of five, I have few memories of my father, and those of my mother are bound up with two outwardly dour but inwardly tender and extremely humorous women, Doris and Maria, who washed and fed and scolded and loved us under Mother's constant supervision. Doris and Maria had been carefully selected by friends in Hanover and Bremen for their strict Lutheran upbringing, and their impeccable North German accents. They were not only friends of the family but its watchdogs, and we children who never feared our parents were very careful not to arouse the just indignation of Doris, the older of the two, a tall spare figure of tireless energy and sardonic character. When Doris finally returned to her home in Germany, she was heartbroken to leave her foster children, but she expressed this secret despair by assuring us that without her firm hand to guide us we were bound to come to no good end.

The austere side of our upbringing — our obedient acceptance of it, and its lasting influence — is something at which I still marvel. It was a curious obsession of our Lutheran parents that the more we disliked doing something the better it was for our soul's salvation. This was carried into the minutest details. We ate what was set before us without complaint even if it nauseated us. As I hated sewing lessons I was incarcerated for an hour every Saturday morning to stitch a hem. If I escaped Maria's watchful eye and shinnied down the gutter to join the boys at baseball, I sewed for two hours the following week. But the real torment of our lives, considered vital to the formation of a sturdy character, was the cold bath into which we plunged every morning, winter or summer. Hot baths were a sensual indulgence which weaklings, who had no real purpose in life, permitted themselves. Only once a week, on Saturday, were we allowed tepid water while Doris or Maria scrubbed us with vigorous thoroughness. The more we loathed these icy ablutions, the more they assumed the dignity of a religious rite.

Absurd as it may seem, the importance of this daily torture impressed itself so firmly upon me that I continued it until as a married woman of twenty-three, traveling in Japan, I tried the natural hot baths at Myanoshita. The fact that the Japanese considered the waters of these boiling springs hygienic, no doubt broke down the taboo with which hot baths were surrounded for me by our puritanical childhood. Finding that my moral stamina did not visibly disintegrate and go down the drain together with the steaming waters of Myanoshita, I finally got the courage to renounce cold baths forever.

It was not until I was six or seven that my father began to loom larger than the women of the house and made himself the light of my life, and the source eventually of its only real tragedy. I could not know as a youngster that he was considered the black sheep in his clerical family because he was less amenable to discipline and had run away to sea at the age of fourteen instead of going to the Gymnasium like my very scholarly uncles. Now that I look back upon my extraordinary Oedipus complex I am well aware that my father was not the luminous personality I loved as a child nor the somber figure that haunted my adolescence like a nightmare. Even now it is liberating to speak openly for the first time in my life of the emotional extremes to which my father-fixation subjected me.

When I first became aware of him he was a hard-working lawyer who supported his family in modest but comfortable circumstances. Money, in fact, was never so much as mentioned in our family. It played no part in our attitude toward life, and the best heritage I was able to transfer to my own children, who grew up in affluence, was this same conviction that dependence upon material possessions inevitably results in the destruction of human character.

The emphasis in our family atmosphere, wholly created by my father's genial temperament, was an appreciation of beauty and achievements of the mind. In spring and summer he would often awaken me before dawn to see the sunrise from a nearby hilltop. We scarcely spoke as we watched the sun gradually appear above the horizon and penetrate the woodland with its delicate lights and shadows. It was when we turned homeward that conversation came to life, my father discoursing on Wagner's *Nibelungen Ring* and the joys that were in store for me in music, poetry and art.

When at about twelve years of age I was finally considered old enough to enter the sacred portals of music, he chose Wagner's *Flying Dutchman* for my initiation and prepared me for its romantic symbolism, its orchestration and leitmotifs, more religiously than most children are prepared for their first communion. Those of us who in earliest childhood received the Wagnerian baptism of fire are marked for life. Years later, when I began to think more historically, I detested romanticism like a disease that saps the marrow of one's bones. But even after this emancipation, if a few bars of Wagner's insidious magic reached my ears, I was ensnared again by this love potion that first opened to me the portals of an illusory heaven. I am not sure that I hated Wagner because I came to hate my father or whether my hatred of my father was intensified by my hatred of Wagner. But God pity anyone who like myself worshiped them both passionately in a dreamlike, ineffable togetherness.

When I was in my early twenties I heard Mozart's *Don Juan* for the first time at the Munich Music Festival. The orchestration had been made familiar enough through concert performances, but a tremor of recognition shook me when I realized that I knew the arias by heart. I had heard them constantly without knowing what my father was singing. When Don Juan intoned the famous *"Reich mir die Hand mein Leben"* which my father had so often sung to me, with ironical gestures, when he invited me to come for a walk or to go into dinner, I who am not given to tears, felt them pouring down my cheek. For by that time the radiant memories of my childhood had become an agony from which I was constantly seeking to escape.

My father's curious mixture of political interests and artistic talent made him a favorite campaign speaker among the German-American population of New York City. He took care that I should have an opportunity to see him in this role. On the platform his tall, broad-shouldered figure, his big features and bald head surrounded by a circlet of soft curls, and the perfect ease with which he handled himself made an appealing impression. He had inherited from his clergyman ancestors a warm tone of voice which he could project without effort to the back of any hall. Instead of resorting to the spellbinding oratory which was usual in those days, he would talk as quietly, confidentially and casually to a big audience as if he were at home conversing with a few friends. It was artful artlessness and nobody admired the performance more than he and I. His charm, intelligence and gaiety captured his audiences with the same ease that he captured the heart of his adoring only daughter.

Our relationship was all the more deep and dangerous because with typical North German restraint, it was never expressed with outward tenderness or words of endearment. We were simply happy together and we each knew that the other knew it. He was the center of my life; and I was the center of his to the extent that anyone can capture the loyalty of a brilliant but mercurial hedonist. In early life I never loved my devoted mother as much as she deserved to be loved because my father eclipsed her milder personality and focused all of my attention and emotion upon his own.

Let no parent who prefers one child to the other think that the children are unaware of the situation. It cannot be concealed. It betrays itself in the glance of an eye, in the tones of the voice, and in all the other irrepressible symptoms of a natural affinity. It is very hard on the other children. It can be even harder on the child who knows himself to be the center of parental interest. An increased understanding of human psychology, which we owe chiefly to Freud, has made modern parents painfully and in many cases so absurdly aware of the dangers of the Oedipus complex that they warn all their relatives and friends not to reflect their own secret preference for little Susie or Jimmie. This of course destroys all spontaneity and is probably worse for the children than the rankest favoritism. When parents really achieve perfect justice in relationship to their children, I am sure life will be saner but it will also be very dull.

As the result of my passionate relationship to my father, I went about in the world with the most irresistible of human instincts, the expectation to be loved. I also perceived that love, to be enduring, must be earned again and again. My delight in achievement, for example, was set in motion because I enjoyed seeing pride and devotion light up my father's face when I returned from school with high marks on my report card. This was merely one aspect of a competitive situation that was very hard on my brother Bill who, though my senior by more than a year, was in the same class at school but felt no such incentive to hard work.

My brother Fritz — Frederic Ernst, who in the spring of 1953 retired as Deputy Superintendent of the New York City Public Schools — was four years older than I and always represented the height of respectability to Bill and me. Some children are born with physical, mental and emotional balance and Fritz was one of them. A good student beloved by all his teachers, he was the natural leader of all our boisterous games. He had the gift of humor which he inherited from my mother, and a keen sense of the ridiculous which often reduced us to a helpless state of uproarious laughter. Under Fritz's leadership we roamed the fields and forests in search of adventure with the sole provision that we must appear punctually for meals. We frequently all but killed ourselves and each other. We fell down cliffs and cut our heads open. We walked narrow planks over a bottomless water tank where a misstep meant certain drowning. We went on snake-killing expeditions in a sand pit that crawled repulsively with copperheads and other species. But unless children are allowed to take care of themselves at an early age, they cannot learn to do so successfully later in life. And if the love of freedom is not ingrained in them in these impressionable years, they cannot cherish it later on as the very essence of life, without which it has no meaning.

When I was ten we lost Fritz's stimulating companionship as he graduated from our local public school and began preparation for college in New York City. The gap in years separated me even more from my oldest brother Carl. But his fate, as I later learned, was of great influence on the lives of us younger ones. As my parents were deeply religious, they were convinced that all their children must go to parochial schools. These institutions may have their virtues, but for Carl they were disastrous. Since the prime object of parochial schools is indoctrination rather than learning, instruction in the secular subjects is inevitably a secondary consideration. Like many parochial-school graduates today, Carl was too poorly prepared to pass the entrance examinations of a first-rate college and was obliged to continue his education in a Lutheran seminary. The pupils in this institution were of three kinds. Those who were really pious, those who pretended to be, and those who were in open rebellion against an overdose of religion. Carl, like most of the others, did not belong in the first group. Too honest to join the second, he was thrown in with the boys whose natural dispositions had been warped by an authoritarian discipline and an impoverished educational system which may prepare its victims for life in heaven but certainly not for a happy, well-adjusted career in this world of realities.

When Carl finally came home and went to work, he had learned to carouse with his fun-loving, hard-drinking friends as a release from frightful inner tensions. The result was constant and acute conflict with our parents that grew all the more bitter as they continued to preach the same religious orthodoxy he had learned to despise at school. Finally he could endure it no longer and fled from home never to return. But before leaving he told our parents frankly that he had had enough religion to last him a lifetime. We younger children knew only that Carl, poor lad, was a "naughty boy." But I felt grateful to him when I was old enough to understand that his sad history saved the rest of us from a parochial-school education.

I was only five when Bill was sent to the public school in Pelhamville where Fritz was already in the fifth grade. Since it was too dull to be left at home alone I insisted upon going along. This meant walking a mile four times a day, as we came home for a solid, well-cooked German meal at noon. We took this rigorous routine in our stride and spent the afternoons playing hare and hounds, baseball, or some other rugged outdoor sport. If I occasionally faltered, my brothers promptly denounced me as a girl and a nuisance. The result was that I learned to ask no quarter from the male sex then or later in life.

As was usual in our country in the late nineties, the village school at Pelhamville, where three teachers taught eight classes, had high standards which every child had to meet or undergo the disgrace of being "left behind," as failure to be promoted was called. The result was that we worked conscientiously and liked it. I am still grateful to the principal, I. C. Hill, a born teacher who had charge of the three highest grades. He let me go my own pace in learning with the result that I passed all my Regents examinations for high school when I was eleven. As we had no local high school, I spent the last year learning algebra, double-entry bookkeeping, and other curious subjects because Mr. Hill happened to like them.

This honorable man would certainly have been shocked if he could see what goes on in most of our elementary schools today. The theory, for example, that everybody has to be promoted, regardless of effort or achievement, would

certainly strike him as maudlin nonsense, bound to soften
up American childhood.

The fact that my brothers and I were the only children
from the other side of the railroad tracks often caused dissension. Several of the village families were far more af-
fluent than ours and had more pretentious homes. Therefore envy was not the cause of these rivalries. But we were
different, and the gang spirit of the village boys would often
break loose and vent itself not on my dignified elder brother,
Fritz, but on my nearer contemporary, Bill. If it was a fight
between him and one other boy, I kept out of the fray. But
if several others decided to help beat him up, an uncontrollable maternal fury took hold of me and I hurled myself
into the battle with a frenzy I can still feel today as something terrifying. Fortunately I was tall and strong and well
able to take care of myself, especially under the stress of
outraged emotions. When we came home battered and
bleeding, my sense of justice was again outraged because
my mother, instead of sympathizing, reproached us for
unseemly behavior.

Even now if my feeling for justice, for fair play, for the
right of the underdog is challenged — especially when little
children meet with unjust treatment — I feel very much like
a tiger whose cubs are menaced. My reports on the ruthless
neglect of childhood in our industrial centers during the
Second World War always had to be written at least twice
before I could achieve a dispassionate style.

My whole attitude toward the Negro race also arises from
this instinctive sympathy for the victims of injustice. An
elderly couple who lived near us had as general helper a
young Negro named Alfred, a city boy who spent his summers with them. He was about fourteen when Bill and I
were about eight and seven, and his attitude toward us was

protective and devoted. As his days were full of chores, we helped him in order that he might be free to play with us. Many a time when I sensed that a fight was brewing between the village boys and Bill, I would rush off and call Alfred to come to the rescue. Instantly he would stop washing dishes and without so much as drying the suds off his hands, would run with me to the field of action. It was his sweet reasonableness rather than his superior strength which eased the smoldering tensions and started us all off again playing together with our customary friendliness and zest.

I am sure Alfred was happy with us because in the country, in contrast to what his status might have been in the city, he was accepted not only as a friend but as a hero. If Americans could understand what a painful, searing experience it is when Negro children first begin to realize that the mere color of their skin is to be the source of a lifelong discrimination, it might do more to end our cruelty toward the Negro than all the preaching on justice and equality. Negro parents try to stave off this tragic period of awareness for their little children as long as they can. But the inescapable and terrible moment arrives when the child says, "Why can't we do this or that?" And with breaking heart the Negro parent is obliged to confess, "Because you are black." Thus the innocent happiness to which all children are entitled is brutally destroyed for Negro children at a tender age, and their whole development is warped. This massacre of the innocents still goes on, unheeded by most white mothers. To me it is a great tribute to the Negro race that the vast majority of Negro boys and girls, in spite of early embitterment, grow up to be able, well-adjusted, loyal citizens.

How recapture for modern youngsters the flavor of American village life before the dubious influence of automobiles, telephones, moving pictures, radios and television? Our favorite haunt after school was the blacksmith shop where it was a high privilege to be allowed to blow the bellows and watch the coals glow in the open grate. Nobody had as yet thought up the dull process called vocational training. It was still something we absorbed as tools and agricultural implements were mended and horses shod. While this was going on we lent half an ear to the leisurely discussion by the grownups of village and national politics, of human tragedies and comedies, of the many decent, homely interests of decent, homely people who then as now were sure the country would go to the dogs unless the Republicans were re-elected.

This predominance of Republicans in our village and county was a terrible ordeal for me. But it gave me very early training in bucking public opinion regardless of consequences. My father, whose ideas were law for his children, was one of the very few Democrats in Pelhamville. He was as romantically democratic in spirit as he was in his politics. He was so enraptured with William Jennings Bryan when Bryan first ran for the Presidency in 1896 that we children were taken on one of our rare trips to New York City to hear that temporary hope of free men make one of his sensational speeches. People have now forgotten what a magic spell Bryan's oratory possessed when he first flashed upon the American scene. A revolutionary fervor against the power of entrenched wealth swept through the country, which re-echoed in our household and many others. Even though this truly democratic ardor soon petered out, weakened by such unsound demands as free silver, it left its effects upon me and upon the country as a whole. But it was anathema in Republican Pelhamville. I felt the cross of

gold on my own little back when I had to return to school
after repeated election days, a defeated, crestfallen, but still
ardent defender of an unpopular cause.

As there was no Lutheran Church in Pelhamville, the
whole family trudged a mile and a half every Sunday, rain
or shine, or blizzards for that matter, to a church in the city
of Mount Vernon. That meant another three-mile walk per
week there and back in addition to the four miles daily
going back and forth from school. When I was about nine, a
trolley line was laid between the two communities. This
was not permitted to change what today would be considered sheer martyrdom by youngsters who jump in an automobile to go around the corner. There seemed to be a general family feeling that our young characters as well as our
religion would be undermined if we yielded to anything so
demoralizing as taking a trolley.

After Sunday school we went to church with our parents.
What's more, church was not the lick and promise one-hour
service of today. If the sermon itself lasted only an hour, we
children felt we were getting off easy. But we loved the
magnificent, militant, uplifting hymns of Luther, Bach, and
later classical composers. To this day I cannot hear "A
Mighty Fortress Is Our God" without a tingling of the
spinal cord. Luther's greatest contribution to Western civilization lay in freeing the human spirit from priestly domination. His next greatest achievement was a translation of the
Bible so beautiful that it elevated the whole history of German literature. But if he had done nothing else for Germany but encourage the love of music, he would still be
one of the greatest benefactors of Western culture. In our
village life, these chorales and fugues were the only good
music we children heard regularly outside of the home until the family moved to the city. They helped to ingrain in

us standards of taste for which I have always been grateful. I must confess, however, that I no longer love organ music, now that it has been vulgarized by electrical players in moving-picture houses and even in churches. My friend Paul Claudel summed up my feeling about it when he said, *"Je n'aime pas la musique gazeuse."*

The whole Lutheran tradition of direct individual relationship to God, independence of thought, love of civil and religious freedom, resentment of State-Church alliances, merged in our young minds with the identical American traditions. Church and school were widely separate in those days. Our respect for the clergy was so great that we children would have thought they were demeaning themselves if, as is now too often the case, they had tried to invade our public school. The fact that the village children went to different churches never affected our thinking nor the unity of school life as it does today. We loved going to each other's confirmation services and observing the differences of worship. We little Lutherans with typical sectarian fervor knew there was but one true church. But we felt a decided inferiority complex when the Episcopal Bishop Potter appeared in his white lawn sleeves, which seemed so much more dashing than the subdued black robes to which we were accustomed.

In our spiritual life the two influences of Church and school reinforced each other. The gap between State and Church only served to heighten our devotion to both institutions and fostered their mutual interaction. It is the happy memory of this truly American atmosphere that now makes me such a positive opponent of sectarian religious instruction within the public-school system and of such divisive innovations as the released-time program. James Bryce was reporting correctly when he said of this country at the very time of which I am speaking: "So far from suffering from the want of State support, religion seems in the United States to stand all the firmer, because, standing alone, she is seen to stand by her own strength." Only by accepting their erstwhile places as the allies rather than the dictators of our democratic morality, can the churches again become the powerful leaven in American life that they were during my childhood years at the turn of the century.

There is no doubt, however, that both religion and education not only during my childhood but even in later years, depended far more upon the family than upon the Church or the school. The church services were nothing more than the celebration of Christian doctrines which were the web and woof of daily life at home. We said prayers when we woke up, when we sat down to meals, when we went to bed. God was not a remote potentate but an omnipresent friend whom we invited to meals when we said, "Come, Lord Jesus, be our guest." Inspired no doubt by an engraving which hung in my bedroom of the two angels at the foot of the Raphael Madonna, formerly in the Dresden galleries, I was convinced that similar *Englein* (little angels) hovered about my bed at night. When the sun shone or the rains fell, it was God blessing the growth of his whole creation. This childlike love of God in nature became a part of my attitude toward the social environment and of my faith in the goodness of all human beings.

The only thing about Luther that frightened me as a child was a certain violence of disposition, which I learned later is essentially German. It was highlighted during my childhood by many stories such as the one when he hurled the inkwell at the devil. I can still see my father's look of startled attention when I announced solemnly, at the family dinner table, that I liked the peace-loving Erasmus much more than Luther. It is a reminder that even at the age of eleven, I was struggling valiantly to control my own savage German temper. Also, this precocious comparison recalls to what an extent our family preoccupations hovered around the period of the Reformation and how closely I identified myself with the historical personalities my elders discussed, again and again, because the great religious schism was, for them, the real beginning of Western civilization.

My struggles to control my temper were, in fact, the nightmare of my earliest years. I can remember muttering to myself when I felt inner rage getting the better of me: "Please, God, don't let me do it, please, please, please," and then bang, I would more often than not lose control until the storm blew itself out. My contrition afterward was abject. Then, like a person recovering from a severe illness, it gave way gradually to the return of my assurance that God enjoyed loving me as much as I enjoyed loving him and that all was well again between us. This God relationship was amazingly naïve but of a beauty which I never wholly lost, although it took me years of education to translate the innate quest for perfection which it implies into more conscious and more permanent values. Its immediate result was that the Lutheran catechism and the long passages from the Bible which we learned by heart, were not mere theory but divine guidance for living. Religion, behavior and culture were closely allied in this Protestant tradition. Yet all these influences would not have taken such deep root if my mother had not lived her Christianity in her relationship to us and to all human beings.

It was due to her charitable nature that our house, situated not far from a main highway, became a favorite stopover for the numerous tramps who roamed the countryside in those days. As those colorful characters have long disappeared from the American scene, it may be necessary to explain that the tramp was not a "hobo"; he was not a victim of society but one who scorned its restrictions. Call them the "professionally unemployed." They were never turned away when they knocked at our door and asked for food, but in return they always had to cut up some kindling wood before the meal was handed out. We children would sit open-mouthed with wonder and admiration listening to these embryo Walt Whitmans as they chopped away in leisurely fashion and discoursed on the advantages of complete freedom and the joy of seeing the world instead of being pinned down to the unbearable routine of a steady job. How we loved them! Nowadays I suppose these colorful, fiercely independent, American characters are sedentary and on relief.

Another feature of American life which fascinated us and which has now disappeared were the numerous gypsies with their brilliant clothing, and their many lovely roly-poly children. Their horse-drawn covered wagons could still be parked almost anywhere on open fields, preferably near a stream or a spring. We never had the courage to talk to them as the rumor that they kidnaped "white" children was firmly fixed in our minds. But this reputation only enhanced their glamour when we stole as near as seemed safe to their evening campfires. Our hearts yearned for we knew not what as we heard in the distance the plaintive music of their violins, their melancholy songs, and the soft murmur of their voices punctuated by carefree laughter.

Like our religious training, our secular studies were reenforced at home. During the summer months, a German university graduate, Herr Thimm, whose cheeks were gashed with dueling wounds, drilled us throughout the morning in European literature, history, languages, and what not. After the noonday meal we went on long walks while Thimm, a born narrator, told us all the Greek, German and Norse myths with such vividness that I can still see them as moving pictures. When we came home, the women had usually finished their chores and the whole household, including a steady accretion of relatives and other visitors, settled down to reading aloud — a priceless habit that has, alas, been destroyed in American homes by the ubiquity of radios and television. We heard much good poetry as well as the great classical prose writers read by people who knew how to read — a valuable training for the ear as well as the mind and the imagination. Nor were we children banned when our elders discussed history, politics, music and life in general. We were made unconsciously aware of cultural roots that went far back into the past of American and European history.

The home in those days was still the fountain of life. I am convinced that our American society will become more and more vulgarized and that it will be fragmentized into contending economic, racial and religious pressure groups lacking in unity and common will, unless we can arrest the disintegration of the family and of community solidarity. I shall never forget the words of a prominent Catholic bishop, who said with infinite melancholy when I was in Germany in 1950: "If we do not succeed in stabilizing the family, the Church is finished." Not only organized religion but the very existence of Western civilization is at stake in this major and extremely difficult social problem.

Those of us who grew up in the native, sound, and cultivated American society which I have tried to describe, were fortunate people, for we gained an ever-expanding faith when faith came easy. Our rural village life was a purifying, uplifting influence that fortified us against the later impacts of urbanization; Church and State, because they were separated and friendly, had spiritual and ethical standards that were mutually enriching; freedom and discipline, individualism and collectivity, nature and nurture in their interaction promised an ever stronger democracy. I have no illusions that those simpler, happier days can be resurrected. But those of us who date back to that fortifying era received a heritage so noble that we are in honor bound to live up to the demands of this present world revolution with the same grandeur of vision which our forefathers achieved during the nation's first no less dangerous revolution.

CHAPTER II
Adolescence

ADOLESCENCE always has its tragic aspects. It is only a question of degree.

In my own case the usual difficulties of transition from the age of twelve to sixteen, from unconscious spontaneity to conscious awareness of life, were complicated because my parents decided to move from the rural environment in Pelham Heights to the complex society of New York City. The parental decision was reached in the interests of our education. Bill and I were ready for high school and my older brother, now called Fred, for college. My father could not afford private institutions and the best high schools and colleges at that time were to be found in the city.

Our new home on 151st Street was on the corner of a block of identical frame houses on both sides of the street, with a sad little patch of grass in front and behind them an occasional bush or tree in what was called a back yard. The very word was new to me as was the designation of a nearby open space with sickly grass and no less sickly trees as a park. There were no mysterious haunts where brooks flowed so clear that we could watch the trout in our secret pools, no endless woods and fields to roam at will.

For the first time I walked on streets of dull uniformity, where I encountered only strangers instead of the familiar

village personalities with whom I had a meaningful relationship. Gone was my sense of intimacy with all the life
about me, the feeling of neighborliness, of being a part of
some intangible wholeness. When I remember how hard it
was for me to bridge this one abrupt change of environment, my heart aches for the millions of American children
who are now hurled about in our nomadic society without
the least concern for the impact of this gypsy existence
upon their sensitive natures. A certain amount of flexibility
in the social structure is an advantage, but the mass migrations now habitual in our nation are disastrous to the family and to the formation of individual character. It is impossible to create a stable society if something like a third
of our people are constantly moving about. We cannot grow
fine human beings, any more than we can grow fine trees,
if they are constantly torn up by the roots and transplanted.

Even our close family life no longer exerted the intimate,
stimulating, happy influence it had been in the country.
We children, armed with a tin lunchbox, went off to school
early in the morning, and did not return until late in the
afternoon. Scarcely had the evening meal been consumed
when we sat down to a heavy dose of homework, which
my parents no longer followed and supervised. The gap that
springs up and steadily widens between parents and children
during adolescence appeared with a sudden shock for me
because it was accentuated by a new environment which
meant nothing but aridity to me. This whole transition period was sheer pain, all the more acute because a child of
twelve, so suddenly uprooted, becomes inarticulate and suffers in silence a spiritual chaos which he cannot understand
and which still defies my adult attempts at retrospection
and analysis.

What puzzled me most was the necessity of being segregated for the first time with girls. Back in Pelham it was perfectly natural for me to play with the boys even during school recess. But now in our "block" the boys and girls seemed to have no common interests. At school they separated by mutual consent. I belonged moreover to no age group. At twelve I was in high school; my contemporaries were in the sixth or seventh grammar grades and to my utter horror played with dolls.

One day when I was playing with a number of girls the local bully, a stringy, pimply lad, decided to torment us. I was as tall as he but I may have looked deceptively mild. When my playmates were reduced to tears, my patience snapped. "If you don't get out of here, I'll punch your face," I said. He fled. But the girls seemed aghast. I sensed for the first time that I was even stranger to them than they were to me.

The next day as we walked to school I talked the scene over with Bill, whose reactions to the bully, I was sure, would have been like mine. But he had made his own observations of life in the city.

"Ag, you mustn't get into fights now that we're in the city."

"But, Bill, you would have kicked him out long before I did. I asked him to leave us alone two or three times, but it only made him laugh. I couldn't let him go on pushing those girls around. What do you expect me to do, just stand there?"

"I don't know," said Bill dubiously. "I just know that in the city girls don't fight."

I said no more about it. How could I? I decided Bill must be right. I would fight no more.

Nevertheless I have my whole long life been grateful for the fortunate accident that I grew up in an American society

which developed in all of its members a fierce independence, self-reliance, and the courage when necessity arises, to
go it alone regardless of accepted ideas, the power of authority, and the stigma which is now frequently placed upon
the individual who thinks for himself. Experience with the
power of some of the major pressure groups that exist in
our country has taught me caution, accuracy and disinter-
estedness when I am obliged to differ with them. I check
and double check my facts before I write or speak out in
opposition. I force myself to use understatement rather than
exaggeration, and I literally pray to God that I may not be
unjust when I feel obliged to clash with the conventional
idols of our country. But, having done that, I have, thanks to
the frank atmosphere of my childhood, no fear of telling
what I consider the truth. After every such experience I
have had the immense satisfaction of discovering anew that
America is largely made up of people like myself, people
who welcome the truth when it is factually supported no
matter whose ox is gored.

As my endeavors for social progress have led to numerous
public battles, even some of my friends think that I like
controversy. I don't. I hate it. It still nauseates me as it did
in my childhood when I saw that Bill and I had to defend
ourselves against superior forces.

As a child, my first contacts with the new and strange conventions of city life were so overpowering that they threw
me back upon myself. I was lost and unable to communicate
what I could not find words to express. From that time for
many years I became more and more a dual personality,
which preserved outwardly the buoyancy of childhood as a
successful disguise for the adolescent turmoil of mind and
emotions. Instead of "boasting" two soul-sides, as Browning
put it, I suffered two soul-sides, one to face the world with,

the other to show on only rare occasions to people whom I loved and trusted.

Fortunately the Morris High School, which my parents had selected for Bill and me, was undoubtedly one of the best college preparatory schools in the country. Most of the teachers had been transferred in a group from the Boston Latin School. These men and women were not only scholarly gentlefolk who knew their subjects but they also knew how to teach. Gradually I forgot some of my loneliness as I became more and more entranced with the delights of learning. School became a second home.

The college entrance course in those days was rigidly confined to Latin, Greek, ancient history, mathematics, one foreign language — French, in my case — and a definitely prescribed outline of English and American literature. Now that the educational world is split over the question of adherence to the classical educational tradition or adjustment to the realities of modern life, I have asked myself what I derived from this antiquated and strangely assorted mental diet to which we were all subjected in the typical college preparatory course. I was exceedingly happy under this discipline because the stretching of the mind was an exercise I enjoyed much as I enjoyed physical exertion. I liked playing games whether they involved intellectual or physical dexterity. As a result I liked mathematics most of all because the rules of the game were precise and failure to play it correctly could be checked with exactitude. I liked to do original problems in geometry the way other people like to do crossword puzzles.

I am grateful for the acquisition of French which, like the German language, opened vast new worlds and vistas greatly to the enrichment of my whole life. I see only with reluctance the sacrifice of foreign languages in the modern curriculum, especially now that we must learn to communicate more readily with other nations; but even more because familiarity with foreign cultures makes us more tolerant of foreign traditions and more critical of our own standards and values. History has much the same desirable effects as languages, of throwing open the windows of the mind and sharpening the sense of discrimination. Perhaps the greatest asset I derived from the love of literature was an increased desire to associate with the best minds whether in books or in life, a passion in which I felt justified after reading that Goethe had the same urge. But this was the only bridge to reality that I discovered in the many texts we consumed. At the time, this critical attitude toward people narrowed my social life to a few friends who were just as egocentric and book-centered as I was, and we were equally persuaded of our superiority to everybody else. Even before I went to college I had lost contact with the little democratic village girl who liked to blow the bellows in the blacksmith shop and listen to the conversations of the country people, the Irish coachmen and the village storekeepers.

Yet my self-centered, artificial intellectualism and my growing aloofness from my instinctive self were no fault of mine. It is positively shocking to remember that our whole education in those days took place in a social vacuum. No efforts whatsoever were made to relate our excellent academic curriculum to modern life. Many of the students, including my brother Bill, for whom this abstract education was meaningless, escaped at the end of the second year from what to them was an empty routine. The youngsters who in those days left school early could still find instructive jobs that frequently helped them to become successful "self-made" men and women. Today when different economic conditions and strict labor laws make it necessary to keep all children in school until they are sixteen or even eighteen, the problem of adjusting the high-school curriculum to the individual capacities and interests of the child has become of paramount importance. Now that education for all is our American objective, rather than for the intelligent minority which was still the rule at the beginning of the century, the public schools are faced with one of the most profound problems that has been created by our endeavors to establish an honest democracy — a democracy which really affords all children an opportunity to develop such talents as they happen to possess.

I am a passionate defender of our public schools, and wholly devoted to their improvement, expansion, and readjustment to new social demands because my own schooling at Pelhamville and Morris High School were of such fundamental importance in my life. The one was all sunshine and gaiety, since it was closely linked to an integrated experience of nature, community and family. The high school was as isolated from the social scene as any monastery, but it was a beneficent refuge throughout four difficult years. It carried me safely through a period of profound spiritual turmoil and prepared those of us who went to college so thoroughly that we pitied the products from the famous private schools. If the private schools are now considered superior to the public schools it is only because the latter have been allowed to deteriorate.

In pursuit of an educational program to suit the bright and the not so bright, we have watered down a rigid training for the elite until we now have an educational diet in many of our public high schools that nourishes neither the classes nor the masses. This is a problem for which the lowest common denominator is not an answer. We must evolve an adjustable curriculum which does not sacrifice the superior student to the drones at a period in our history when we need highly trained people in ever increasing numbers to solve the vast and complex problems which destiny has placed upon our shoulders.

Aside from the public-school system, the only other institution that gave me a sense of the continuity of life after we moved to the city was the church. Here we sang the same beautiful hymns, heard sermons on the familiar Bible texts, and forgot all temporary disillusionment in the contemplation of what, to our whole family, were eternal verities. We missed the friendliness of a smaller congregation whose members had known each other for many years. Like most city churches the people came from far and near and therefore lacked the sense of neighborhood, of mutual assistance, of common interests and purposes. But we were hardened to this by the same absence of neighborly relations in our daily lives.

Then came the time when Bill and I were sent to confirmation classes for instruction in the real meaning of church membership. Our city clergyman was far more intelligent than our country pastor, but he was a Prussian type of Lutheran, a martinet and strict disciplinarian of anything but Christian character. What the other children thought of our tempestuous classes in religion I do not know, as we saw them only during these trying sessions. Bill and I despised this authoritarian drillmaster and laughed heartily over his rough and ready methods of education that were such a contrast to the far more intelligent, liberal, and kindly spirit that reigned in our public high school.

As Bill was older than I, he came out of this ordeal with his spiritual wings badly singed. But I was still so young that the sincerely religious influence of our home life could not be obliterated by this unfortunate experience. I still recall with what dedication of heart and mind I heard my German Biblical text which is given to all Lutheran children at confirmation as a guide to life: *"Die der Geist Gottes treibet, die sind Gottes Kinder."* In the King James version, this sentence of Saint Paul's reads: "For as many as are led by the spirit of God, they are the sons of God." Which one may be the more accurate, I do not know, but Luther's translation has in the word "treibet" (driven) more of the immanence of God to man than the gentle word "led." The *"Kinder"* (children) is not as contemptuous of the female sex as "sons." I have always cherished this admonition as to what constitutes spirituality, especially on the many occasions later in life when it became my buckler and shield against the narrowness of the various man-made Christian orthodoxies and against the destructive rivalries and hatreds which they have aroused throughout the ages in otherwise decent people.

My own religious development as a high-school student was intensified by the opportunities city life afforded me for the first time to hear great music greatly rendered. For all Lutherans the complex music-religion is an inseparable entity. Is that not the chief reason why from Bach to Mozart to Beethoven, to Brahms to Gustav Mahler, German music reached a higher and more continuously uniform level than that of any other country? This escape from what was then to me the sordid aspects of an urban reality was all the more important as the rigid orthodoxy of Lutheran fundamentalism gradually lost its hold upon my imagination. The powerful appeal of Christ as a glowing tradition-shattering personality never ceased to influence me. His message still means to me that we must constantly re-create the forms and formalities of religion if we are to learn what it means to live by the spirit. This conception already appears in a letter I wrote as a college senior to a friend who was trying to impress me with his skepticism: "As for the divinity of Christ at which you scoff, what does it matter one way or another? When sectarian Christianity has gone the way of all man-made institutions, Jesus will probably be known very much better, and after Jesus as God we shall come back to faith in the God of Jesus."

I am especially grateful that I grew up with an intimate knowledge of Luther's translation of the Bible. It has a greater intensity than the King James version because its musical language is redolent of one man's passionate faith. As for modern translations, I find their cold accuracy repelling. It is sad if only for cultural reasons that modern youth is so ignorant of Biblical lore. Yet the clergy are pusillanimous when they blame this ignorance upon our secular technological society. Their narrow dogmatism has done more than modern rationalism to dim the light the Bible can throw upon the path to holiness. If we told our young people that the Bible is on the whole the most beautiful single record of the growth of the human spirit, instead of constantly emphasizing its contribution to righteousness, redemption and salvation, I am sure young Americans of today would show less resistance to it.

In my own development, the Bible played a part long after interest in the supernatural and in the clerical emphasis on life as a mere steppingstone to a problematical hereafter, had fallen off my shoulders like an outworn garment. I can describe my state of mind in Emerson's words: "Of immortality the soul when well employed is incurious. . . . Higher than the question of our duration is the question of our deserving. Immortality will come to such as are fit for it and he who would be a great soul in the future must be a great soul now."

Yet the older I have grown, the more I traversed "the terrifying path toward myself," the more I learned how inescapably I am the child of my clerical forebears and of my Protestant upbringing. How explain the deep influences of that heroic amalgam called Protestantism? The ardent devotion to freedom of mind, the unending quest for truth, and the constant struggle with doubt and despair, these three elements leap to mind at once. They imply a resolve never to compromise the ideal under the pressure of social realities and never to force one's own truth upon others. The willingness to sacrifice truth for a higher truth as soon as it is glimpsed, at however great a distance — this is the link of the true Protestant rebel with a compelling mysticism. Thomas Mann borrowed a word from Goethe as the key to *The Magic Mountain*. It is *Steigerung,* one of those untranslatable metaphysical German concepts, which describes the simultaneous elevation and intensification of life's significance. This quest for self-development stretches the imagination whether in the realm of social activities, in scientific research or in the appreciation of the arts. Morality and music — the interaction of reason and imagination, of knowledge and faith — what other tradition has pierced the human breast more deeply with these creative polarities? They are the quintessence of Protestantism with all its many shadings of light and melancholy that still dominate my life.

It was preordained, therefore, that I should turn to music as the source of the *Steigerung* which I had once found, but could no longer find, in religious orthodoxy. My heart still warms with gratitude when I remember Walter Damrosch at whose children's concerts, like thousands of my contemporaries, I was initiated into the mysteries of orchestral composition and its thematic structure. Dr. Damrosch may not have been one of the greatest musicians, but he was a great teacher and thereby contributed perhaps more to the thorough musical education of Americans than the famous stars of this celestial firmament. He rescued his pupils from the banality which still besets music in our country, of confusing the realm of music with mere technical instrumental proficiency which leads to a mob worship of "big names" in the American musical world and an unwillingness to encourage the beginner and to support such esoteric delights as chamber music.

Now began for me an inner tug of war, which I was incapable of understanding at the time, between the intoxicating, overpowering, voluptuous charms of Wagnerian opera which swept me off my feet and the very different more intellectual delights which I experienced in their highest manifestations as I was drawn more and more not only to orchestral concerts but to the magic performances of the Kneisel and Flonzaley quartets. What I unconsciously resented in Wagner's music was the something excessive, the violence, the love of catastrophe and death, that yielding to the senses which I feared in myself since my earliest childhood battles to control my volcanic eruptions of temper. The whole tenor of the Wagnerian mystique reflected my father's German emotionalism which our close relationship had encouraged in me as contrasted with the profoundly civilizing restraints of my American democratic childhood and our Lutheran traditions. "In Wagner's work and world," says Thomas Mann with his exact critical insight, "the great and only thing is emotional primitive poesy, the earliest and simplest, the pre-conventional, pre-social — only this seems to him at all suitable for art. . . . What is German? . . . The German spirit is, socially and politically, essentially uninterested."

The *Nibelungen Ring* is not only antisocial, it is anti-Christian barbarism disguised by the most seductive sounds the world has ever heard. My final release from bondage to its magic spell took place during my European student days in the summer of 1909. I could not resist going to Bayreuth as I had never heard *Parsifal*. After a year in the critical, clear-eyed, rational atmosphere of Paris, the sudden transition to the false, theatrical and sensual religiosity of *Parsifal* acted like a lightning flash of revelation. The melancholy of sudden insight was appalling, deepened moreover by the cloying sentimentality and crass materialism of the Bayreuth audience. Hardly had the curtain slowly closed upon the holy-unholy strains of the Grail music at the end of the second act when a fat South German sitting in front of me growled to his wife: "Now hurry up Guste or all the fried sausages will be gone." While everybody devoured huge plates of these succulent sausages with sauerkraut, Siegfried Wagner followed by a court of simpering, adoring females circulated among the crowd. The opera, the people, Bayreuth itself, reeked with vulgarity and decadence. It was a real Twilight of the Gods for me — a permanent one. But this debacle was the culmination of a long, slow, painful process. From my fourteenth year until I was twenty, I still succumbed to the antisocial German tradition so completely that I felt music as the secret life of the soul, as withdrawal from actuality and its vexations, as spiritual compensation for the joys of childhood which were now receding more and more into a dream world.

Throughout my four years in high school, with their social isolation, my relationship to the adored father of my childhood days had been steadily deteriorating. What actually happened to transform the model parent whom we children knew when we lived in the country into an ever more irresponsible human being has always remained a mystery to me. Years after my father had died I was told that even before we moved to New York, he had become emotionally involved with a beautiful young woman who was one of his law clients. Mercifully I knew nothing of this as a child; for even as an adult this revelation still had the power to tear open wounds I thought had been cicatrized by time. Perhaps this experience started him on the downward path. Perhaps the rigors of family life and heavy professional responsibilities had always been too exacting a burden for so artistic a temperament. Perhaps the city offered my father more opportunity to live the self-indulgent life that now absorbed him more and more to the neglect of his law practice, his wife and his children.

Whatever the reasons, my growing realization that the idealized father of my childhood was a myth of my own making had a disastrous effect upon me. What aggravated my almost hysterical reaction to this disillusionment was the worry caused my mother by his Bohemian ways and by his growing indifference to his law clients and to the fact that butcher and grocer bills must be paid. Instead of earning a living for his family, he wrote books and dramas that were incredibly amateurish. One was a play about the German revolutionary, General Peter Muhlenberg, which was actually produced. In the last act the entire American and British forces seemed to be gathered on the stage. My brother Fred and I commented to each other that if there had been as many people in the audience as there were on the stage, the event would have been a success. Such experiments created mounting debts to which my father was sublimely indifferent. Failure after failure only encouraged him in the idea of being a misunderstood genius.

As an adult, I can appreciate the comedy of this development and realize that I took the situation too tragically. My poor mother, who should have been far more affected, could invent the most elaborate excuses for his conduct and even shared his illusion that an overwhelming artistic success was just around the corner. But it is one thing to read a Dickens novel and quite another to have a Micawber in the family. Because my father had been for me a knight in shining armor, I could make no compromise between my youthful hero and the harsh reality. For several years I still hoped that his metamorphosis was just a terrible nightmare from which we would both wake up and begin our common life anew. But when his irresponsibility became more and more pronounced, my love turned into an exaggerated burning shame that haunted me all the more because I was too proud and too deeply wounded to confess it even to my brothers.

What finally broke the golden cord that held me to him was the dawning realization that he no longer wanted me to go to college. He never expressed it in so many words, but from my mother I gleaned that he would be freer to pursue his fantastic mode of life, if I should begin remunerative work sooner than would be possible if I continued my academic career. The thought that the father who had inspired in me the love of learning was betraying the very ideals he had taught me to cherish was the chief cause of the deep wound in my soul that took so many years to heal. And then it healed only on the surface. For there are such things as mortal blows to which the heart can reconcile itself but from which it can never wholly recover.

To understand the anguish with which I lived for years

afterward, it is necessary to remember not only my profound emotional involvement with my father but my Lutheran up-bringing in a warmly religious household. The command-ment "Honor thy father and thy mother" had been graven into my being not through the memorizing of mere words but through the happy family life I had lived as a child. This moral imperative was shattered and I was aghast. I was ashamed not only of my father but of myself.

I was also haunted by a sharp awareness that my father and I were two of a kind. In my heart I realized that I loved complete freedom and hated work, continuous effort and discipline as much as he did. This insight terrified me. He, on the other hand, was tortured by the knowledge that his only daughter, whom he could not help loving and pro-tecting, had his own passionate nature and uncontrollable love of life. He suffered acutely, if unnecessarily, when some young man brought me home late at night from wholly in-nocent expeditions to the theater or concert or the most decorous parties. The scenes between us, when he tried to exert an authority which I was no longer willing to accept, were all the more searing because the distance, formality and restraints that had been so habitual between us as long as we understood each other, now broke down and gave way to the violence of emotion that was characteristic of both of us. And like all people who are "well brought up," these occasional bursts of temper left us both exhausted in mind and body and sick of ourselves and life in general.

Yet our silences, the things we never said, the fact that our eyes no longer met in glances of mutual understanding, these transformations tortured me and I am sure they tor-tured him more than the few open clashes that were my fault more than his. Occasionally my nerves were stretched to the breaking point, ordeals from which I recovered only because I was physically robust, and because my childhood sense of security had given me an indomitable love of life. But the lonely battle for self-control and survival was a heavy load for an adolescent youngster.

Years later I acquired a certain skepticism as to the perspicacity of psychiatrists when I spent a day entertaining the famous Dr. Jung. He interspersed his amusing conversation with questions that invited confidences. As I parried all of them, he finally beamed his radiant personality straight at me and made one last effort to conquer my reticence: "You show no wounds," he murmured. "Certainly not," I replied calmly. "I don't understand it," said the great healer of neuroses. Thereupon I turned toward him as if at last I was about to confess all and said in my most confidential manner: "I'll tell you why, Doctor. It's because, like a healthy dog, I licked them all until they got well."

Yet the estrangement that grew up between my father and me had an immediate effect of a salutary nature. Since he no longer really wished me to go to college, I refused henceforth to accept any financial assistance from him. That meant I had to win scholarships and earn enough money to pay all my expenses. It was the first sensible idea that I had had in four years. It brought me down to earth from my bookish and musical ivory tower at least now and then. It did more to strengthen a character that had all my father's weaknesses than anything else that happened to me throughout the next four years of college life.

CHAPTER III
College Days

WITH A SCHOLARSHIP earned by high marks in my entrance examinations, I went to Barnard College in 1903 as if I were going to heaven. What after all were high schools for, with their rigid academic programs, if not to serve as a kind of purgatory to prepare their pupils for the seat of real learning — college — college with its illustrious faculty, its great library, and its carefully selected group of students?

As I had a great love of mathematics, I decided to specialize in mathematics and physics. The three professors whose courses I chose had all just obtained their Ph.D.'s from famous American and European universities. One of them is now among our most distinguished mathematicians. But none of them had the slightest concept of teaching beginners, and none of them was aware of us as anything but ignorant little females. After the brilliant teachers to whom I had become accustomed in Morris High School, these scholars first baffled, then annoyed, and finally bored me by their fuzzy conduct of classes. Because of my naïve frankness this soon became apparent to my professor in solid geometry, trigonometry, and calculus. I enraged the poor man, who knew I had come to college with high marks, by paying no attention to our daily stints. When it came time for examination, I carefully reread all my textbooks the night before and handed in papers which were perfect, as I well knew. He nevertheless gave me a D, the lowest mark next to failure, and explained that my "attitude" was wrong. As this mark, if it stood, made it impossible for me to renew my scholarship the next year, I objected vociferously but all to no avail. Dean Gill (predecessor of the very different Dean Gildersleeve) and the members of the faculty who decided the question of scholarships, labeled me as too "irresponsible" to deserve a scholarship, and knowing that I could not afford the tuition, they probably thought this was a good way to get rid of somebody whose flagrant independence of spirit, so unbecoming to an impecunious student, proved that I was not "college material."

My disillusion with the quality of college teaching is a commonplace experience. I reacted violently only because I had expected too much. It is still a custom in many of our institutions of higher learning to let the young Ph.D.'s cut their educational teeth on the freshmen, whereas the incoming classes should have the great teachers that can be found in every university. But at Barnard as elsewhere the shining lights of that institution such as Charles Beard, Shotwell, John Dewey, William Peterfield Trent, Franz Boas, William Shepherd, Crampton, Montague, Giddings, James Harvey Robinson and others taught only the upper classes. The science departments were still feeble in the women's college of that era. Though I clung to my passion for mathematics two years more, I gave up physics after freshman year because I had to pursue it with the same charming but ineffectual instructor. Thus I turned more and more to such subjects as philosophy and literature because the faculty was stronger in those departments. This was the worst thing that could have happened to so introspective a youngster as myself. But there was no one to advise us, no one in-

deed who took the slightest interest in our choice of subjects.

Our colleges have made great progress in student guidance since those days, including my own Alma Mater. But
these efforts are too often unsuccessful as the various college departments still teach far too much in proud isolation
of one another's often closely related subjects, and pay too
little attention to the unity of the learning process. Yet
the greatest hurdle toward a genuinely integrated scholarship for the average student is the young college professor's
lack of educational techniques. The cultural split between
means and ends, science and the humanities, between expert and lay leadership that runs all through our civilization, is beautifully illustrated by the fact that our public-
school teachers have educational techniques but little
learning, and our college professors are steeped in learning
but rarely have experience in arranging this material for the
encouragement of thought.

Fortunately there was one young professor who compen-
sated me during my freshman year for the many disappointments. Clayton Hamilton, whom Brander Matthews called
his most promising student, was our English teacher. In his
early twenties, he was as beautiful as a Greek god and as
mad as a March hare. When he asked us to write our first
theme on a subject of our own choosing, I was determined
to make an impression on this brilliant and attractive young
lecturer. I did an enormous amount of research and handed
in a paper on "The Position of Woman as a Measure of
Civilization." When I breezed into Hamilton's study for
consultation on my magnum opus, carrying a tennis racket
and wearing my most becoming sweater, I felt that I was
irresistible. So did Ham, and therefore took all the more
delight in handing me back my theme marked "D." My

self-satisfaction exploded audibly. How could such a magnificent effort be thought unworthy? Clayton Hamilton thereupon delivered a lecture on writing that was of profound influence upon me. Its sum and substance was, write about things you have experienced and don't try to bluff your readers.

It took years before I really learned that sound lesson thoroughly. In fact I am still trying to learn it. Once the pursuit of truth begins to haunt the mind, it becomes an ideal never wholly attained. From that moment Ham and I became lifelong friends. But I always regretted that his later success in Hollywood and the large amount of money he earned there in a short time weakened his ambition to become the superb critic and essayist which, judging by his promising early work, he might well have been.

Another enchanting memory of this first year is a brief encounter with Mark Twain. We youngsters were so in awe of his white suit, his beautiful shock of white hair and his fame that we were tongue-tied in his presence. In our little theater he entertained us with a discourse, the theme of which was that he had a twin brother — one of the twins died in infancy and nobody ever knew whether it was he or his brother. He embroidered upon this for an hour so hilariously that we were reduced to helpless laughter, laughter so uncontrolled that I feared our rather plump professor of economics, Mr. Moore, would burst asunder or suffer an attack of apoplexy. His theme would seem to prove that Mark Twain, himself, was conscious of the dual personality which many modern critics have emphasized.

The Barnard faculty members who condemned me as an irresponsible character were more than justified in their opinion. As I did not enjoy the work for which I was best fitted, I was extremely unhappy at college and even more unhappy at home where my mother's loving care and devotion could not compensate for the strained relations with my father. Instead of hanging my head in shame and misery, I plunged into all sorts of extracurricular activities. As Charles Surface in the *School for Scandal,* in white wig, white satin eighteenth-century costume, and a dashing red cape, I was the recipient of much adulation, which I thoroughly enjoyed. As center on the basketball team, and pitcher on the baseball team, I was in my element. The Columbia undergraduates who climbed on the roof of Brinkerhoff Hall to watch our baseball games laughed so hard at our antics that they all but fell off their perch. Because I could pitch curves, the college paper referred to me as Barnard's Christy Mathewson.

How could the dean and the faculty be expected to know that I was a very distraught child of sixteen, making the best of a very bad situation at home and of keen disappointment in my studies? I distrusted most of the faculty in my freshman year and they distrusted me. My relation to the authorities never improved as long as I was in college. My mood of rebellion continued because the academic atmosphere made me feel as if I were at a perpetual funeral service without being able to discover who was being buried or where the corpse was concealed. All I knew was that the whole place smelled of death and that the faculty was rather inept at conducting the obsequies.

I have only to enter the halls of a college to feel at once whether the place is alive or dead. In the latter case I still shiver with the same revulsion that terrified me as a youngster during my undergraduate days. No wonder good old Mrs. Liggett, our Barnard bursar, who used to lecture me

on my "irresponsibility," gave me up in despair and told
me I was a hopeless case.

At Barnard College where this irresponsible undergraduate is now a responsible trustee, I have done my best to
make college education more vital, and more closely integrated with the realities of modern life. My only lasting
contribution to these objectives was made when Helen Reid
and I sat on Millicent McIntosh's doorstep until she consented to be the successor of our distinguished retiring Dean,
Virginia Gildersleeve.

Like all adversity, my failure to get a scholarship for the
sophomore year was a salutary influence. Instead of moon-
ing over my troubles, as I was inclined to do, I had to get
to work and earn enough money for my tuition and other
expenses. During the college year, I could make enough
money to pay for my clothes and meals by tutoring students
in algebra and geometry for the college-entrance examination. But the $150 I had to have to enter college in my
sophomore year was a sum so formidable in 1904, when the
dollar was worth a dollar, that even my obstinate soul was
dismayed.

That summer I worked twelve hours a day not counting
an hour's subway ride to work at seven in the morning and
home again at ten P.M. It was on the whole one of the
happiest experiences of my college days. In the morning
and early afternoon I was principal of a Baptist summer
school. From six to ten P.M. I had charge of the Hudson
Guild lending library where I enjoyed the friendship of the
universally beloved Dr. Elliott. With a sinking heart I calculated that all my earnings would fall fifty dollars short of
the needed sum. But again my kindly fates watched over

me. The superintendent of the summer sessions announced at our second weekly meeting that two men principals had been driven out of one of the schools in Hell's Kitchen, then the toughest section of the city, and he called for volunteers to take the position at double pay. As I would gladly have undertaken anything short of murder for double pay, I volunteered and got the job.

When I arrived next morning in the basement of a church on West — I think it was — Thirty-sixth Street, pandemonium reigned. About one hundred fifty boys between eight and fourteen were fighting, laughing, rolling among the Sunday-school benches while two assistant teachers looked on with desperate expressions. I watched this hullabaloo quietly and not without sympathy. After all, I was just seventeen and had been an obstreperous tomboy not so long ago. Soon I perceived that one little blond-haired demon of about fourteen — our age limit — was directing the battle. Without a word, I marched into the fray, took him by the back of the collar, dragged him the length of the room, and threw him past the iron gate into the street. Instantly one half of my pupils marched out with him. I let them go and slammed the gate. When I came back an awed silence had fallen upon the remaining youngsters. "Why did those other kids leave the room?" I asked the nearest boy. "Jesus, teacher," he stammered, awestruck, "you trew out de leader of de tirty-sixt street gang and de rest went on strike." "Well," I replied calmly, hearing the boys outside clamoring for readmission, "it isn't a strike any more. It's a lockout."

I discovered that all the boys who had remained belonged to a rival group, the Thirty-seventh Street gang. "Who's your leader?" I asked. "Me," announced another big boy, very proudly. We went into conference. "We can have a lot of fun here, Jimmie," I explained, "if you and the leader of the Thirty-sixth Street gang will help me run the show." He volunteered to deliver the message. The two young rival leaders appeared before school the next morning and agreed to "knock the block off any bloke that spoiled the racket." From that time on my difficulties were solved and my double pay assured. Weeks later I asked Jimmie how he had persuaded the leader of his rival gang to come to terms. He blushed as only fourteen-year-old boys can blush, even the toughest of them. "To tell ye the truth, Teacher, he wanted to come back because you're de dead image of his goil."

When the superintendent of the summer schools appeared unheralded two days after my peace treaty was signed and sealed, to find out whether I was still alive, he found a lot of boys making hammocks, doing carpentry, and thoroughly enjoying themselves amidst an orderly confusion and gaiety. Stunned by this transformation he asked me how our Bible-lesson period was going. It seems the Bible lessons had finished off my two male predecessors, both young divinity students. "Oh, wonderful," I replied nonchalantly. "They love it," but failed to add that Bible stories like that of David and Goliath had never been so jazzed up before. "How did you do it, Miss Ernst?" he queried in puzzled admiration. I intimated that Christian charity had triumphed over the forces of evil. "There's nothing to it." I ended with calculated indifference. "You just have to like boys."

But, on the whole, my answer was not so far out of the way. No doubt the gangs of young hoodlums who now terrorize our major cities are tougher lads than my two groups. Everybody is tougher today. Why shouldn't they be? If these gangs of boys and girls found greater understanding in

our schools and were given constructive outlets for their energies before they get to the criminal stage, we could save
these children and the money we now spend on programs
of rehabilitation. But piecemeal attempts such as my summer school are not enough. Our huge cities must be broken
down into small neighborhood groups with the public schools
as the hub of an integrated and continuous welfare, health
and educational program. The teachers, social workers,
guidance experts and recreation leaders needed for such a
program must be specially trained for their arduous task,
and rewarded if not with double pay, as I was, with salaries
that will make such jobs attractive. Nothing less than such a
comprehensive community program will do, because nothing less will make these city boys and girls feel that they are
a part of a meaningful democratic world in which everybody, poor or rich, counts as much as and no more than the
next fellow.

When our summer session ended there were prizes to be
awarded. I announced to my whole group of ruffians that
the first prize would go to a shy little fellow named Billy,
who belonged to neither gang and had persevered in coming only because I had protected him. Thereupon our good
Baptist superintendent informed me the prize could not be
given to Billy as he was a Catholic. I was dumfounded.
This was my first encounter with religious intolerance. To
make amends, I called on Billy's mother to explain that I
was helpless in the situation and brought him a prize purchased with money I could ill spare. This wise little woman
looked at me pityingly and said: "Don't worry about it.
That's the way things are. If a Baptist went to a Catholic
summer school, he wouldn't get a prize either." Today I
worry about religious intolerance more than ever. It pains
me more than any other human infirmity.

When I returned to college in the autumn, one of the gentlest, kindliest of my teachers, Miss Hirst of the Latin department, stopped me on the stairs and informed me that the faculty had decided to give me a scholarship after all. This was like manna from heaven. But I had been too long in a rebellious mood and also I was too deeply moved to show my benefactor the slightest gratitude. "Thank you," I replied coldly and walked on. Yet many dire problems had been solved for me by this windfall. I could now help my mother pay the household bills to whose urgent reality my father was becoming ever more indifferent. I had time to think rather than to rush about tutoring lazy or stupid youngsters who couldn't pass their exams.

What puzzled me was why I had worked so hard to come back to college when I was in such revolt against the whole pedantic atmosphere. I had, after all, been far happier matching wits with my tough and lovable young gangsters. I could not think my way through to the obvious fact that I had given my whole self to these desperate youngsters and that I was rigidly withholding myself in most of my college contacts. I had worked long and hard to come back to this abstract world that had no relationship to reality partly as a matter of pride but mainly out of a deeply ingrained moral obsession that whatever has been begun must be completed.

Then the final catastrophe happened that justified my rebellion against the academic world. I was taking a daily theme course under the idol of Barnard intellectuals, William Tenney Brewster, affectionately called Billy by the students. Without realizing it, I poured my heartaches into these daily bits of authorship because writing was my only emotional outlet. In midterm Billy announced that he would read two sets of six themes. The first series consisted of admirably written humorous vignettes of city life, objective, realistic, very entertaining. The next group was immediately recognized by the fierce legibility of the handwriting as mine. They were melancholy, introspective, nostalgic yearnings for the evanescent beauty of childhood, the pathetic revelations of all my hidden grief. No doubt they were full of "slush," as we used to term sentimentality. But a more humane instructor could have been of real help to me if he had criticized these pitiful outbursts in private. My classmates who knew me only as a hail-fellow-well-met, life-of-the-party character roared with laughter over these unexpected revelations. Billy licked his chops with cruel delight as he announced that the first writer was interested in the world, the second — well, mainly — and he paused unctuously — mainly in herself. If I had been stripped naked in the middle of Madison Square I could not have felt more humiliated. How could I ever live down this ruthless exposure of my inner preoccupations and travail? "How's your soul today, Ag?" was a common quip. The class yearbook always had a satiric quotation for each member. Mine was "Fortunate he who discovers a new continent, more fortunate he who acts as the Columbus of his own soul."

But I was not the only member of Barnard 1907 who was going through secret tortures. With one of my classmates, then called Juliet Points, which she later spelled Poyntz, I had a friendly-hostile relationship. We were rivals in the debating society, athletics, and other activities chiefly because we resented and feared each other at first sight. But I was also attracted to Juliet as she was far more brilliant than most of the girls. Always a model student, she was nevertheless supremely unhappy and maladjusted. She could not hide as I did that she was in a bitter conflict with her home. Her father was a policeman. Juliet felt this as an in-

surmountable social stigma. She felt that her mother, a former schoolteacher, had married "beneath herself." Here
was a perfect example of the corroding influence due to the
split in our society between those who work with their heads
and those who work with their hands. My conversations with
Juliet revealed that this was the source of her hatred of our
democracy, which the aloofness from all honest social orientation of our intellectual college atmosphere was bound to
exacerbate. Juliet's history proves how dangerous it is to develop the intelligence without at the same time developing
the moral and social consciousness that can guide it to noble
and constructive uses. Her story reveals with tragic and
even comic clarity why so many of our rootless intellectuals
became Communists or fellow travelers during the depression.

Juliet and I argued eternally. She knew that I was working my way through college and tried to arouse in me her
own feeling that we were economically underprivileged.
When I pointed out that in other countries girls without
means could not possibly go to college and that I enjoyed
earning my way in the world, Juliet's hatred of me became
a livid fury which I could not understand. What annoyed
her most was my indifference to money and my irrepressible
gaiety. She reproached me savagely for being frivolous. As I
sensed a powerful irrationalism in her disposition, of which
I had more than enough myself, I began to avoid her.

I never saw Juliet after graduation but learned that she
took out her grudge against the rich, the socially secure,
and the injustices of life in general by joining the Socialist
party. Morris Hillquit, the able leader of Socialism at that
time, recognized her ability as well as her zest for power. He
tried to discipline her by giving her rather routine duties.
She became impatient as she felt that she was not getting

ahead fast enough in the Socialist party to satisfy her egotism, wounded pride, and vaulting ambition. She then went
to London and there, I was later told by people who were
very close to her, became a bona fide member of the Communist party. When she returned to New York City, she
had married a German whose political affiliations were ob-
scure. Some of her friends maintain that Juliet then refused
to carry out some of the Communist orders she received.
They surmise that she tried to rescue herself from the toils
of the party. In any case, she left her apartment one morning
in June 1937 to go to work as usual and disappeared without
a trace. The police investigated the case fruitlessly for years.
The supposition is that she knew too much about Communist activities to be allowed to break with the party and
was murdered by members of her own Communist cell. She
was declared legally dead in 1944.

Anyone who knew Juliet's furious rage at society and her
insatiable will to power during her college years has no difficulty in recognizing the inevitability of her history. In the
course of my social studies, I have met several American
Communists who, like Juliet, were pathological mentalities
largely because they could not reconcile themselves to a sordid and embittered childhood. But much as I pity these
warped personalities, I am convinced that there is no such
thing as reconversion to American democracy from this pathological Communism unless through profound psychiatric
treatment. Americans who are willing to betray their country will also betray their Communist brethren if this second
betrayal promises their sickly egos greater rewards. And
how can we tell that this process of betrayal stops at the second phase? Why don't we realize that these converts may
still be avenging themselves upon our society by sowing
confusion with their unsubstantiated slander of innocent

people, some of them our highest public officials? As for the ex-Communists who become ardent Christians overnight, they remind me of the Chinese proverb concerning enlightenment: "He lays down the butcher's cleavers, and immediately becomes a Buddha." When our usual common sense reigns again in this land, we shall all be ashamed to remember that we allowed these Communist renegades and their Fascist allies to poison public opinion, determine legislative reprisals, and create an hysterical fear of Communism here at home while we should be planning how to handle the Communists in China and Russia.

Although I was on friendly terms with many of my other classmates, I saw far more of the girls in my sorority, Alpha Phi, than of the others. We were a congenial lot and enjoyed ourselves thoroughly at the meetings, dances and other social activities. But since we were also thoughtful youngsters, it began to bother some of us that the girls who were left out of these secret societies suffered from being excluded. I was particularly disturbed by the fact that all the Jewish girls were ineligible — it was my first introduction to anti-Semitism. In reaction I made a deliberate effort to befriend the Jewish girls I liked. The whole situation began to get on my nerves to a point where I drifted away from the narrow sorority atmosphere. Several years after graduation when some of our professors had the good sense to start a movement for the elimination of all the sororities at Barnard as undemocratic, I supported them enthusiastically and helped win the battle. I am sure Barnard has been a happier place for the whole student body since these organizations for the cultivation of snobbishness were banned.

It was not until my junior year that my involvements with the opposite sex became almost an obsession. It is heady business being an attractive young girl, and nobody was more thoroughly spoiled by male adoration than I. If somebody was not head over heels in love with me, I found life very dull. Yet nothing was further from my mind than marriage. I valued these passionate friendships as sheer poetry. Many of my earliest "crushes" have remained my lifelong friends. When I look back, it seems clear that we were, boys and girls alike, as chaste a generation as any culture ever produced.

I also enjoyed the mere sense of power a young girl derives from general popularity. There is no flattery more subtle to woman than this feeling that she can give pleasure by merely being who and what she is. Alas, this early realization of the magic gift made me conceited and self-centered to an unbelievable degree. I was told so often by men who in other areas possessed critical acumen that I was the greatest woman on land or sea that I accepted the verdict as self-evident. For several years to come I was in love chiefly with myself, an ecstasy that cost me and others much pain before life cured me of this intoxication.

During my senior year at Barnard I had only two hours of formal study to complete. I was not permitted to include these in my junior program as nobody was allowed to desecrate the holy routine by completing it in three years. It was also a misguided attempt to chastise a wayward youngster of nineteen who had never shown much respect for the academic atmosphere. Many colleges are more sensible today and let their students maintain their own pace as long as the required total number of courses have been completed. But it would be far better if we telescoped the college curriculum and also that of the high school into three years. The bright students can accomplish this with ease, and those without an aptitude for book-learning would be far better off if they were prepared for active life and work at the end of high school or of the junior community college. It is an absurdity, an appalling waste of time and energy, to insist upon the regulation four years of high school and of college, whereby most students cannot begin their professional training or their business careers before they are twenty-two.

Although I returned to college reluctantly, it was a blessing in disguise. For I met John Dewey, whose philosophy became one of the most enduring influences in my life. I was not sensible enough to elect one of his courses. I knew nothing about John Dewey when, as president of our Philosophical Society, I happened to invite him to address our group. For the first time a college professor spoke to all that was native in the saner aspects of my character and all that my other college work had left untouched after I gave up mathematics and physics — to its love of reasoning from facts rather than from abstract concepts, to my childhood happiness in human associations as the richest and widest manifestation of life. I had had several courses in the history of philosophy with Montague and Woodbridge which I enjoyed as mental calisthenics. Now for the first time I encountered in Dewey a deep and moving philosophy that was based squarely upon the empirically manifest instead of upon the occult. Here at last I found myself upon a path that I had unconsciously sought, a path to knowledge grounded upon observation and experience rather than the futile juggling of a priori suppositions.

Dewey also encouraged my love of freedom and my intuitive drive toward self-development for he brought the two together by his teaching that freedom is in reality the power to change one's disposition and character through intelligent choice and discrimination. This was a salutary lesson for a

rebellious youngster whose rash impetuousness was henceforth kept in check at many critical moments by Dewey's
cool reminder that freedom increases only if we weigh the
consequences of any course of action through intelligent
appraisal of the possibilities involved. What he gave me was
an inner gyroscope for the tempestuous seas upon which I
lived.

How could I not love and revere a teacher who had
brought such a genuine, constructive, modifying discipline
into a lonely, unguided young life torn by strong and conflicting desires? Obviously I could derive only a mere inkling
of Dewey's immense range of thought at this immature time
of life. By good luck his daughter Evelyn was a college
friend of mine and invited me occasionally to come home
with her for dinner. Dewey's modest, almost shy personality and his granitelike yet sensitive features, struck me as
the highest type of native Americanism that I had ever encountered. Never will I forget the picture at the Dewey
dinner table where half a dozen youngsters made a cheerful
conversational din while at the head of this gathering sat
Dewey, so lost in thought, so unperturbed by our talk and
laughter that I wondered what was going on behind his
domelike forehead without ever daring to interrupt his
meditations. For John Dewey I felt that sense of admiration
and awe which my nature needs and which I consider the
highest spiritual influence in life.

It is but natural, therefore, that I am outraged by the stupid attacks now made upon Dewey's educational theories and
upon his philosophy by people whose statements prove
that they have not read his books and could not understand
them if they did. The most absurd of these accusations is that
Dewey's progressive theories of education would fasten Socialism upon our schools. This flies in the face of everything

that Dewey preached over and over again. Here is just one of the many shafts he hurled at educational indoctrination, Socialistic or otherwise: "A genuine energetic freedom will manifest itself in a jealous and unremitting care for the influence of social institutions upon the attitudes of curiosity, inquiry, weighing and testing of evidence. I shall begin to believe that we care more for freedom than we do for imposing our own beliefs upon others in order to subject them to our will, when I see that the main purpose of our schools and institutions is to develop powers of unremitting and discriminating observation and judgment."* That kind of freedom is, to be sure, anathema with people who in a period of world-wide revolution still hope to preserve the *status quo*.

Other traditionalists who claim that Dewey is antireligious, betray similar ignorance of his innermost nature. Dewey is not religious if we confine religion to the various Christian orthodoxies. But he is beyond a doubt the most religious of contemporary thinkers if religion is interpreted as an intelligent and persistent search for the highest human values.

Dewey's confession of faith was put on record in his essay "The Religious in Experience," which contains an inspiring definition of God: "It is the active relation between ideal and actual to which I would give the name 'God'. . . . But the function of such a working union of the ideal and actual seems to me to be identical with the force that has in fact been attached to the conception of God in all the religions that have a spiritual content: and a clear idea of that function seems to me urgently needed at the present time." Said long ago, this admonition was never more important than in this era of religious ambiguity and spiritual darkness.

What Dewey has done continuously over a long span of

* *Philosophy and Civilization*, page 297.

years is to point out the emptiness of doctrines that are put forward as basic truths in separation from systematic consideration of the method by which the alleged truths are arrived at. Basic truths have been treated by the most influential philosophy as if they were direct deliverances of a faculty called reason or intellect in complete separation from the experiences by which they are reached. Dewey insisted upon the inseparability of all doctrines that are entitled to rank as truths, a conviction for which life itself affords ample proof.

What Dewey calls the religious element in experience — arriving at truth through the interaction of the ideal and the actual whereby new values are realized which serve, in turn, to create still higher ideals and so on continuously — points the way to a religiosity of the most promising and elevating nature to a society in flux. Dewey has neither the overoptimism of the nineteenth century that scientific knowledge would lead automatically to the development of human goodness and social progress, nor has he the pessimism of this postwar era as to human nature which has led to a revival of the doctrine of original sin. But his moral science, which uses physical, biological and psychological knowledge to illuminate and guide the activities of men, represents a happy balance between the overweening pride of the nineteenth century and the tearful self-abasement of the present. His philosophy creates a basis for reconciliation of religion and science, which Whitehead has termed the crucial problem of modern civilization.

It is therefore a sad commentary that many people fail to understand the reasons for the pre-eminence of this greatest of contemporary American thinkers at a period when they need his guidance more than ever.

Little do these critics know, and little did I know as a

mere schoolgirl when I first encountered this great genius, that here is the man who has built a foundation for democracy which will never crumble, who emphasized what we so sorely need to remember in this corrupt age, that the world in which we live and strive, succeed and are defeated, is preeminently a qualitative world, and that life itself without quality of thought, feeling and action is meaningless.

When I spoke at the dinner in celebration of Dewey's eightieth birthday I had already been active in public service for many years. I was proud to confess that his quiet voice, with its call to freedom, social conscience and public service, had reverberated in my ears throughout years of egotism and introversion until its summons became compelling, and reinforced by related influences, broke down the last walls which separated me from a life of conscious devotion to my community, and eventually to my country. I had a long way to go before that happened. Only then did I become a serious student of the many works which Dewey had published during the interval. With far more awareness of what he called "the religious element in experience," I was better able to understand and to live his admonition that "those goods approve themselves whether labelled beauty or truth or righteousness which steady, vitalize and expand judgment in creation of new goods and conservation of old goods." *

This ultimate endeavor to live life on the high plane which Dewey revealed to his students, reconciled me eventually to all the many frustrations, hardships and disappointments of my college years. But that is a small part of the debt of gratitude I owe him. I believe I would never have married the man I did — the greatest good that ever befell me — if Dewey had not counteracted my *Sturm und Drang* with his inspired common sense. I still wonder how, in

* *Experience and Nature,* page 417.

the midst of all my mental and emotional confusion, I ever had enough of the sacred fire he called discrimination to recognize and accept wholeheartedly the one teacher among all our learned teachers who was the most truly learned of them all and who has kept the learning process alive in me until this very day.

CHAPTER IV
New Horizons

When I announced to my family just before graduating from Barnard that I intended to do newspaper reporting, my mother wept and my father said solemnly: "I would rather see you dead." In those days women who had to earn a living rarely thought of any other occupation but teaching or clerical work. And teaching to me was anathema, chiefly because it would condemn me to a world of petticoats. In the newspaper profession at that time there were only some half-dozen women, and most of them were "sob sisters" who did feature stories for the sensational press rather than straight reporting. My conservative parents were not the only persons who saw me headed for a hazardous career when I got a job on the *Morning Sun,* at that time one of the most literate and brilliant papers published in America.

In 1907 the *Sun* had on its staff such famous journalists as Will Irwin, Frank Simonds, Frank O'Malley and Al Thomas. Never had a woman set foot in the city room. It was well known that the *Sun* would have none of them. Chester Lord, the distinguished editor, broke this rule for me, I think, only because it appealed to his lively sense of humor. During my senior year the constant need to make money led me to call upon Mr. Lord to suggest that I report college news items for him. He ran most of my stories about Barnard, but later when I asked him for a regular job, he replied: "We don't employ women on the *Sun*."

"That's why I want to work for you," was my rejoinder. This amused him. "All right," he said. "You're on space, five dollars a column. You won't get any assignments from me. Go ahead and see what you can do."

But I did get assignments every now and then, especially to interview people who had refused to see a "real" reporter. If some recalcitrant bank president who had admitted me out of politeness looked over his spectacles and said in fatherly tones: "Aren't you very young to be doing work of this kind?" I knew I was going to get my story.

I took good care not to get underfoot in the stuffy, battered old city room of the *Sun,* for fear of losing my job. If I had a late story, I wrote it in a little six by eight cubicle that served as anteroom with all the traffic going back and forth. The men who did not ignore my existence treated me as a harmless joke.

The *Sun* seldom sent more than one person to cover stories for which the A.P. would detail half a dozen crack reporters. My ignorance was so complete that I would have come to grief over and over again, had not the men from other papers gone out of their way to help me. Mr. Lord had let me cover the voluntary charitable institutions probably because nobody else wanted to bother with them. When Governor Hughes decided to inspect all these organizations soon after I received this assignment, I suddenly had a job on my hands with which I was unfitted to cope. But the other reporters recognized how green I was and frequently wrote my story as well as their own, taking care to make the two versions sufficiently different. I particularly remember one semi-intoxicated, battered old fellow who sat next to me at the press table when Governor Hughes made his final speech at Carnegie Hall. Realizing my ignorance of the subject, of how to handle the political angles involved, and how to write the story, this kindly creature marked the passages in the Governor's speech that I had to use and outlined my whole piece for me before we left the hall. It was the best schooling in journalism anyone could have had, but the danger I constantly ran of ignominious failure was a terrible strain.

My uneven earnings were another source of worry, as I was anxious to keep down the family indebtedness to which my father had grown ever more indifferent. In a good week, my maximum earning was $40. To make this I fell back on illustrated Sunday features such as the dog cemetery in Hartsdale, which even in those remote days was one of the hackneyed pieces of which people never seem to tire. Or I would fill in by braving snake charmers in apartments crawling with reptiles or tracking down stories at the insane asylum on Ward's Island. Nothing daunted me, if only it promised additional income. But in the worst weeks, when I got no assignments and found few that suited the city desk, I would draw next to nothing from the nice old paying teller who always tried to comfort me when he handed me the humiliating sum of five or ten dollars.

My zeal to discover curious people who would make good copy led me to explore a new gallery where photographs were considered art, a revolutionary thought in those days. I remember walking into a little attic room on the top floor of 291 Fifth Avenue, the door of which was marked PHOTO-SECESSION. A slightly built man, with beetled eyebrows, named Stieglitz introduced me to another young chap named Steichen. Though I was supposed to do a number of other things that day, I forgot all about them and spent six hours, from 11 A.M. to 5 P.M., discussing the future of photography versus painting with these ardent young rebels. Thereafter if life seemed too dull or too discouraging, I would repair to "291," as this famous institution was later called, and refresh my spirits with discussion of the battle that Steichen and Stieglitz had begun to wage against the academic smugness then prevalent in the American world of art. A gusto for life and beauty, a flouting of accepted traditions and relief from the ex-cathedra pronouncements of professorial pundits was what delighted me in these two new friends. It seems Stieglitz's passion for perfection had given him the idea of publishing the finest American photographs in a magazine called *Camera Work* and exhibiting them at 291, where Steichen had a one-room studio. He had tried lithography as a commercial venture but so much of the product had been thrown out as unsatisfactory that his father finally said, "Alfred, you'd better retire. I can't afford to keep you in business."

It is not difficult to explain the lift these two independent thinkers gave my troubled spirit at this precarious period of my life. I was rebellious without knowing why, and lonely in my discontent. When Stieglitz launched his humorous thrusts at the sterile teaching of the art schools, I found my antagonisms toward the equally conventional academic atmosphere of my college days explained and justified. I felt at 291 that my sails were filled by the free air I craved.

But my spirit of rebellion did not extend to the political or social fields. Mr. Lord had relented and given me fringe assignments such as the coverage of Socialist meetings. The chief orator at my first Socialist dinner was Elizabeth Gurley Flynn, recently arrested as a leader of Communism, who was then a "girl orator" of sixteen or thereabouts with long black corkscrew curls that were a part of her act. Her romanticized appearance and her vague emotional diatribes about the poor and the oppressed were of a piece. She had little education and no common sense, but a flowing and inexact vocabulary which aroused boundless enthusiasm in her audience. From this and similar orgiastic meetings I developed a contempt for American radicalism from which I have never wholly freed myself.

At that time the Socialist party had men of character and intelligence among its leaders, such as Eugene Debs and Morris Hillquit, but I encountered chiefly an ill-assorted group of psychopaths, of whom the Flynn woman was typical, with nothing in common except their rootlessness and discontent. It is a curious fact that most reform movements in our country have been cursed by a lunatic fringe and have mingled sound ideas for social progress with utopian nonsense. The Socialist crackpots, effeminate men, and masculine women, who were very much in evidence at the meetings I covered, invariably shouted for the centralization of power in the Federal Government and the nationalization of industry, instead of emphasizing the saner aspects of the Socialist program. Remembering my father's support of Bryan and his free-silver plank, I was revolting not only against the same fatuous left-wing extremism but also against the sound liberalism which was far more characteristic of my now rejected father influence. In fact I began to look upon all political activity as a sorry mess with which I could not be bothered.

As regards social problems I was equally indifferent. My regular assignment, coverage of the State Charities Aid Association, the Charity Organization Society, and the Association for Improving the Condition of the Poor, bored me profoundly. I had not the slightest feeling of sympathy for welfare programs nor for some of the distinguished leaders like Edward T. Devine and Homer Folks, who guided them and who years later became my friends and co-workers. To be sure, I had taught summer schools in the slums of the city. Year after year I spent two months in close contact with social conditions far more appalling than any that exist today. These experiences left me with nothing but a feeling of revulsion. For my activities were undertaken simply to earn money, and work undertaken for that purpose never gets under the skin.

If I was indifferent to the poverty of others it was partly because my own family situation had deteriorated economically. My brother Bill was working in Montana and Fred was married with family responsibilities of his own. That left me to cope alone with our household expenses and with my oversensitive and overcritical attitude toward my father. "Why worry about the poor?" was my frame of mind. I, too, was not only poor but always hopelessly in debt, as my father at this time was spending money much faster than he or I could earn it. That there were impoverished millions who were contending with long working hours and low pay, as well as horrible conditions of labor in sweatshops and mining areas, found no trace of sympathy in my egotistical young mind. The devil take them. I had my own problems to think about. We are still bringing up too many youngsters, capable of better things, to exactly that frame of mind.

This ignorance of social problems was fairly general among my contemporaries. It was due not only to our academic education but to the social climate of the period, which discouraged progressive, to say nothing of radical, social ideas. I need only point out that before World War One no Western governments had as yet accepted the responsibility which has now become their major concern, of raising the standard of living for the masses, and of shap-

ing a better life for the people as a whole. The right to
private property was still so sacrosanct that one coal operator
stated during a coal strike which took place shortly after my
graduation: "We own the mines and we shall do with them
as we please." Economically it was the day of ruthless exploitation of national resources and of labor, with much
grim poverty taken as a matter of course. Minority problems were ignored. The Negro's economic and social status
was appalling. Yet the first time I heard our treatment of
the Negro mentioned as one of America's greatest injustices
was a year later when I was living in Europe. In other
words, my asocial frame of mind was not unique but characteristic of the majority of Americans.

In spite of my political and social aloofness, I had a distrust of our country's preoccupation with material progress
which was characteristic of my romantic father. I was not interested in "getting ahead in the world." In response to a
canvass made by one of our professors during senior year
as to our future plans, I startled the good man by replying:
"I want to know and to be and to do." My questing soul
wrestled anxiously with this vague program.

I liked my newspaper work. I liked its freedom from
routine. I enjoyed reporting facts in such a way that a
higher truth shone through the surface of reality. I enjoyed
being able to help pay the family bills. Yet with all this I
lacked a sense of direction. I was playing with life and
I could not understand why I was so restless and discontented.

Then one day I met a Barnard classmate. "You're just the
person I need, Ag," she greeted me. "I'm giving a ball next
week with all sorts of amateur performances for entertain-
ment. The girl who is dancing the 'Merry Widow Waltz' has
a jealous husband and he won't let her do the part with a

man. You've got to help me out and play the part of Prince Danilo."

The night of the ball I was cavorting about in my dashing uniform, when a young man I did not know came up and spoke to me. "Didn't I see you at the American Galleries on Lincoln's Birthday?" I admitted that I had been there to look at an exhibition of Japanese prints. "I thought so; now you have to meet a friend of mine," he said.

"Oh do I? Why?" I asked, intrigued by his eagerness.

"My friend and I saw you there and we promised that the one who met you first would introduce you to the other. It's up to you to help me keep my promise."

The following Saturday this young man gave a theater party at which I met his friend, my future husband, Eugene Meyer.

Echoes of their conversation came to me later. While they were examining the Japanese prints, Eugene said to his companion: "Do you see that young girl over there?"

"Yes, what about her?"

"She looks interesting. I'd like to meet her."

"Well, in that case, you'd better speak to her or you may never see her again."

"If I speak to her now," said Eugene, "she won't like it. I'm sure one of us will meet her."

So these two made an agreement that the one who met me first would introduce me to the other. In the vast city of New York I met the friend within a week and Eugene the following week.

But nothing was further from my mind than serious interest in this new friend or any other. I had decided to go to Paris to do postgraduate work at the Sorbonne. Europe was my real objective and the Sorbonne merely a respectable excuse.

I chose to go to Paris rather than Germany partly, I am sure, as a reaction against something passionate and uncontrolled in the German nature as illustrated by my own father. By leaving home for France, I was trying desperately and consciously to escape from my own unruly disposition and father complex. I was sorry to leave my mother alone with her household cares, but I knew that my father would never again face his own financial responsibilities as long as I was there to foot the bills.

As I had not been able to save any money at the rate of five dollars per column, I borrowed $500 from a friend, fully confident that I could pay the debt when I returned. I also promised the Sunday editor of the *Sun* a number of feature articles which I hoped would stretch out my capital indefinitely.

As things worked out I had a traveling companion, Nancy N., one of my college friends, who had made up her mind to come along just two days before we sailed. In my farewell talk with Eugene Meyer I happened to tell him that Nancy was just as eager as I to try her wings in Europe but had decided she couldn't afford it. "How much have you got for this expedition?" he asked. He laughed heartily when I said five hundred dollars. "How long do you think that will last?" "Oh, six months at least, but I shall earn more by doing interviews for the *Sun*." "Well, you tell your friend that somebody will lend her five hundred dollars, who doesn't care whether she pays it back or not." I told Nancy the news without mentioning the name of the benefactor and, presto, she accepted at once.

Not until I had married Eugene did he confess that he hated to see me start my Odyssey alone and had suggested this loan to make sure I had a chaperone. I had as good reason as Nancy to be grateful for this generosity. It made the first months of adjustment very much easier and gayer.

We sailed on August 4, 1908, on the *Rotterdam*. Embarked upon the high seas, I began to feel rather lonely. At our table sat Dr. Harrigan, Director of the Massachusetts Board of Health, who was seeking relaxation in Europe after a heart attack. He had the deep wisdom and the humor that is not unusual in experienced medical men. I was always unconsciously looking for father substitutes, so he adopted me for the voyage and encouraged me to pour out my confidences. Dr. Harrigan's sympathy for my hopes and fears was mingled with a salty realism that acted upon me as a tonic. He called me "Angelface," ironically. "Never," he declared, "have I seen such shrewd innocence." I wish he could have known what courage he gave me when I was in dire need of reassurance. I never forgot his parting shot. Half in jest, half in admonition, he said: "Angelface, you will always find your way. Never fear." It was like a blessing—which became all the more sacred when shortly after arriving in Paris, I received news of his death.

CHAPTER V
Europe

As I look back it is startling to remember how little good art there was in our country at the beginning of this century. The Metropolitan Museum had not yet been enriched with the innumerable important private collections that have been left to it since that time. The Frick Gallery did not then exist in New York, nor the National and the Freer galleries in Washington, nor the many excellent museums of various kinds that have sprung up in our cities from coast to coast. The competition among American millionaires in the acquisition of great masterpieces was to prove a major contribution to the cultural development of our country, which can best be appreciated by those who date back to the time when there was little opportunity to feel the historical and aesthetic stimulus of great architecture, painting and sculpture.

Never did a neophyte accept his spiritual revelations more religiously than I, when by slow degrees I became initiated into the artistic traditions of Europe. It was a homecoming, a recognition that life to be life must know from what it stems.

Paris, the very streets of Paris, were like music to my starved senses. As I crossed the Luxembourg Gardens every morning on my way to the Sorbonne, from a little flat in the

Rue le Verrier which I shared with Nancy, the form and color of this enchanting little park enlivened by the playing children never ceased to act upon me like a revelation of perfect harmony. All history sprang to life from the medieval architecture of the Cluny Museum, Notre Dame and the Sainte Chapelle to the eighteenth-century façades of the royal palace at Versailles. In the Louvre and Luxembourg galleries, I saw and studied and drank in like a thirsty child the color and beauty of form that I had never seen in America.

And the theater! The Comédie Française was still in its glory. Mounet Sully made Sophocles' *Oedipus Rex* an experience all the more searing because he was almost blind in his old age. George Behr recited the verses of Théodore de Banville with the lilt of genius. Coquelin and Réjane at the Porte Saint Martin brought the comedies of Molière to life. Sarah Bernhardt's voice still rings in my ears with the despairing shriek: *"Que m'importent les autres? C'est lui que j'aime."*

By standing in line for hours, we Latin Quarter students got tickets for the first night of the Russian ballet, that incomparable dream of loveliness then making its debut in the Western world. Pavlova, Karsavina, Fokine, Nijinsky and Mordkin were at the height of youthful grace. But these great dancers were just a few among many. It was the discipline of the whole group under Diaghilev's direction that created the vision of perfection. The Bakst settings heightened the fairy tale and legendary atmosphere. Who has not seen the Russian ballet between 1909 and 1912 has no concept of what ballet can be.

When at a later performance the tall figure of Chaliapin walked upon the stage in the golden crown and imperial jewel-studded robes of Boris Godunov loaned by the Czar for this first appearance, the audience was awed into a solemn stillness. And when his unbelievable, fresh and sonorous voice poured out into the hushed silence, something between a gasp and a sob issued from that sophisticated, enraptured Parisian audience.

Another artistic treat that could be had for nothing was attendance at some of the High Masses at the Madeleine or Saint Sulpice which on special occasions were sung by members of the Opéra. I wrote my mother an enthusiastic letter about a certain High Mass at Chartres. We entered the cathedral on a snowy day and the combined beauty of the music, the nobly arched Gothic interior, and the iridescent light that filtered through the stained-glass windows made such a deep impression on me, that my mother wrote back at once and warned me "against the aesthetic seductions of the Catholic Church!" I became so entranced with the clear diction of the French people, especially the singers and actors, that I took lessons in singing to place my voice correctly, and in diction to speak French with more precise enunciation—lessons which were to help much later in my as yet unanticipated career of public speaking.

How could lectures even by professors as brilliant as Seignobos, Debidour, or Bergson compete with these vivid artistic impressions? It merely amused me then that Debidour's passionate lectures on the need for the separation of Church and State should raise ructions in the classroom and violent outbursts in the streets between Royalist and Republican students. It seemed to me as to all Americans of that era a dead issue. I know better now.

I went faithfully to the Sorbonne and to the Collège de France until spring, but in my memories those purely intellectual impressions are all but wiped out by the art and the artistic personalities I met.

After a week at the American Student Hostel, Nancy and I moved into a comfortable little apartment of four rooms and kitchen. Together with food, laundry, and all minor expenses this cost us each $36 a month. We made it a favorite gathering place for students of every nationality, most of whom lived in primitive *pensions* or in dilapidated, poorly heated studios. Our conversations, which often lasted through most of the night, were gay and stimulating. Oh, the faith, hope and optimism of those days in 1909! The friendliness between the Russians, Germans, Poles, French, Italians, and the welcome they gave to us Americans, was in itself something to be remembered and cherished.

And yet there was a shadow over this European mentality, as we discovered when Emperor William rattled his saber in the spring of 1909. My Austrian friend, Mary K., whom I called "Alt Wien" (Old Vienna) because of her irrepressible good humor, came in tears one morning to see me. Had I heard Kaiser Wilhelm's threatening statement? No, I hadn't. Nothing was further from my mind than politics. Mary was shocked by my ignorance. For her the Kaiser's saber-rattling meant that her two brothers would have to go to war at any moment. "Mary, you're insane," I gasped. "People don't go to war any more. We're too civilized for that nonsense. Reason and diplomacy are the tools of nations today, not violence." This categorical statement was no comfort to her. I was just an impetuous American who could afford to be ignorant of European tensions because we had the Atlantic Ocean to protect us. And yet my blithe dismissal of the whole war scare finally calmed her nerves.

My indifference to the tenseness of the European international situation and to politics in general, which this conversation betrays, was so complete that in retrospect it is dif-

ficult to excuse. In the interviews which I sent home for the
Sun I talked not only to the literary and artistic personages
of the day but to political leaders. I must have written my
interviews like an automaton. Madame Pichon-Landry,
whose father was a former prime minister, made several efforts to interest me in the women's movement for equal
rights and in other social battles of which she was a militant
leader, but all in vain.

I had enough personal experience of the frightful poverty of my fellow students at the Sorbonne, and of
the French working class in general, to awaken the social
consciousness of anyone not totally blind to such questions.
But I wrote home in noncommittal fashion that the *femme
de ménage,* a woman with a family, who cleaned our apartment one-half day per week, received as current wages thirty
cents in American money of which five cents was a tip. So
preoccupied was I with the artistic superstructure of society
that I could not see the rotten timbers in its foundation
which were soon to bring the weakened edifice tumbling
about our ears. And the people with whom I associated were
just as unaware of the deluge to come.

Though I avoided most Americans in Paris, as I had not
gone abroad to remain at home, I loved to visit the family of
my friend Edward Steichen on the Boulevard Montparnasse
and the apartment of Leo and Gertrude Stein on the Rue
de Fleurus. Steichen and I had met at "291" when I visited
that gallery as a reporter for the *New York Sun.* My friendship with Steichen has ripened over the years as few early
friendships do. My children have loved this warm, great-
hearted man since earliest infancy. He has become a part of
our family history which he has recorded over the years in a
superb series of photographs. Today he and his lovely wife,
Dana, live not far from us at Ridgefield, Connecticut, in a

fascinating modern house of his own design, overlooking a lotus-filled lake framed on the opposite shore by steep, wooded cliffs. Here Steichen grows even finer delphiniums than those I admired in his garden at Voulangis, France, forty years ago. The world has changed since we became friends in our turbulent youth and we have changed with it, but these outer and inner transformations have only served to strengthen the multitude of common interests which first brought us together and which have expanded as we ourselves became more mature and more sensitized by experience. New friends are like a fine champagne, sparkling and delightful, but old friends are like a rich old Burgundy that has ripened slowly into perfection. In October 1950, at my husband's seventy-fifth-birthday dinner, to which many old friends came from far and near, four of them made short talks: Bernard Baruch eulogized his business acumen, General Bradley his public service, Joseph Pulitzer his career as a newspaperman, but Steichen, as the last speaker, captured the hearts of all with his tribute to the family.

In 1908 and '09 Steichen was still alternating photography with painting, but his doubts as to the function of easel pictures in our modern society had already begun, an inner turmoil that resolved itself soon after his final return to America by a complete renunciation of painting in favor of photography. What helped him arrive at this momentous decision, was his service during the First World War in which aerial-reconnaissance photography by its practical contribution to the human struggle for survival, gave him a new sense of the close relationship which art must maintain with the contemporary social scene.

During my Paris year I came to feel a real sympathy for Leo Stein and genuine respect for his artistic judgment. But I was hampered in my relations with Leo because I conceived an immediate antipathy for his sister Gertrude. It is no doubt one of my limitations that I have always distrusted masculine women, and found their self-assertion distasteful. Gertrude Stein also offended my aesthetic sense, for in her middle thirties she was a heavy woman who seemed to squat rather than sit, her solid mass enveloped by a monklike habit of brown corduroy.

Most of the visitors to the Stein apartment in 1909 paid little attention to Gertrude. The center of attraction was Leo's brilliant conversation on modern French art and the remarkable collection mostly of contemporary paintings which he made at little cost with the aid of his independent and exacting judgment.

Leo was cruelly shut off from easy communication with others by his inner conflicts. But his extreme sensitivity, introspection and overly severe self-criticism aroused sympathy rather than aversion. When we looked at his collection together, he spoke little, but his occasional words and the intensity of his feeling revealed the modern paintings one saw with him in their highest significance. Leo Stein was the only one of the many contemporary art critics I have known, not excepting Berenson, Roger Fry, or Meier-Graefe, who achieved complete integrity in his relationship to aesthetic values. It is a great loss to the world that Leo never acquired until late in life the facility of these other critics in expressing his more profound ideas on the relationship of art to life.

What hampered him was his passion for honesty, clarity and exactitude. Though both he and Gertrude have been vague as to the ultimate reason for their eventual estrangement, what must have contributed to their separation more than anything else, was Gertrude's indifference to all the honest values that were most sacred to Leo. For Gertrude was and remained, in my opinon, a humbug who lived when I first knew her in 1909 on what she could assimilate from Leo, and later, on what like a busy magpie she could glean from other artists and intellectuals among the avant-garde thinkers in Paris.

Fortunately I also met ultramodern artists of the most profound honesty and simplicity. One of these was Brancusi, the Romanian sculptor who fought his way laboriously from realism to a high concept of abstract form which never lost its earthy roots. There was no "blague" in Brancusi's development, no levity, none of the sleight of hand or superficial cleverness in which Picasso indulged. His evolution was as natural as the growth of a tree, because it was guided by his thoughtful, imaginative and original nature. My friendship for Brancusi was later shared by my whole family and has lasted to this very day, because we all, including every one of the children, love the man's quizzical, witty and profoundly honest temperament as well as his art.

I cannot remember when I first met Darius Milhaud. But I owed him my introduction to contemporary French music, and in the postwar years, to some of the members of Les Six, a group of ultramodern composers among whom Milhaud, Honegger, and Poulenc are best known to American audiences. Their leader, Erik Satie, was the chief inspiration in those days of these highly gifted men. Satie's peculiar genius, his sense of the ridiculous, his staunch independence in art as in life, his extreme poverty due largely to a fierce and defensive pride, his loving and lovable nature, can still make my heart ache with the fervent wish that our sad contemporary world could produce more artists of Satie's integrity.

At one of our gay suppers in Brancusi's studio, in July 1929, when I revisited Paris, the hostility that existed be-

tween the modernists and the classicists was brought home
to me. Despiau had just completed a bust of me which was
purchased by the Luxembourg Museum. I had kept it a
deep secret from my good friend Brancusi that I should allow a pupil of Rodin's to do a portrait of me. Not knowing
this, Milhaud called to me across the table, "I think
Despiau's bust of you is superb." Brancusi looked at me as
if I had driven a dagger into his heart; he fell into an op-
pressive silence which ruined the remainder of the evening.
When I bade him good night he gave me a look of defiance.
"I'll show you what a portrait of you is really like," he murmured sadly. Two years later he had finished the black marble abstraction which he called "La Reine pas Dédaigneuse."
His indignation over Despiau's more realistic sculpture had
produced another masterpiece.

The only woman in Paris who made a deep personal impression on me was Madame Curie. I used to meet her twice
a week when we took fencing lessons at the same Salle
d'Escrime as the best exercise for busy people. Our instructor, Monsieur George, informed me that she was a physicist
who worked all day in a laboratory with her husband. This
impressed me, but less than her personality, a mixture of
feminine sensitivity, high seriousness, and a rapt intellectual
preoccupation such as I had never before encountered in any
woman. I was puzzled by a feeling of awe in her presence.
"Who is she?" I asked myself. Her own shyness made me
almost speechless. She raised my conception of what the female character could be. Here, I said to myself, is a woman
to emulate. It was the first time an ideal of femininity had
touched my imagination.

During the spring vacation I went to London, which
seemed a gray and cheerless place after the brilliant be-

flowered gardens of Paris. But it was an epoch-making visit. While examining the collections in the British Museum, I wandered by chance into a small room where some delicate paintings were exhibited the like of which I had never seen. Sensitized by my concentration upon the arts in Paris, I was no doubt well prepared for what happened. That at any rate is the only rational explanation I can give for the fact that I fell in love at first sight completely, hopelessly, and forever with Chinese art. It was, as the French express it, a *coup de foudre*. Here I felt was my spiritual homeland, here was a fineness and vitality of line, a subtle division of space, a rhythm and a sureness of vision that transcended reality and transformed it into its highest significance. Here was an attitude toward life I vowed there and then that I must explore to its uttermost depths. It was a vow faithfully kept. It determined the main direction of my intellectual activity for the next eleven years. To this day Chinese art from the Shang to the Ming Dynasty, a stretch of four thousand years, remains for me the most exalted continuous record of the human spirit.

After my return to Paris, spring burst into full bloom and my heart danced with animal joyousness at the sight of the world's most beautiful capital under a sun that is nowhere more brilliant nor more welcome after the long gray days of winter. I spent much time with Rodin, whom I had met through my friend Eugene Meyer. Rodin took me under his wing because he enjoyed my eagerness to learn. A curiously warm friendship sprang up between us which I had to defend now and then against his sensual attitude toward all women. Nothing I could say ever explained to him in convincing manner why I was unwilling to pose nude on horseback with javelin in hand for a statue of Boadicea which he had in mind, but we became even warmer friends as the

result of our argument. The time and attention he devoted
to my education moved my heart with eternal gratitude.
Often we would wander through the Luxembourg Museum
or the Louvre while he explained in meticulous detail why
this sculpture was good and that inferior. Unforgettable was
his admonition to see beauty beyond surface manifestations,
as we stood in the Luxembourg Museum in front of his own
sculpture of the desiccated body of "La Belle qui fut Heaul-
mière." Sometimes we would repair on a Sunday afternoon
to the gardens of the Palace of Versailles when the foun-
tains were playing, and Rodin would evoke the great *fêtes
champêtres* of Louis XVI with such vividness that I could
see the whole magnificent panoply of the French eighteenth
century rising before my eyes. I met many of his distinguished visitors at informal luncheons at Neuilly. Of them
all I was most grateful for seeing Gustav Mahler at close
range for several days, when Rodin invited me to be present
while he worked on a bust of this composer who had genius
stamped on his nervous features more distinctly than almost
anyone I have ever known.

One day a slender, pale, blondish young man whisked
through the room and gave me and the Duchesse de Choiseul,
a great friend of Rodin's, such a hostile stare that I asked the
cher maître who he could be. "Oh," he replied, *"C'est un
poète allemand qui m'aime beaucoup. Il s'appelle Rainer
Maria Rilke."* The name in 1909 meant nothing to me but
with my naïve American ideas about the relationship between men I received a distasteful impression of this now
famous poet, which his whole subsequent life and works
have only increased. His subservient adoration of Rodin was
repulsive, and his ill-suppressed jealousy of the beautiful
women who came and went in the studio, struck me as
venomous. He was obviously an embarrassment to Rodin,

though like all artists Rodin enjoyed the ardent worship he received from Rilke.

When I left Paris, Rodin gave me a superb drawing of the great Japanese actress, Hanako, in a brilliant red kimono, sinking to the ground just after committing hara-kiri in one of her most famous plays, the name of which I no longer remember. This drawing with a warm dedication, *"en souvenir et en attente"* written by my great teacher, now hangs in my bedroom as one of my most treasured souvenirs of the happy and fruitful months I spent in Paris.

As several European friends had asked me to visit them during the summer, I planned to leave Paris in the middle of June. Nancy had left for home in February because her funds were exhausted. But I had earned almost enough to pay my $36 per month of living expenses, and with the help of small sums which my mother insisted upon sending me now and then I still retained the greater part of my initial loan of $500. I had given up our apartment after Nancy's departure and taken a room on the sixth floor of a *pension* opposite the Seminary of Saint Sulpice, where board and lodging cost me only $30 a month *tout compris*. These living quarters had neither bathrooms nor heat. We could get a tepid bath for ten cents at the American Student Hostel. Never in my life have I shivered with cold as I did in Paris. Yet I was indifferent to all discomforts because I lived wholly in a realm of ideas. The stark outlines of European history, with which I had come to Paris, were coming to life as an artistic and cultural continuity of incredible splendor from the earliest Egyptian sculptures at the Louvre to the nineteenth-century paintings at the Luxembourg Museum. This was a revelation so intoxicating and ennobling that I was radiantly happy unless the thought of my return to what seemed a drab America thrust itself into my consciousness.

These aching premonitions I resolutely pushed aside. After all, the summer would cost me little but third-class railroad fares, which meant that I could plan a visit to Italy during the autumn. When I said good-by to Rodin, he gave me a rambling lecture on what I was to see in Florence and Rome, analyzed with rapid pencil sketches the geometrical balance of some of the famous sculptures, and promised to continue my art education by letter. It is typical of my careless youth that I kept only a few of these drawings and the many illustrated letters which Rodin sent me during my Italian visit. I was so spoiled by the incredible kindness of the great and the lowly that I accepted everything with delight but without a shade of awareness that I was singularly fortunate. I was too happy to be grateful, too preoccupied with an exalted strain of music singing itself within my breast.

When my train pulled out of Paris, I watched the dome of Sacré-Cœur fade into the distance with a sadness and regret such as I have seldom felt at any rupture with the past. The tears flowed and flowed down my cheeks. Gradually I became aware that the strains of Dvorak's "Humoresque," then not the hackneyed piece it is today, were reaching my consciousness through my painful reflection that one can come to Paris for the first time once and never again. I turned from the window to the only other passenger, a young man softly playing a superb violin. "Excuse me for intruding on your sorrow," he murmured, still playing, "but I felt this was the only thing I could do to show my sympathy." He was the second violinist in Ysaye's famous string quartet. During the next two hours he diverted me with his music, and such personal charm that I forgot my melancholy and we were gay friends when he had to change trains for Brussels.

My three weeks in Munich were hilarious, thanks to the introductions of my friend Alfred von Heymel, whom I had met in New York through a German friend, O. J. Merkel. Von Heymel was a character such as could only develop in the pre-World War One European international world. Brought up by a wealthy Bremen mercantile family, he was obviously not wholly of German parentage for in appearance he might have been a twin brother of the Spanish king, Alfonso XIII. He was a brilliant, cultivated, undisciplined, utterly charming aristocrat with catholic tastes that flew in all directions. On one occasion, hearing that I was arriving at the Bremen station at 7 A.M., he insisted upon meeting me; he had just finished translating Marlowe's *Edward II* into German. So entranced was he with his own artistic handiwork that I was forced to sit down on a baggage truck in the cold gray dawn of a North German winter while Alfred read me his version of the second act. He had reason to be enchanted with himself. It was the best of his many literary efforts. But besides fancying himself as an author, von Heymel deserves the chief credit for founding the famous Insel Verlag publishing company. He made several excellent art collections and was famous throughout Europe as a crack gentleman steeplechaser.

Reinhardt, the German theatrical producer, who was at his creative best in those early days, put on a performance of Aristophanes' *Lysistrata* that summer, which was Greek comedy as the Greeks themselves might have experienced it. The whole action took place on a flight of steps, which ran the width of the stage; the humor had lost none of its bawdiness in the German version, and the acting, costuming, lighting were a miracle of artistic achievement. I was also enraptured by Moissi, then in his early twenties, as Hamlet. He was the most convincing Hamlet I ever saw, and the translation of Schlegel so euphonious in its faithfulness to the original that some passages became clearer to me in their psychological bearing on the hero's development than ever before. How wonderful the stage was then the world over! And how disciplined! In New York many years later when dissipation had hurt Moissi as an actor, I heard him read the lovely German translation of Hans Christian Andersen's "The Princess and the Pea." His diction was still intact and I would go a long journey, on foot if necessary, to experience such artistic perfection today.

In the Munich of 1909 Hugo von Hofmannsthal was the central literary figure around which one devoted group rotated, whereas another coterie despised von Hofmannsthal and burned its incense before Stefan George. I knew members in each camp. If von Hofmannsthal wrote a new poem, Rudolf Alexander Schroeder, a young poet, wrote a critical review, and Count Harry Kessler would follow with an appreciation of Schroeder's appreciation of von Hofmannsthal. Then von Heymel would publish all of these productions in superb editions de luxe with comments of his own. It was all very ingrown — a matter of utmost seriousness to the people involved, and very entertaining to this observer. Nevertheless these highly cultivated people around von Hofmannsthal were great humanists with standards of taste that have never again been attained in Germany by a literary coterie. Von Heymel died early in the First World War, and the work of von Hofmannsthal suffered from his inability to adjust himself to the postwar world. But Schroeder grew steadily in stature, made an excellent translation of Homer's *Odyssey* and is still celebrated as one of the few

German poets who lived through the Nazi debacle without losing his personal standards and values.

But the George crowd, especially the women, had a morbid, self-abasing veneration for the *Meister,* which set my teeth on edge. I was told I could see but not meet him. Nobody who was just passing through Munich could expect to meet this deity. "Even we hardly ever speak to him when we are in his presence," they assured me solemnly. "It is enough for us to see and adore him." George was, to be sure, a gifted poet, but to my democratic nature, this psychopathic hero-worship smelled of decadence and of something which in later life I would have called Fascism.

I was not sorry to leave the hothouse atmosphere of Munich for the Austrian Tyrol, where I spent a month climbing mountains with Mary K. and her circle of Viennese friends. Her brother-in-law was Dr. Julius Tandler, the famous professor of anatomy and Socialist leader, who, when Minister of Health, built the workingmen's apartments in Vienna that were later their stronghold during the revolution of 1929. In those happy prewar days we were so gay together, swimming in the lake of Seeboden while the white-capped mountains towered around us, that I feel a profound melancholy when I think of the tragic life that lay in store for this genial scientist and friend of the people. My slab-sided build looked so absurd among the buxom Austrian girls, that it became the source of many off-color witticisms. "Jonny" (all my Austrian friends call me Jonny), "as an anatomist I can assure you you have a handsome skull but otherwise you are what I can only describe as a double Amazon," was one of Tandler's more respectable jokes at my expense. After the First World War when we met again for a mountain-climbing expedition in the Jungfrau region of Switzerland, Tandler told me that he had been asked by the

Austrian Government to build underground bombproof and gasproof shelters. I felt as if I had not heard right. "What for?" I gasped. "For the next world war, of course," he said. "But, I refused. I told the officials that another world war would ruin civilization and that I had no interest in preserving a few specimens of the human race."

Tandler became so morose after the workers' revolution failed that he went hopefully to Russia on the invitation of Stalin to build a nation-wide health system for the U.S.S.R. There he died of heart failure. I heard it may have been hastened by the fact that he had become as thoroughly disillusioned with Communism as with the authoritarian governments of Western Europe. For the liberal humanitarians and Socialistic idealists like Tandler, there was no balm to be found during the interval between the two World Wars. They saw with broken hearts the growing triumph of evil men like Mussolini and Hitler, and the degradation of human character which these tyrants brought about.

While we were climbing in the Tyrol the Chinese landscapes which had made such an overwhelming impression on me in London would rise before my eyes time and again, especially when the bases or tops of the highest peaks were obscured by a bank of mist. These recurrent fogs were responsible for one of the most hilarious international evenings. We were high in the region of the Ampezzo Valley when suddenly impenetrable clouds obscured everything but the next step. Tandler, who knew every foot of the way, guided us safely to one of the nearest mountain huts that are scattered over the European ranges. It was built to accommodate eight people, but on that perilous evening about thirty people converged upon it. As sleep was impossible we broke the hard and fast rule of the Alpine Clubs that silence must fall at ten o'clock. Women in those days toured the mountains in long skirts. I became a sensation when I changed my wet clothes to trousers and a white turtle-neck college sweater. If the guestbook of the Hanover Hut still exists there is a poem in it to an American girl called Jonny. This motley crew of various nationalities, who did not know each other's surnames or stations and cared about neither, then settled down to an evening of music, laughter and dancing characteristic of the free, decent, cultivated people who love the ever-present dangers involved in mountain climbing, and the rarefied air of what Nietzsche called *Hoehenluft.*

The Florentine painter in the Louvre had caught my imagination and aroused a strong desire to see their work in its native environment. So I bade my gay Austrian friends farewell and traveled by way of Venice toward the Tuscan hills. In Florence I lived for $30 a month in an old palazzo at the corner where the Ponte Santa Trinitate crosses the Arno, then called the Pensione Piccioli. After I had studied the Italian arts and language all day — I was reading Burckhardt's *Renaissance* and Dante's *Paradiso* — Rudi, an American friend who was studying voice, and I would take our supper to the hillsides of Fiesole. While the monastery bells tolled the hour or called the saintly brotherhood to prayer, and the moon shed its quiet splendor over the enchanted landscape, Rudi would sing Mendelssohn's *"Auf Fluegeln des Gesanges,"* and other German *Lieder.* No wonder my letters to my mother at this time reported "the world is really a very nice place."

When Italy was Italy, the trains assuredly and happily did not run on time. On one occasion the habits of Italian engineers nearly cost me my life. I was going from Rome to Siena on a belated express train which was dashing along at terrific speed to make up for lost time. The heat was intolerable. So I left my seat and stood in the corridor between the cars. As usual I was reading. The train suddenly rounded a sharp curve, the door next to me flew open and I pitched out head first. I grabbed for a brass handle, missed it, and when my head was some two feet over the roadbed, a man who had been standing next me caught my extended left arm and hauled me safely back onto the platform.

I arrived in Siena at noon. Before doing any sight-seeing, I consumed a good lunch with a bottle of Orvieto wine which the waiter recommended. It was new to me, and as every connoisseur knows, it is deceptively light. When I got to the cathedral I was much surprised to find that the columns were wheeling around the empty nave in black and white circles. Gradually the wheels stopped and I discovered that the alternate layers of black and white marble in the columns for which I was not prepared and the heavy Orvieto wine with which I was well prepared, had played a trick on me.

The primitive painters of Siena, and especially the Byzantine frescoes at Ravenna, served to inflame my curiosity to see more Oriental art: I find in my letters home that I asked my mother whether she would mind if I returned to America by way of Japan, where I wished to study the famous collections at Nara Temple and other Buddhist shrines. Fortunately she reminded me that I had promised again and again to be home by Christmas. What helped me to keep my word was my low exchequer. The small sums of money I had earned in Paris by writing for the *New York Sun* petered out during my subsequent travels. Also, my poor mother had written me desperate letters about the behavior of my father and my brother Bill, who had a habit of falling in love with one girl after another —

each of whom, with good reason, seemed to my mother a highly undesirable addition to the family. The double duty to pay off my indebtedness and to look after the family left me no alternative but to say farewell to ecstasy and to shoulder the grim responsibilities of everyday life.

When I finally sailed for home it was with deep misgivings. The return from Parnassus to the dusty routine of common days was difficult for all young Americans in those days. The surface of American life offered no stimulus to a sense of history and to a cultivated love of beauty such as had become to me the very breath of life. Like most of the self-exiled Americans, I too had little feeling for the native American scene. I could not, like Walt Whitman, hear America singing in every home and village its strong melodious song of love and faith in democratic ideals. I was caught between two great traditions and after a year and a half in Europe belonged neither to the one nor the other.

But I was happy when I thought of seeing my family and my friends. While I was in Europe Eugene Meyer had come over for two memorable visits. He became an institution with my Latin Quarter friends. The gaiety of his personality was memorable as he took flocks of them to dine at the Tour D'Argent, whose succulent feasts none of us could otherwise afford. Occasionally he would organize automobile trips to see the nearby chateaux and cathedrals. My Paris friends adored him. *"Quand est-ce que votre type va revenir?"* they asked frequently.

During the home voyage, always in the back of my mind was the apprehension of seeing my father again and of living once more under the shadow of our conflict. Christmas was the usual festive occasion it always had been in our family, with affectionate memories of childhood days in the ascendant. But the next month at home was so emotionally confused and stormy that I began to regret that I had ever left my beloved Europe.

I was torn between my much older relationships to some of my devoted artist friends and my far greater confidence in Eugene Meyer's character and personality. They threw me into such emotional confusion that I decided I needed time to weigh my feelings away from the impact of these totally different masculine temperaments. The only chance to do that in peace was to put the ocean once more between me and them. While lunching with Eugene at the old Waldorf Hotel, I confided my half-formed decision to go back to Paris, where I could straighten out my inner confusion.

"I have decided to get away for a bit myself," said Eugene. "I'm going to take a trip around the world, starting next month."

"Why, how long are you going to be away?" I asked in hurt surprise. "Oh, at least six months," he replied casually.

The thought that he was about to disappear for such a long time made me feel as if the ground were caving in beneath my feet. For several minutes I was silent. Then I heard what seemed to be my voice saying very quietly: "I'm going with you."

"I know," replied Eugene. "I have your tickets."

Three weeks later, on Lincoln's Birthday, exactly two years after our chance encounter in the American Galleries, we were married. We spent two weeks at Eugene's farm in Mount Kisco, which is still our real home, and then left for a trip around the world.

CHAPTER VI
The Female Egotist Gets Married

Our leisurely honeymoon around the world brought to Eugene and me an ever-increasing respect for the Oriental peoples, that grew as our knowledge of their ancient culture deepened. As we knew that it was impossible to see the fine collections of Chinese art in the country of its origin, we made an effort to see in Japan as many of the temple museums and the private collections as possible.

The Japanese are apt to withhold their finest objects from those who have no real appreciation of art; but they take all the more delight in sharing their treasures with anyone in whom they discern a genuine love of beauty. Their courtesy to us still lingers in our memories like a delicate fragrance. The Temple of Nara, the Imperial Palace at Kyoto and the Sumitomo bronzes were highlights of our visit. We were almost as grateful for the ceremonial atmosphere with which these courteous people surrounded our visits to their temples and homes as for the education we derived from the magnificent bronzes, potteries and paintings, both Chinese and Japanese, whose quality exceeded our highest expectations and fixed our determination to continue our study of these great civilizations. It will help Americans to understand the Oriental attitude toward Americans if I narrate one experience with Count Okuma. While drinking tea in his superb garden, Eugene asked him to explain why the Japanese were quicker to take advantage of our Western achievements than we were to learn what Eastern culture has to offer us. Count Okuma evaded the question at first, but when pressed for an answer replied: "Because it is easier to acquire material than spiritual knowledge."

We journeyed to Korea, Manchuria, Siberia, Russia and Europe, before returning to New York City where we took a house in East Fifty-first Street, and where I was obliged to concentrate upon the intricacies of housekeeping, for which my academic and artistic education had given me not the slightest preparation.

Incredible as it may seem, it had never occurred to me until I became engaged to Eugene that it would have been impossible for me to marry anyone who was not well-to-do. For the only dowry I had to bring a husband were my father's debts and my own. The fact that I could confess to Eugene the perpetual nightmare of my relationship to my father was a release from deep inner tensions. It gave me the sharpest realization that I was no longer alone in the world and the added blessing that henceforth I would be free of a crushing burden of debt. Let no one undervalue the importance of economic independence. If wealth is not allowed to dominate the individual's thought and action, it can be the greatest boon. It affords leisure for the enrichment of the personality; it affords freedom of speech in times such as these, when people are apt to lose their jobs if they offend any of the powerful authoritarian groups, social, economic or religious; above all it brings the joy of helping others quickly and efficaciously.

Even more than my own freedom from money troubles, I enjoyed the fact that my mother could now lead a happier life. Not that her worries or mine were wholly removed as far as my father was concerned. They merely changed in nature after my marriage as my father's ideas of grandeur and munificence expanded; for it can be said in his favor that he was as free in giving when he had money as he was in borrowing when he had none. When he died in 1913, I could not mourn him. But the tragedy of this indifference was a torture far more acute than is the suffering of children who have lost a beloved and respected parent.

It is all the more humiliating to admit that I repeated my father-pattern and rebelled inwardly and outwardly against the suddenly imposed responsibilities of marriage. During the first few years of marriage I behaved as if the whole world were in a conspiracy to flatten out my personality and cast me into a universal mold called "woman." So many of my married college friends had renounced their intellectual interests and lost themselves in a routine of diapers, dinners, and smug contentment with life, that I was determined this should not happen to me. I wanted a big family but I also wanted to continue my life as an individual. The problem was not without its complexities, in an era when most married women were not supposed to look beyond domesticity.

At the time I saw no other outlet for my intellectual curiosity than more academic training. I had just sense enough to realize that my undergraduate work had been too abstract, and therefore I chose factual subjects, biology, economics and history. In the last field I chose James Harvey Robinson's famous course at Columbia entitled "Mind in the Making." The book which he later wrote with that title is only a faint reflection of his momentous impact as a lecturer. He had a humorous obliqueness in the presentation of human frailties and absurdities that led us imperceptibly toward the cultivation of intellectual freedom and the criticism of established mores, habits and ideas. In this reactionary period when clerical authoritarians seek to replace the will of the people as the foundation of our secular society with "the will of God" and its clerical interpreters, it is salutary to remember that Robinson traced the blind acceptance of authority back to its primitive roots and warned us that the past does not furnish us with reliable, permanent standards of conduct and public policy. "Is not the moral overrating of the past our besetting danger?" he would query the class. "We have the great task before us" — he answered his own question — "of gradually replacing archaic beliefs, tastes and scruples by others which will conform more closely to our accumulated knowledge and the actual conditions in which we live. Otherwise our struggle toward the good life must perforce be feeble, which indeed it is."

We seem intent today on repeating another piece of human stupidity against which Robinson warned us. "As animals and children and savages, we are all naïvely and unquestionably intolerant. But the present-day attempts to eliminate by force those who wish to reorganize social and economic relations are just as hopeless as the attempts of the Inquisition to defend the monopoly of the medieval Church." He was then speaking of Socialists as the "heretics" of the period, but his admonitions are now relevant to our reaction to Communists. Robinson was emphasizing the obvious truth that punishment of heresies, now such an obsession with some of our political leaders, is futile. Bad ideas he insisted, such as Socialism or Communism, can be defeated only by good ideas which capture the loyalty of people not by force but by persuasion.

It was through my acquaintance with Robinson that I met Charles Beard, who together with his wife, that staunch scholar, Mary Beard, later became good friends of ours. At this time, about 1915, Robinson, Beard and Dewey began to discuss the need for a free and liberal university, talks which laid the foundation for the New School for Social Research. I caught their enthusiasm and not only helped in a modest way with financial contributions toward the establishment of this important institution, but also worked in psychology classes when in 1919 it opened its doors on West Twenty-third Street.

Dewey, Beard and Robinson were empirical idealists with a profoundly hopeful attitude toward the future of American democracy. But Veblen, whom I also met through Robinson, repelled me by his black pessimism and an emotional instability which seemed to me to affect his thinking. Nevertheless I recognized that his insistence on the importance of studying the connection between economic institutions and other aspects of our culture was of far-reaching influence on American scholars. These four men together with Justice Holmes, whom I was to meet later in Washington, dominated the thinking of America for over twenty years. They created the country's intellectual climate until the financial crash of 1929 and the subsequent depression broke the courage of many superficial, utopian liberals and tempted them into an intellectual and moral surrender to Marxism. Through fear they lost the ability to criticize objectively the debacle in which they were enmeshed.

The apostasy of these men of little faith proves that the intelligent control of social situations which is basic to democratic progress will always be endangered in periods of acute emotionalism such as ours. Only the most secure mentalities have retained the truly American liberalism which these five men initiated in philosophy, law, history and economics. They were statesmen of ideas who gave our country the best integrated democratic system of thought it has evolved since the days of Jefferson and Madison.

Aside from these academic interests, I took a lively part during the first years of marriage in the struggle to interest New Yorkers in modern French art which Alfred Stieglitz was carrying on in his little hole in the wall at 291 Fifth Avenue, Edward Steichen's New York studio. Here it might be just as well to set straight the record that Stieglitz was solely responsible for this entertaining and important cultural development. It was Edward Steichen who, on his return from Paris, gave Stieglitz the idea that he should supplement the campaign they had been conducting on behalf of photography by educating Americans to the importance of the contemporary arts both in France and at home. It was Steichen who discovered John Marin in Paris and sent over his water colors together with the works of such other American artists as Edgar Maurer, Max Weber, Arthur Carles; French painters and sculptors such as Cézanne, Rodin, Matisse, and the exquisite drawings of Gordon Craig's stage settings which had such a revolutionizing effect upon the art of the theater from Moscow to New York.

It was not Stieglitz but his later sycophantic admirers who built him up into a lone David fighting the American Philistines of art singlehanded. In his youth Stieglitz was too American not to be a truly co-operative genius. He loved without as yet patronizing the small group of artists and amateurs who made the impact of "291" so truly creative and influential in its early days. While I was in Europe, Stieglitz with typical kindliness had sent me every number of *Camera Work*. Now I was again taken into the brotherhood as "The *Sun* Girl," the name Stieglitz had given me when I first went down to interview him for that paper.

"291" was an invaluable antidote to the artistic aridity of New York and took the place of the Bohemian student atmosphere that I had found so congenial in Paris. We were a motley crew and not the least charming was a man named Arthur Lawrence, an interior decorator who occupied the back of "291." His quarters were constantly invaded and his sample chairs worn out by all sorts of curious people who had nothing better to do than to sit around and argue out their conflicting views of art, philosophy, and life in general. The personalities changed but the excitement was constant. Big Bill Haywood, the I.W.W. leader, and the violent but sincere rebel, Emma Goldman, dropped in occasionally on the theory that in our own way we were fellow revolutionists. Hutchins Hapgood was a frequent visitor. Poetry was represented by Carl Sandburg and the more inarticulate, exquisite personality of Alfred Kreymborg. Marsden Hartley, Arthur Dove, Max Weber, Walkawitz, Picabia and other newcomers to the artistic scene were given a chance to show their work. Mabel Dodge, now Mabel Luhan, created a flurry of interest. She gave parties which the "291" crowd enjoyed; but they also resented her. She played with life as if it were a game in which the stakes were not very high.

In those days Stieglitz did not take himself so seriously and joined heartily in the pranks we played on the public. On one occasion Steichen painted a fake Cézanne water color to see whether anyone would spot it amongst the real ones, a jest that got somewhat complicated by the fact that it was the most popular picture in the exhibition. Stieglitz also encouraged the crazy experiments Marius De Zayas and I made in illustrated "stream-of-consciousness" writing, which was supposed to weld together the plastic and literary arts in a depiction of various levels of a total state of mind. We were on the track of something only dimly understood before the crucial analyses of Freud and the works of such successful explorers of the unconscious as Virginia Woolf and Joyce became popular. In its gay and unpretentious way "291" in its garret days had much more influence on the predominantly conservative artists, critics and dealers than did the formal rooms which Stieglitz later called "The American Place."

This outlet for the continuation of irresponsible habits I had formed in Paris created a lively tug of war between my desires and my duties, made all the more acute by my absurd lack of preparation for motherhood and for the social responsibilities of marriage. During the first months after our return to New York City I would come home and throw into the wastepaper basket the calling cards that had been politely deposited by our friends. I took care not to look at the names so that my rudeness to all these people would not be individualized. This was my idea of simplifying life, whereas it created the most unpleasant complications both for my long-suffering husband and for me.

When my first child was born in 1911, I insisted upon nursing her, but would often forget to go home at the hour for feeding the poor child if I happened to get too deeply involved in one or the other of my extramural activities. Reminded by over-flowing breasts that I was neglecting my infant, I would rush back, conscience-stricken, to find the nurse walking the floor to comfort a baby screaming with hunger. Why my husband did not quietly murder me and call it a day is more than I can now understand. When I told Eugene recently that I was writing this quasi-sociological biography, he said with ample justification: "What a pity you have already used the proper title for an earlier book" — that title being *Journey Through Chaos.*

Eugene's gift for seeing the ludicrous side of my outrageous behavior may well have been his most effective educational method. I recommend it to all desperate husbands. Luckily I had one good quality that is essential to any wife. I always found my husband's humor enchanting, especially when its barbed shafts were aimed at me. In my later and wiser years I, like many other heavy-handed writers, have produced some solemn lucubrations on marriage in an effort to stem the divorce rate. None of us, I fear, has sufficiently emphasized the central difficulty. Most husbands and wives take each other's shortcomings too seriously and their own not seriously enough.

In my own case it was the resurgence of traditional forces that came to my rescue and brought about a gradual acceptance of family responsibilities. It was the instinctive return to my happy childhood memories of family life, the strong family feeling of the numerous Meyer clan — Eugene's dignified and handsome parents and their eight children — together with the disciplinary influence of a husband whose character has always set a high standard of behavior. But I was so imbued with my own importance that the gradual turning of my eyes away from self and out upon the world was an agonizing ordeal.

In the spring of 1914 when I had been married four years and had two children, I still felt so rebellious over what I interpreted as the crushing of my personality that my wise husband, who would not leave the U.S.A. because he smelled the coming of war, encouraged me to revisit my beloved haunts in Europe on my own. I went first to Germany as I had never seen the Japanese collections of the Berlin Museum nor met Otto Kümmel, one of the finest connoisseurs of Oriental art, whose life later became a tragedy, when he succumbed to the lure of Hitler's promises and became an enthusiastic Nazi. He was not the only good man whose judgment went astray as a result of years of unbearable poverty, insecurity and suffering.

In Paris, Raymond Koechlin, Director of the Amis du Louvre, a highly discriminating collector, and young Bing, whose father had been the earliest importer of first-rate Oriental art, became my boon companions and showed me the otherwise inaccessible private collections of the Parisian eccentrics. A visit to the Louvre Museum with Koechlin after closing hours is enshrined among my memories. In the tomb-like silence of the great galleries, the beautiful record of the ages became far more poignant. All the delicate objects seemed to breathe more freely and project their loveliness throughout the whole atmosphere. Eumorphopoulos, Oscar Raphael, and Sir Herbert Read in London were also members of this little international group of Oriental enthusiasts who vied in amicable fashion to outdo each other in the acquisition of art treasures. In America, of course, Charles L. Freer, of whom I shall speak later, was the most daring explorer of the hidden mysteries and glories of China and probably the most cultivated among this highly cultivated group of people. What fun we all had together!

The last really carefree, happy week I spent in Europe was at the end of July 1914 at Voulangis, where Steichen had a peasant house and lovely garden in which he was hybridizing and cultivating his marvelous delphiniums. Here Brancusi, De Zayas, and the American artists Katharine Rhoades and Marion Beckett, two of the most beautiful young women that ever walked this earth, joined us. Mercifully unaware of impending doom, we enjoyed each other and the lovely French countryside whose tranquillity was so soon to be shattered.

I had promised Eugene to come home on a Dutch steamer which sailed on July 31. Again I was fortunate. It was one of the last boats to leave the European shores before the First World War broke out and destroyed forever the Europe I knew and loved. When the Germans threatened a few weeks later to break through at the Marne not many miles from Steichen's house, he was too near the front to know what was happening and cabled to Eugene for advice as to what he should do. "Suggest immediate orderly retreat," was Eugene's cryptic reply. Steichen lost no time in retreating with his family to our farm in Mount Kisco where they spent the rest of the summer.

The voyage home from Europe was a turning point in my life, not only because World War One erupted while I was still on the high seas, but because I had a terrible nightmare that gave me an insight of permanent influence upon my life. I dreamed that I was watching the sunrise, an experience that I had often in childhood shared with my father. Gradually the sun was eclipsed by the face of my father which looked straight at me with an expression of sadistic triumph. He did not speak. It was unnecessary. The expression said more clearly than any words: "I've got you. You are just another me. And you are doomed to go the way I did." I awoke in terror. My agony, guilt and self-contempt were so acute that I can feel them today. I could not help but realize that in escaping from my home responsibilities, I was repeating the self-centered, irresponsible conduct of my father which had cost his wife, his children, and especially his only daughter such bitter humiliation. The Bible does not take modern psychiatry or just plain human intelligence into account when it says that the sins of the fathers shall be visited upon the children unto the third and fourth generations. These sins can be a source of a profound conversion if they are not deliberately buried in the unconscious and allowed to fester away like an undiscovered cancer. Like all conversions, mine had its moments of spiritual aridity and relapses from grace. The victories in a battle with the self are few and far between. The defeats are numerous and tragic. But henceforth I was not so much dedicated as caught in a process of regeneration from which there was no escape for the rest of my life.

In June of the following year my third child was born, my only son. With surprise and a feeling of guilt toward the two older girls, I realized that I now felt a ridiculous sense of achievement. Warned by the dangers of my own father-fixation, I determined not to tie my son to me as I had been tied to my father. If anything, I have been more severe in my attitude toward him than toward my daughters because nothing seemed to me more abhorrent than a mother's boy. My generation was, moreover, haunted by Dr. Freud's psychoanalysis, which by this time had become the latest rage among the intelligentsia. I feel sorry for the modern mothers who have not one but a whole swarm of famous psychiatrists to confuse their thinking and spoil their fun by reminding them constantly that love is a dangerous business. What with the women who reject their children and those who bring them up with a thermometer in one hand and a book on psychology in the other, many American children are having a hard time.

When the United States declared war in 1917, my husband closed his banking business at once and went to Washington as a dollar-a-year man, to serve on the Advisory Committee of the Council of National Defense, later the War Industries Board. At the time my conscientiousness did not reach beyond my own family circle: I took care of our chil-

dren, now four in number, settled the various houses we
rented in Washington and helped my husband by making
our home a center for the social gatherings which in Washington are an extension of the working hours. But I was so
engrossed in translating Chinese texts and in writing a book
on the philosophy of Chinese art that it never occurred to me
to make any active contribution toward the war effort. In
plain truth I sat out the First World War.

Soon after my marriage I had met Charles L. Freer, who
discovered Oriental art for America and who founded the
beautiful gallery in Washington that bears his name. Unlike the other industrial magnates to whom we owe our
many splendid collections of European art, Mr. Freer was
an aesthete in every phase of life — in his home, in his appreciation of good food and good wines, above all in his love
of beautiful women. He had many friends and many enemies as his emotions were strong and he never suffered
fools gladly. His capacity for enjoyment was as boundless as
his sensuous response to beauty, whether in the realm of art,
of nature or of human nature.

His interest in the Orient was first aroused by Whistler
to whom his whole museum is a tribute. Although the Chinese and Japanese collections fill most of the galleries, they
lead the visitor inevitably to Whistler's famous Peacock
Room which has now been restored to its pristine glow of
gold and blue. Whistler never lived to see the more exquisite paintings, bronzes and jades which Freer eventually discovered and brought to this country. Whistler's hunch as to
the probable existence of this vast as yet unknown art world
was based largely on the Japanese prints, ceramics and costumes which the China trade first brought to Europe and to
New England, and it is all the more credit to his artistic
perception that he sensed the existence of older and finer

works. There can be no doubt that Freer would never have
devoted himself with such unswerving faith to the search
for early Chinese art, had he not been infected by Whistler's
enthusiasm for the color and form, the delicacy and vitality,
above all the exquisite refinement of the various Japanese
products that he and Mr. Freer examined together.

Often when Eugene and I visited Mr. Freer while his collections were still housed in his home at Detroit, he would
read us letters from Whistler which revealed the close
friendship which unlike some of the other friendships in
Whistler's stormy life, was never troubled by misunderstandings and dissension. Both of these great Americans, one a
famous artist, the other the early creator of one of our great
industries, the American Car and Foundry Company, were
the products of a period in our history which still valued the
development of the mind and the spirit above everything
else that life has to offer.

From January 1913 until his death in 1919 in New York
City I had the privilege of studying Mr. Freer's growing collections under his guidance, and not infrequently we divided
the new shipments which were forwarded by his personal
representatives in China. As we unpacked shipment after
shipment of bronzes, jades and paintings, good, bad and indifferent, we were thrown back upon our own judgment of
their quality. Often we made costly mistakes. But this exercise
in discrimination was a profound education. It brought us
closer to China's ancient culture than the usual approach
to an unknown civilization through the study of its historical records. To the extent that his busy life permitted it,
Eugene took an active and helpful part in this exhilarating
pursuit.

At that time the whole thinking of the Western world
as to the origin of Chinese painting was dominated by the

distinguished scholar Fenollosa, who had studied in Japan under Buddhist teachers and who had become a convert to that religion. With the usual zeal of converts, he accepted what no doubt was the honest belief of many Japanese priests that Chinese painting was not Chinese at all, but had been inspired by the introspective Zen sect of Buddhism, a faith brought from India in the early sixth century.

As more and more objects were added to Mr. Freer's collection, we both became convinced that an imported religion, and particularly so introspective a religion as Buddhism, could never have evolved so deep a sense of nature's significance as is revealed in Chinese landscape paintings. We felt that only a slow and cumulative growth of the native influence could have created paintings with such power and profundity as were now coming to light in ever greater profusion.

Since the Western literature on the subject was under the domination of Fenollosa, it seemed imperative to us to examine the Chinese texts. From 1911 to 1913 I studied Chinese with Professor Friedrich Hirth at Columbia University and then with the aid of a Chinese scholar, Mr. T. Y. Leo, I spent the next five years amassing the research materials needed for an analysis of the respective contributions of Confucianism, Taoism and Buddhism to the development of the great paintings of the T'ang and Sung dynasties.

To keep this enormous task within bounds, I chose one of the most celebrated of the Sung artists, Li Lung-mien, as the object of my study and made a catalogue of all his known works together with the descriptions and comments in the Chinese art catalogues. I discovered that the life and interests of one Chinese artist was bound up with those of his great predecessors and many who suceeded him. The works of every Chinese artist, whether in the plastic or poetical arts, have the same abundance of historical overtones as their language because the unity of this great culture was never broken. Of its own accord the story of Li Lung-mien's significance spread out until it touched the first dim years of China's history, and illumined many things that the Chinese think and feel to this very day.

This sounds rather remote from the realities of American life during a great world war. Yet Chinese history and philosophy have a far more important contribution to make to democratic thinking than Americans have as yet generally realized. Chinese art helps us to find new ways of looking at life that are closely akin to our own native philosophy from Jefferson to Emerson, to Walt Whitman, to William James, to John Dewey.

The Chinese are the only civilized people of whom it may truly be said that they were at home in the world. From their earliest beginnings they put the center of gravity where it belongs in the universe instead of placing it, as Christian culture did, within the human breast. They observed the order of the cosmic mechanism with considerable astronomical knowledge, and tried to establish in human relations and the social order, the same harmony which they perceived in the rotation of the stars and the progress of the seasons. They never formulated supernatural beliefs and consequently avoided our Western preoccupation with metaphysical and theological abstractions that for centuries have eaten the tissues of the muscular Western mind like a cancer. As they were not torn between fidelity to this world and the next, they became integrated personalities who used their careful observations of nature to create order in their philosophical conceptions and in the art of day to day living.

The continuity of Chinese history from the sixth century B.C. to the end of the Ming dynasty was due to the powerful hold of Confucianism on the Chinese mentality. The Chou dynasty was nearing its end when Confucius was born; China was disrupted during his life (551–478 B.C.) by as much warring, treachery, murder and social disorder as exists today. He therefore set himself the task of codifying the ancient texts as the groundwork for an ethical system that could rescue his nation from moral and social chaos. The Han-dynasty scholars expanded his work into definite regulations for human conduct and for all human relationships, from those between the Emperor and his subjects to those between the father and his family and between the people as a whole. Moral standards had no reality except as they were translated into definite patterns of human behavior. Like our democratic philosophers, Confucius believed that people must live as they think and think as they live. Our own Henry James translated this into aesthetic terms when he said: "Form is content to such a degree that there is absolutely no content without it."

Lao-tzu, the contemporary of Confucius, states in the opening of his great work, the Tao Tê Ching: "Before the beginning of time, there was a Divine Principle, ineffable, unnamable. While it was unnamable, it conceived heaven and earth. When it had thus become namable it created all things." This is very different from our Genesis in which God creates the world and remains remote enough to see that it was good; for the Chinese the divine power becomes namable, tangible, becomes the world itself, so that whatever there be of the spiritual and eternal must be sought in the world and not beyond it. Thus the Chinese, though they built great engineering projects to protect man from the ravages of flooded rivers, never sought to conquer nature but to understand it and considered that man's highest wisdom was to be derived through identifying himself as an integral part of the universe.

Though Confucianism and Taoism were both based upon the "universal becoming" to be observed in nature, their aims differed in that the Confucians were mainly interested in the application of natural laws to group life, whereas the Taoists sought to define the law itself, and emphasized the importance of an unbroken contact with nature and nature's laws. Whereas Taoism continued to emphasize the freedom of the individual and the importance of individual contributions to society, Confucianism absorbed, preserved and developed these contributions for the good of the community and the nation. Thus these two systems, not unlike our classical and romantic traditions, were complementary and through their interaction created, not only one of the highest and most enduring civilizations the world has ever seen, but bronzes, jades and eventually paintings, especially landscape paintings, whose purity and beauty are unexcelled by those of any other people.

Emerson was very close to the character and thought of the T'ang and Sung philosopher-painters when he said: "The test of the poet is the power to take the passing day and hold it up to a divine reason till he sees it to have a purpose and beauty, and to be related to astronomy and history and the eternal order of the world. Then the dry twig blossoms in his hand. He is coalesced and elevated."

But how can I explain all that my years of study in the fields of Chinese art, literature and philosophy meant to me? The introduction to my book on the subject makes the claim which has become even more apparent today than when it was written thirty years ago, that Chinese life and thought, of which Chinese art is the sensitive record over a period of 4000 years, has an especial value for the Western world under present historical circumstances. In spite of all our scientific discoveries, the lessons of actuality and the methods of science have not yet been incorporated in our scheme of human behavior. Romanticism, abstract philosophy, and the speculatively religious patterns established by our scholastic ancestors still hold us firmly in their grasp. Chinese life, on the other hand, was founded upon a highly developed understanding of the universe, which, though lost at times, was ever recaptured and reinvigorated by later teachers who saw the value of that early wisdom.

From the point of view of my Lutheran orthodoxy this was revolutionary thinking. Like a strain of solemn music, the wisdom of the Chinese sages lifted me outside the self and taught me to look upon man and his environment as a superb, unending, continuous whole. I was released from the bondage of seeing myself as the center of my private universe and from preoccupation with the salvation of my own soul.

I was also rescued from that wider egotism which has isolated the Western mentality and hampered it from profiting by the magnificent cultural achievements of the Orient. I was freed from the prejudices of race and religion and the sense of superiority which mar the thinking of the white Christian world, and from the consequent authoritarian habits of mind which are to blame more than we have realized for the cruel exploitation of peoples the world over, known as imperialism. The chief message of my book was a call to Western man to abjure an exaggerated introspection, to renew his faith in scientific knowledge as a guide to life and to distrust all philosophical ideals that are not used as a lever for the improvement of human relations.

An interesting link between the Chinese and early American thinking was pointed out to me by Albert Schweitzer who has traced the direct influence that Confucius and his followers had upon the leading philosophers of the eighteenth century who in turn influenced our Founding Fathers. My gratitude was renewed to Jefferson, Madison and other writers of the Constitution who founded our democracy not upon the dogmas of the religious sects, but on the principles of brotherhood, respect for individual rights, for the human personality, and for democratic human relations which were instilled in these great men and renewed in the Christian tradition itself by the humanitarian faith of the eighteenth-century Enlightenment. Greater understanding of Chinese ethical humanism would not only renew our faith in our democratic principles, but furnish the basis for a valid internationalism in which Christians, Buddhists, Mohammedans, and the multitudes of no faith can all meet if the sectarian groups transcend their theological differences and emphasize the autonomy and universality of the moral world.

Thus the lesson to be learned from China's Confucianism could never be more significant for us than it is now. Its ethical aspects are a reminder which our Christian civilization needs if we are not to stand before the world as hypocrites who preach love while practicing the bitterest hatreds toward rival orthodoxies and toward peoples whose skins are of a different hue. We shall, in fact, dig the grave of Western civilization unless we implement the faith that Confucianism and democracy have in common, namely, that ethics has its roots in man's relation to the universe, that morality comes into being through honest, clear-cut human relationships and cannot endure unless it is reflected in the patterns of daily life.

All through these preoccupations with the art of China, I recalled the closely related admonitions of John Dewey which had been reinforced since my college days, fifteen years earlier, by constant reading of his later works. Dewey's philosophy contained the same message of selflessness and service, the same emphasis on the interaction of the natural and social environment as comprising the wholeness of life, the same belief that thought without action is incomplete, the same attitude toward experience ripened by discipline as carrying the universe onward by arduous, slow but imperishable accretions. I felt as if my beloved Chinese sages were alive once more and waking me from "a vast somnambulistic egotism" when, reading John Dewey's *Experience and Nature,* I hit upon the following passage:

> Fidelity to the nature to which we belong, as parts however weak, demands that we cherish our desires and ideals till we have converted them into intelligence, revised them in terms of the ways and means which nature makes possible. When we have used our thought to its utmost and have thrown into the moving unbalanced balance of things our puny strength, we know that though the universe slay us still we may trust, for our lot is one with whatever is good in existence. We know that such thought and effort is one condition of the coming into existence of the better. As far as we are concerned it is the only condition, for it alone is in our power. To ask more than this is childish; but to ask less is a recreance no less egotistic, involving no less a cutting of ourselves from the universe than does the expectation that it meet and satisfy our every wish. To ask in good faith as much as this from ourselves is to stir into motion every capacity of imagination, and to exact from action every skill and bravery.

And yet people say John Dewey cannot write!

My book, *Chinese Painting as Reflected in the Thought*

and Art of Li Lung-mien, was published by Duffield and Company in 1923, and was well received. To my surprise the first person to praise it was that famous iconoclast, H. L. Mencken. That year it won the individual award of the American Typographical Society; the popular edition sold out, but the edition de luxe containing the catalogue of Li Lung-mien's paintings and many reproductions was so expensive that its circulation was largely restricted to libraries and collectors.

I deeply regretted that Mr. Freer to whom it was dedicated did not live to see it in print. But he knew its content; "Agnes," he said to me once, "you are really on the track!" And his approval kept me close to the arduous task of its completion. My introduction ended with the words:

> His [Mr. Freer's] was the clearest vision of what China has yet to give us. I feel what I have done here as nothing but a dim reflection of his great light; founded upon his teaching and insight, it is but the beginning of that unending quest upon which he has started all who shall rightly see the Oriental treasures he has amassed — a quest not for a new world, but for this same ever present world which the Chinese knew and loved so well — a quest on which I travel happily and hopefully without the pretense of having arrived.

Even before the date of publication, my quest took an unexpected direction. Now that my ears had been attuned to receive the message, I was called upon "to throw my puny strength into the unbalanced balance of things," and to devote myself with weak powers but ever-growing courage to what John Dewey calls "the coming into existence of the better."

CHAPTER VII

Boss Ward—the Last of the Barons

OUR LIVES are not as individual as we would like to think. As a young woman my college classmates fixed their impression of me in one of our yearbooks by quoting Henley's poem:

> I am the master of my fate;
> I am the captain of my soul.

It described the overconfident pride with which I faced the world in order to conceal the doubts that haunted my adolescence. As a far more humble adult, looking back on a stormy life, I am convinced that no human being is master of his fate, and that we are all motivated far more than we care to admit by characteristics inherited from our ancestors which individual experiences of childhood can modify, repress, or enhance, but cannot erase.

When Eugene and I became engaged, it was as great a surprise to his family and friends as it was to mine. Dire prophecies that the union of two such tempestuous and independent people would not last six months were freely expressed by several of our mutual acquaintances. My circle of artistic friends, whose pet name for me was Gloria, hung out the crepe because I was throwing myself away upon a mere businessman. One of them gave me a gold vanity case as a wedding present marked *Sic transit Gloria*. Eugene's friends, who looked upon this brilliant, highly respected young banker as the catch of the town, were aghast that he should waste himself upon a penniless harum-scarum like me.

But eyebrows were raised with the greatest disapproval by the many people who looked askance at mixed marriages, which were not as common then as now. My Lutheran mother thought the world was falling apart because her daughter wanted to marry a Jew. Eugene's parents accepted me as they accepted everything their surprising son did, with philosophic resignation and with the generosity of spirit that was one of the most charming traits of this dignified couple.

These are what I termed the surface reactions to our marriage. What neither our friends nor we ourselves thought about at the time, is that Eugene's ancestral background and mine were startlingly similar. Several of his forebears and near-relatives were Jewish rabbis. His great-great-grandfather had been Preposé des Juifs, the administrative head of the Jewish population in France under Louis XV. His great-grandfather was one of the rabbis appointed by Napoleon I to the Sanhedrin, a congress called to determine the legal status of French Jews. As a result of their findings Napoleon I gave to the Jews of France and of countries then occupied by France full civil rights. His uncle, Zadok Kahn, was Grand Rabbi of France in more recent times. These learned men handed down to him the same almost puritanical spirit, the same regard for the sacredness of family life, the same moral fervor and adherence to principles that motivated the Hanoverian Lutheran clergymen in my own ancestry. We were both to discover, as we met life's problems together, that common ethical ideals are probably the most essential bond that man and wife can possess, aside from a certain level of cultivation which may be a concomitant.

I do not recommend mixed marriages if one of the partners entertains the primitive belief of orthodoxies that claim there is but one path to truth and that those who do not accept it are headed for eternal damnation. It cannot be comfortable to look across the breakfast table at a spouse who is certain to enter the jaws of hell. But for more civilized people a different sectarian background is less menacing to a successful marital relationship than differences in moral, mental, and spiritual aspirations. To put it another way, it is less important that both man and wife should belong to the same orthodoxy than that they should both be religious. My own marriage has helped me to realize what a tolerant, universal religious spirit could arise in our country if there were more intermarrying between the feuding sectarian groups and between Christians and Jews. For my husband's far more intense spirituality has been a constant challenge to me, and a constant reminder that the Jews made the covenant with God, whereas Christians as a rule have more complacent souls because we merely inherited it.

If only Christians would realize how much we owe not only to the ethical but to the religious genius of the Jewish race, anti-Semitism even in times of deep insecurity could not become so acute as in recent years. For the creative religious spirit is a gift, just as artistic genius is a gift, possessed by some people and not by others. Americans are almost devoid of it and even the Jews amongst us are affected by our religious tone-deafness. The English are no more gifted in this direction than we are. As a purely speculative occupation those courageous dreamers, the Germans and the

Jews, have revealed the greatest sensitivity to religious thinking. Goethe saw both races as the salt of the earth. He
maintained that the Germans were dangerous in the mass
because they lack self-control, but that they could become a
greatly needed leaven in society if they, like the Jews, were
scattered over the earth.

As one who has experienced the Jewish problem from
within, I am convinced that many American Jews have a
morbid tendency to exaggerate their handicaps and difficulties. I, too, occasionally suffered the cruelty meted out to
Jews by anti-Semites. It hurt me to discover what it means
to be treated not as an individual human being but as a
nameless member of a race. There is no doubt that the Jew,
for example, has to be twice as good as the average non-
Jew to succeed in many a field of endeavor. But to dwell
upon these injustices to the point of self-pity is to weaken
the personality unnecessarily. Every human being has handicaps of one sort or another. The brave individual accepts
them and by accepting conquers them.

I do not know what is meant by an ideal marriage. If it
implies that both partners become a mush of concession, our
marriage does not meet the definition. Eugene once said to
me: "You have often irritated me, but I confess you have
never bored me." The lightning has flashed and the thunder
reverberated in our household. On the surface it was as
hectic as it was interesting. Paul Claudel after spending his
first week end at Mount Kisco, which happened to coincide
with one of my huge county music festivals, wrote me a
bread-and-butter letter saying he felt like a cat that had
been thrown into an electric fan. He added that Eugene and
I were the calm imperturbable center of the vortex to which
he had been exposed. Thomas Mann, on the other hand, who
loves his comfort and who also was a frequent guest at our

country and city homes, declared that I ran the best hotels on two continents. Both discerning artists felt that the apparent chaos of our lives was founded upon a peaceful and orderly continuity. I am convinced that the perpetual ferment that enlivened our family atmosphere was the main reason why we developed a strong sense of solidarity. The canker at the heart of family life today is sheer boredom for lack of common interests between husband and wife and between old and young.

Our five children contributed their share to the general turmoil. Since all five of them were encouraged to think independently at an early age, they soon learned to hold their own in our lively debating society. The family dinner table became famous among our friends because we were apt to ignore the opinions of our guests if we happened to differ violently with each other. When the argument threatened to become confused, my husband would constitute himself chairman of the meeting and call upon each child, regardless of age, to rise and state his case. Their greatest joy as they grew older lay in out-arguing Daddy. If he tried to extricate himself with some logical sleight of hand, he was greeted with a chorus of "boos" and hilarious laughter. To this very day we enjoy differing with each other and agreeing with each other far more than with anybody else. But the ranks close and the fur flies if any outsider tries to intimate to any one of us that some member of the group is not perfect.

We felt it important to encourage the children to bring home their friends. They did — in droves. As their tastes were very different the mixtures were sometimes hilarious. On one Mount Kisco week end Florence, the eldest, had invited Chaliapin, the great Russian basso and his whole family; whereas Bill and Katharine, who were at college, and interested in social problems, contributed some of their serious-minded left-wing classmates, who reacted to Chaliapin's joyous exuberance as if it were a personal insult that a White Russian should be so self-confident, charming and lighthearted. In the country we often sat down eighteen strong for meals week after week. I managed to keep domestic help only by painting their duties in darkest colors before engaging them.

Although Eugene and I were often away from home during the winter months, we tried to compensate for these absences by sharing the children's recreations on the farm, on occasional trips to Europe en masse which were reminiscent of the Sanger circus, and on other journeys by land and sea. What the children still cherish as their richest memories were our hair-raising pack trips in the Jemez Mountains of New Mexico with Indian guides and perilous expeditions through the Kern and the Kings River Valley of California and in the Canadian Rockies. But I never succeeded in making any of them a devotee of my favorite sports, fishing and mountain climbing. On one occasion in Switzerland when I took three of them up the Jungfrau on a day of incredible beauty after a fresh fall of snow, I thought I had captured their love of mountain peaks forever. But as soon as we got back to the hotel at the Jungfrau Joch, they refused to go on to the Monk and the Fischerwand as I had planned. "One mountain a year is enough, Mother," they declared firmly. "We're going back to the tennis tournament at Mürren." Nevertheless these shared adventures helped to make them all excellent friends, which included the in-laws as one child after the other married. This sense of belonging that pervades the second generation — so much so that the in-laws occasionally stage a rebellion of what they call "In-laws Inc." — seems to have captured the grandchildren as well. When

Bill's wife, Mary, asked their son, aged nine, who were his best friends at school, he mentioned two names but added: "Of course, I don't like them as much as my cousins."

This family solidarity was a by-product of parental solidarity. Thus, when the First World War ended and I had hoped to return to the old continuity of life in our real home at Mount Kisco, I acquiesced without question when Eugene after a year's interval decided that he ought to remain in Washington to cope with postwar problems. Eugene having suggested the need for the financing of exports, Congress had extended the powers of the War Finance Corporation into that field. Our family life, therefore, continued to rotate between our house in the nation's capital and our new house in Mount Kisco, which we had planned and built with the sensitive co-operation of Charles Platt, one of America's outstanding architects.

Early in the year 1921 I had one of those curious summons of fate that have played such a decisive role in my life. Women had finally won their prolonged struggle for the vote in 1920. The following spring I was invited by the Republican Women of Westchester County to attend their annual luncheon. I accepted somewhat skeptically as I still had an antipathy for exclusively female activities and felt no particular urge to join any political party. At this function I was introduced to William L. Ward, who for twenty-five years had been the boss of the county. I had the usual American prejudice against political bosses, and I confess I was surprised to see this very tall broad-shouldered, aristocratic, eagle-eyed gentleman. "Young woman," he asked brusquely, "what are you doing for your county?" "Nothing," I replied, "Why should I?" "Do you mean to tell me that you can live in this beautiful county and not try to do what you can to improve its government?" I dodged by confessing that I didn't know where to begin. "You begin at the front door," was his emphatic reply. "Your town of North Castle is one of the few townships that has been Democratic. The women are voting now. Why don't you help get out the women's vote and elect a Republican supervisor?"

"What's the use making it Republican?" I asked, still unwilling.

"I'll tell you why — because we have a lot of work to do for this county. We have to improve the welfare services, we have parkways to build, and we have to straighten out the county finances. And we can't do any of those things unless the Board of Supervisors will go along with me on the program."

I had heard women grumbling that the Boss would not trust them; so I said: "But the women claim you don't give them a fair break."

"They don't know what they are talking about," he came back bluntly. "They're new at this game and think they can assert themselves before they've even done the spadework of getting out the women's vote. There is only one honest use of political power — to make things better. Anybody who wants power for the sake of power is on the wrong track. Remember that." He turned away.

"Power not for the sake of power but to make things better." Those words might have come from John Dewey. Coming from a political boss they were a revelation. Here was a summons which without knowing it I had been waiting to hear ever since finishing my book on Chinese art, and it came from what I had always dismissed as the sordid world of politics. I discussed the new challenge with Eugene. Buoyed by his confidence in Mr. Ward, I enlisted.

Let me try to draw a picture of this extraordinary man to

whom I owe my political education. William Lukens Ward was born in 1856 in Greenwich, Connecticut, the son of cultured, hard-working and respected Quakers. When he was seven, his family moved to Port Chester in Westchester County where he continued to live for the rest of his life in a great stone castlelike structure which his father built in 1871. An engineer by training, he devoted his youth to his father's nut and bolt factory, Russell, Burdsall and Ward, which he made one of the most efficient manufacturing companies, with branches in various parts of the country. When he went into politics at thirty-seven, Westchester was known as a safe Democratic county. With a native genius for leadership he fought his way up in the rough and tumble of politics characteristic of the day and became Republican County Chairman of Westchester in 1896, a position he held until his death in 1933.

Together with the famous Republican chieftains who ruled the country until Wilson's election — Mark Hanna, Tom Platt, Boies Penrose and others — he helped to determine the Republican Presidential candidates at every national convention. But his chief interest lay in developing Westchester County which he ruled with the absolute power of a benevolent despot. He was often called the Duke of Westchester by the newspapers. This fighting Quaker crusader was the only one of the famous Republican political bosses who died without being stripped of his power. He made Westchester so overwhelmingly Republican that it gave huge Republican majorities even to the most unpopular state and national candidates.

Of all the Republican leaders I have ever known, only Mr. Ward had that deeply human quality to be found more frequently even in the coarsest of Tammany ward heelers. It arises out of the politician's need to evaluate human character, to work with the worst and best people and to use them accordingly. In Mr. Ward, however, this sympathy for all kinds and conditions of men was combined with scrupulous integrity, the highest objectives, and a ruthless but astute capacity for nipping skulduggery in the bud. On one occasion when I expressed admiration for the honesty of a certain politician, he remarked dryly: "He's virtuous just as long as my shadow falls across his path."

For those in Boss Ward's organization who really studied what made him tick, the tenderness, the humility and the sheer loveliness of the Quaker expression "to have a concern" took on a new meaning. He was a shy man, as Quakers often are, who covered his sensitive awareness of the intangibles by translating them into the most realistic parables. He smiled tolerantly at evil without sacrificing his major concern to make the good appear the better cause. For he knew that evil lurks in every human heart and that nobody can become a leader of men without a knowledge of evil and the ability to forgive and transcend it.

Boss Ward had two rules. Everybody came to Mohammed at Republican headquarters in White Plains, the county seat. Never did Mohammed condescend to go to the mountain unless there was trouble. The other rule was equally adamant. No politician was allowed to set foot in the Boss' old turreted stone house at Port Chester unless he was also an old associate like young Teddy Roosevelt or Jim Wadsworth. His home was his castle and he refused to have it invaded by anyone but his personal friends. There was something in Mr. Ward's stature that was over life-size as if his physical being were a monument to his large nature. When I saw him in conference with his subalterns, they looked like a lot of schoolboys interviewing a formidable headmaster. The most characteristic thing about him was the force, the velocity with which he moved, especially when he wanted to get away from people who bored him. His aloofness was protected by a slight hearing difficulty which seemed to disappear at will and by a mysterious, intimidating splendor that defies analysis even in retrospect. His whole concept of life, his carefully selected clothes of excellent cut and material, his colorful neckties chosen to match the seasons, his perfectly run household, his love of good food and drink, were all part of his aristocratic nature. His living rooms were always full of flowers which he selected and grew in his extensive greenhouses — chrysanthemums of every shape, huge double French carnations, and deep red roses. "If you are ever in doubt about people," he said one day, "look at their shoes. Self-respecting folks always have well-kept footwear." His own were made to order by the best English bootmaker. I myself used to call him "the last of the Barons."

Mr. Ward was a perfectionist in the minutest details. Nothing but the best was good enough for him and he respected the rights and the dignity of others so sincerely that he wanted the best of everything for them too. Like the most enlightened of reigning monarchs, he devoted his intelligence and gift for leadership to bringing about ideal living conditions in his Westchester principality. He literally transformed social conditions in the county and doubled property values with a magnificent network of parkways, the first to be constructed in America, with numerous beautiful parks, public golf links, picnic grounds and beach resorts. One of our residents in Tarrytown used to have a large sign on his property: "A part of William L. Ward's almost perfect world." But Mr. Ward's world was not confined to external advantages. Over the years he worked for a higher concept of the moral responsibilities of government and built up the most efficient, humane and comprehensive county welfare system that exists in our nation. He was ever conscious that his example would raise the quality of local government throughout the nation. "Girl," he said to me one day — he called us all "girl" regardless of age — "if we do a good job in Westchester, the others are bound to copy it."

When I got to work and became acquainted with the local leaders of North Castle, my township just north of White Plains, I found the women frustrated. The resistance of the embattled political male that existed all over the country when women first got the vote, was strong in North Castle. But I soon discovered that word had gone out from the Boss that I was to organize the women in North Castle. His word was law. Though the opposition continued, it was always carefully concealed.

We began ringing doorbells from house to house. What sounded like dull work soon began to fascinate me. Sometimes we were all but thrown down the front steps by irate husbands who shouted that woman's place was in the home and not in politics. But the women would drop their housework, ask us to visit and to explain to them why it was important to vote. I listened to family problems of the most intimate nature. I had to give advice as best I could on matters tragic or trivial — from the treatment of wayward husbands to the selection of a new stove. I lost one vote because I was asked: "How do you keep your fruitcake?" and gave a flighty reply out of the depths of my ignorance on this vital topic: "I don't keep it, I eat it." I who knew so little about women, was moved by their need to unburden their hearts if only to a stranger. My never-ending education in human sympathy had begun.

But this desire to be frank and friendly, to pour out everything that relieves the lonely human heart in our complex
society, is characteristic not only of women. It is true of
most Americans in every walk of life. All they require is
someone who is willing to listen. Many a time when I have
explored communities torn by sharp conflicts, I have gained
more flashes of insight into the situation from men and
women who happened to sit next to me in a drugstore, from
the janitors of apartment houses, or from groups of street
urchins than from the responsible civic leaders. These people have only to feel that they can trust you not to betray
them, to pour out all the conscious and the unconscious re-
sentments that they would not confide to their most intimate friends.

And what an admiration for the American people one
gains from these chance encounters! I cannot understand
why our novelists continue to be so obsessed with the obvious weaknesses of our society and our democratic civilization. The need to overemphasize the shortcomings of our
nation is past. Now is the moment to hold aloft for all to
see and feel the quiet heroism, the self-sacrificing public
service of little people in every local community, and the
zest for social progress that pervades our whole population.

As we women made headway in North Castle, the local
Republican leaders got uneasy. Where was the feminine
invasion going to end? Would their power wane? A few
weeks before election, they called my attention to a certain very poor-looking district in our town that I had not
covered. I was grateful and went to work. There seemed to
be a great many women in every house. What a find, I said
to myself. No, they had not thought of voting but would
like to. I explained the paper ballot and taught them how to

mark it. Would they vote Republican? Of course, they'd love
to vote Republican. We were very gay together. I never felt
more popular.

When election day came these latest friends of mine were
the first at the polls. I swung North Castle into the Republican line by a majority of fourteen out of some twelve hundred votes. Not until six years later did I learn that the men
had sent me through the red-light district. They assumed
that I would be insulted by this experience and desert politics forever. But my one-track mind was so concerned with
its educational mission that I thought of nothing else. My
political converts took such delight in my obvious naïveté
that they could scarcely wait until the polls opened to express their gratitude. Without their help the election would
have been lost.

After I had learned to organize a township, I was rewarded by being sent as a delegate to the Republican convention at Cleveland in 1924. I was also promoted to
county-wide responsibility for the women's vote but without
any official position in the Republican organization. Somewhat later I was invited to the highest state position for
women, vice-chairman of the Republican State Committee.
By that time the women also wanted me to run for Congress
from Westchester County. The Boss called me down to
headquarters and said: "Girl, you have to make up your
mind whether you want to be an officeholder or a boss. You
can't be both at the same time. I tried to combine them
when I was young and fool enough to let my organization
send me to Congress. I soon found out that a political boss is
in an ambiguous position if he wishes to profit by his own
power and run for office. Take my advice. If you really want
to serve your local community, don't look for public positions, gratitude or other rewards." The answer for me was

simple. "I don't want the steady responsibility of state or federal political positions because my husband and my family must come first; and besides Eugene would put his foot down."

Many Americans who believe that married women have the same right to a career as men will take exception to that flat statement. The question has two aspects, individual and general. Speaking as an individual I have always subordinated my activities to those of my husband because his work, whether private or public, has always been far more important to the nation and to our family than any endeavors of mine. Therefore I considered it not only a matter of loyalty but of simple intelligence to help him by supplementing his activities as best I could, whether in his public work or by taking all household worries off his hands and keeping the home running joyously, smoothly and efficiently. This meant that I could never take a steady job of any description which would conflict with Eugene's interests.

Speaking generally, it seems obvious, career or no career, that the wife who wants to hold the family together should accept her husband as the head of the household and teach her children to regard him as such. Democracy or co-operation should exist in every family, but even democracy must have leadership from the Presidency right down to the conductor of the village choir. Whether the wife has a career or a job is not the determining factor, unless it tends to neglect of the children. For the wife who loves and respects her husband can preserve his dignity as the head of the family even though, to take an extreme situation, he becomes an invalid who has to be supported by his wife. If, on the other hand, the mother is a domineering type and preempts the leadership of the family, the children's relationship to their parents is thrown out of balance and their psychic development upset. They are apt to become emotionally disturbed, and frequently very sick people.

Not only as a politician but as an old-fashioned Quaker, Mr. Ward thoroughly approved of my renunciation of public office. "All right, that's fine," he said. "Then I'll teach you how to be a boss. Sit down and get your first lesson. Harry M. is coming in to tell me he wants to be a judge. He's not ready for it. If I tell Harry that, I've made an enemy. If I get Harry to tell me that, he remains loyal and grateful. Sit down here and see how it's done."

Harry came in, sat down and told the Boss what was on his mind. I listened attentively as this astute leader of men manipulated the conversation back and forth over Harry's political ambitions and his present position in the organization. I nearly fell off my chair when after twenty minutes of discussion as to Harry's qualifications, I heard him say: "You know, Mr. Ward, I think I'd better wait awhile. I don't think I'm ready for that job just yet."

With such practical examples of applied psychology, Boss Ward guided the thinking and activities of his whole organization. We got into the habit of checking with him on every new problem and thereby saved ourselves many serious mistakes. With the acute perception of a great novelist, he taught us to observe the weakness and the strength of human nature, and how to move about among people with respect for their innate dignity and with tolerance for their frailties.

The Boss had one ever-recurring theme to his psychological analysis of leadership: "Keep your mind simple." With this admonition he tried to protect us from becoming entangled in details. It is the interrelationship of facts, he always insisted, that alone gives them meaning and makes possible the over-all vision that is the source of creative action. The test of action and the value of leadership justified themselves in his opinion only to the degree in which they increased human happiness and rendered life more reasonable. He despised random action, however well-intentioned, that had no clear-cut attainable goal in view. At the same time he was a bold experimenter when experiment was based on accurate knowledge guided by carefully formulated ideas and flexible use of all the administrative agencies involved. He reminded me of the indomitable, practical faith of men like Franklin, Jefferson and Madison, that humanity can make its own future a happy one through intelligence, courage and persistence.

When I remember how carefully we had to observe the Boss's maneuvers to understand what he was doing, and the subtle reasons for his actions, I despair of the verbal instruction in group "dynamics" that is given in our educational institutions by people who have never so much as led a Sunday-school picnic. It is the subtlest of democratic arts, which, like all arts, takes long practice to master. It can be learned only in action and by analyzing every mistake. The constructive leader is a growing personality who involves other people in opportunities for human growth. Only if the leader learns and imparts his own learning process to his followers, as Mr. Ward did, can he avoid becoming a dictator who seeks to force a closed ideology upon his adherents.

Creative leadership like that of Boss Ward is therefore a matter of reciprocity, a giving and taking of ideas that makes for mutual respect, confidence and moral development. The destructive leader, on the other hand, is an arrested personality who prevents the growth of his followers by imposing upon them his own fixed conclusions and prejudices.

Unfortunately, there are multitudes who hate to think for themselves and are grateful to the person who does their thinking for them; as a result destructive leadership is a far easier and far more rewarding task especially in a period of mental confusion such as ours. The art of leadership is one which the wicked, as a rule, learn more quickly than the virtuous. This is one of the main reasons why our big-city machines are so corrupt and why spasmodic reform movements led by political amateurs are so evanescent. Concerning New York City's government Mr. Ward used to say: "Given the indifference of the average voter, the wonder is not that it is so bad, but that on the whole it is so good."

With the eagerness of youth for pat solutions, I asked Mr. Ward one day: "What is the principal quality needed for success in politics?" "I'll give you the wisest answer to that question I ever heard," he replied. "When I was a young man just entering politics, I saw the great Tammany boss, Richard Croker, sitting alone at the race track. I didn't know him but I picked up my courage and sat down next to him. I told him I was going into politics and asked him just what you asked me: 'What does it take?' Without looking up from his race card or taking his cigar out of his mouth, he snapped back: 'Patience.' That didn't seem to me very exciting, so I said: 'Oh, yes, of course it takes patience, but what else is necessary?' Croker looked at me with the expression of a weary titan and said with finality: 'More patience.' "

Mr. Ward's own patience was inexhaustible and a greatly needed lesson for all of us. He knew with how little wisdom or honesty the world is governed, but it never caused him to despair.

Sometimes my political education in Westchester County had amusing repercussions in Washington. For several years during the prohibition era the New York City water works had a force of some hundred or more laborers working in North Castle under a Tammany henchman. Let's call him "Pat McGinnis." He had probably been given this out-of-town job because he had an uncontrollable impulse to get very drunk every so often. Annoyed by this solid bloc of Democratic votes in our Republican township, the local men decided to get rid of Pat by closing his favorite speakeasy whose owner took good care of him whenever he passed out. I did not know Pat. But when the local women told me of this plot, I was sorry for the man and announced that we would have to close all our speakeasies or none. As that was a hopeless task, Pat's routine was allowed to continue.

This was in 1927, when Boss Ward was trying to pass a charter in Westchester to simplify and improve our county government; among other provisions the charter eliminated a host of minor local positions. For the first time the Boss had his own organization against him as politicians are not given to abolishing their own jobs. On election day I was motoring from one election booth to another to try to carry the charter with the women's votes. As I was driving along the Kensico Lake Road, a man signaled to me to stop. "Mrs. Meyer, I want to introduce myself. I'm Pat McGinnis," he said, removing his hat with a flourish. "I've not forgotten what you did for me and I'm wantin' to know if there's anything I can do for you?" "There certainly is, Pat," I replied. "I'm trying to carry the charter and the men are double-crossing me. I need your votes." "Leave it to me," said Pat. With the help of Pat's entire working force, North Castle was one of only two electoral districts that carried the charter. As long as Pat remained in the county I could depend on his votes at every election.

In Washington early in 1931 my husband's confirmation as Governor of the Federal Reserve Board was being held up by the hostility of Iowa's Senator Brookhart to what he vaguely termed "the interests" which my husband represented in the Senator's confused thinking on economics. Senator Wagner, though he owed no loyalty to the nominee of a Republican President, came to the Senate subcommittee hearings and choked off many of Senator Brookhart's inane attacks on Eugene's record.

Not long after Eugene was confirmed as Governor of the Federal Reserve Board, I sat next to Senator Wagner at dinner. Immediately I told him how generous it was of him to go out of his way to do justice to my husband. "That's all very well, Mrs. Meyer," replied the Senator, "but don't forget, I'm up for re-election this year. What I want to know is — what are you going to do for me in Westchester?" So I told Senator Wagner about Pat McGinnis and his Democratic votes. "This year, Senator," I said, "you can have your own votes."

Politics in New York State were conducted on a high plane in bipartisan matters of importance when Al Smith ran the state. Our huge Republican majority in Westchester County was a thorn in Al's flesh, and we fought each other in every campaign with no holds barred; but when the campaigns were over, the Democratic women in Westchester would forget about their annual defeats and work side by side with us for our extensive welfare program. If Boss Ward needed Al Smith's help to get enabling legislation through the state legislature, he always found Al ready to cooperate in any worthy cause.

This knightly behavior went out of the window when Franklin D. Roosevelt became Governor. Throughout Mr. Ward's reign there had not been even a suspicion of dishonesty or scandal concerning the activities of the county political machine or the Board of Supervisors, although millions of dollars were involved in Mr. Ward's princely transactions and expenditures for county improvements. In August 1929, Governor Roosevelt ordered Samuel Untermyer to investigate a $948,000 purchase of land by the county supervisors for the new County Office Building at White Plains, intimating that the taxpayers had been robbed. Mr. Untermyer's accusations released to the press were meant to influence that year's election. Mr. Ward stepped into the picture and said he had ordered the supervisors to buy the land cheaply without condemnation proceedings, and if any accusations of dishonesty were to be made, they must be made against him. Untermyer thereupon called the Boss on the telephone and said he would subpoena him for questioning before the jury. "Sam, you can subpoena me if you want to," said the Boss, "but you'll regret it to your dying day." That was the end of the investigation. When Mr. Ward soon after was re-elected by the organization for the thirty-third time as Chairman of the Westchester County Republican Committee, his speech of acceptance consisted of the statement: "You have done a wise thing." The following November the organization brought out 20,000 votes above the normal Republican majority, just to show Governor Roosevelt that his plan to undermine the faith of the people in their Boss had misfired.

Franklin Roosevelt's continued feeling of bitterness toward Westchester County became evident after he went to the White House. When the depression came, Boss Ward at once organized made-work of a constructive nature for the

unemployed, bringing order into the county files, and sup-
plying labor in the park system and in numerous other departments. When Harry Hopkins organized his W.P.A.
with centralized control, one of his appointees who met me
in the county courthouse, said to me frankly: "Mrs. Meyer,
what we're goin' to do to your Republican organization is
nobody's business." With this punitive attitude, Boss Ward's
relief work was canceled. The office of the W.P.A. put the
worst type of down-at-the-heel ruffians in charge of our local
work programs; they handed out the soft jobs to enrolled
Democrats and the disagreeable ones to the Republican unemployed with the express purpose of breaking down the
county Republican control. By this time I was out of politics as my recreation work, described in the next chapter,
made active participation in politics unwise. But this dis-
honorable behavior of the W.P.A. in our county was more
than I could stand. I gathered the shameful record together
in three articles and published them in the *Washington Post,*
by that time my husband's paper, and in the *New York
Herald Tribune.*

I wrote these stories in my recreation office in the County
Office Building in White Plains. My friends all over the
county brought in the lists of bootleggers, speakeasy owners,
and other disreputable people who controlled W.P.A. jobs
in their communities. While I was out to lunch, a W.P.A.
employee sneaked into my office to read my material. As
my story was soon going to press, the W.P.A. officials shook
up their organization in the town of Rye, so that they could
blow up my records by proving that my names for Rye
were incorrect. But these smart boys did not know our
county grapevine. My friends in Rye immediately telephoned me about the plot and gave me the new list of
people who were no more respectable. I caught the stories in

time to tell what had happened and gave the new list as well as the old. As none of the facts I reported could be denied, my articles were a bombshell in Washington and I became anathema with the New Deal and Harry Hopkins. Yet there was no personal or political animus in my attacks. I was trying to defend the independence of local communities against the destructive overcentralization of government in Washington. This is the basic principle of our democracy which the New Deal undermined so thoroughly that the independence of our states, our localities, and our people was seriously weakened.

The final explosion took place when I was asked to defend my position on the importance of local government in a debate on the relief problem over "Town Hall of the Air" in February 1935 at which Mrs. Roosevelt presided. With my unconquerable faith in justice, truth, and the democratic process I did not yet know that you can't beat a central government when it is handing out billions of dollars to desperately needy people. But if I was naïve in my belief in principles, I was wily enough in the ways of politics. It was not in vain that Boss Ward had taught me: "Never go into a meeting unless you know what's going to come out of it."

I was lucky to have as my opponents three New Deal men who as speakers were hopelessly dry and dull. The audience was almost asleep when I got up and began taking the National Youth Administration apart on purely moral grounds. At once the Democratic New York City audience came to life with a bang. The catcalls and whistling got more and more violent. When I said that relief money should not be given high-school students but should be given to their parents if it was an absolute necessity, the noise was so great that I could scarcely be heard. Either I had to act quickly or be run out of the hall and made to look like a fool before millions of radio listeners. I began to pull out my ace in the hole. "Who do you think is the latest missionary sent from Washington to Westchester County to tell us how to bring up our children?" I shouted over the din. "Our latest N.Y.A. missionary is a female real-estate agent." The audience sensed that a bombshell was coming and grew quieter. "This real-estate agent is going to get $6000 a year to tell us how to bring up our children." That huge stormy crowd suddenly became so silent that I felt vindicated, and waiting a breathless instant for the audience to feel the oppression of its own silence, I said quietly: "She's Harry Hopkins's sister, Mrs. Aimee." There was a gasp of surprise, dismay, indignation. Nor was there another sound while I flayed the New Deal, the N.Y.A. and Harry Hopkins for another five minutes. I did not enjoy offering Mrs. Aimee up for sacrifice in this fashion as I knew she had formerly been an able social worker, but she had laid herself and her brother open to criticism and self-defense is the first law in any political battle.

I was also sorry to do this in Mrs. Roosevelt's presence. We were political enemies for the time being, but even on this occasion we took care to shake hands when we said good night. The thing that even Mrs. Roosevelt's most hostile critics cannot take away from her, is her womanly dignity, that quality of self-control which in more civilized days entitled a woman to be called a lady. In spite of our differences, whenever I asked Mrs. Roosevelt to help in some of our nonpolitical Washington activities, she invariably cooperated graciously and generously. In recent years our common interest in public education has overshadowed our political thinking. There is no woman whose advice I value more than that of Mrs. Roosevelt.

But the lesser New Deal lights were often insolent in their heyday. After the Town Hall broadcast, Herzog, the State W.P.A. Administrator, and his assistants surrounded me, crowded me up against the wall and demanded threateningly: "Do you mean to tell us, you're not going to co-operate with Mrs. Aimee when she comes to Westchester?" "You political amateurs," I laughed, "if you had any sense you'd know that Mrs. Aimee isn't coming to Westchester." The White House was so deluged with telegrams of indignation during the next two days that Harry Hopkins informed the press his sister had refused the appointment.

This sensational evening was my last attempt to stave off the evil effects of New Deal relief methods. For many years I suffered acutely in Washington while young New Deal whippersnappers for whom I had no respect strutted around as if no American had ever before raised a hand to make our society more truly democratic. The self-righteousness of the atmosphere was repellent. Rebeca West, who came to see me in the midst of the orgy, remarked: "When I hear them talk, I can't make out whether they are drunk or sober." "They're drunk all right," I replied. "Drunk with power." When the Roosevelt administration made havoc of our Federal, state, and local relationships, I felt as if a lot of savages walking down a beach had found a delicate piece of machinery among the driftwood and were hitting it with a club to find out how it worked.

It must be conceded, however, that the New Deal gave great impetus to the pristine democratic principle that the happiness and welfare of the people is a major responsibility of the government. The most lasting monument to President Roosevelt is undoubtedly the Federal Security Administration. But Roosevelt's temporary relief measures would have had a more lasting influence and would have developed greater local initiative if they had been carried out by the people rather than for the people.

The problem of unemployment, for example, was never solved. It began to pile up again because the superficial jobs of the W.P.A. made no fundamental contributions to the revival of our economy. There were among the New Dealers, as in every other administration, many honest, hard-working, able people who did their best to be effective amidst all the administrative confusion. Secretary Ickes's P.W.A. did much constructive work with a minimum of wasted money and effort. But only the war with its vast industrial revival saved our economy from collapse. The chief lesson of the depression years should never be forgotten. Even our liberty-loving American people will sacrifice their freedom and their democratic principles if their security and their very lives are threatened by another breakdown of our free enterprise system. We can no more afford another general depression than we can afford another total war, if democracy is to survive.

I endured the havoc created by the New Dealers in our orderly county and in other local governments with equanimity because we were making steady progress in other important local problems. One of the achievements in which Mr. Ward took the greatest satisfaction was the work of a new health department which he had established in 1930. His method of doing this was typical. He telephoned one morning to Ruth Taylor, at that time Deputy Commissioner of our Department of Public Welfare, that she was to appear at his house at three o'clock that afternoon. This was very inconvenient for Ruth, as she was busy packing to leave on her vacation the following day. But Ruth, like all the rest of us, did as she was told, not out of fear but out of affectionate respect. When she arrived at Mr. Ward's home, he had not returned from a golf game, his favorite pastime. Finally he entered the sun porch where Ruth was waiting and thrust a sheaf of papers into her hands. "You're going on vacation?" he asked, looking at her with more than customary fierceness. "Yes, Mr. Ward." "Well, I want people to live longer, healthier, and happier lives in this county," he barked at her in his gruffest voice. "Study those papers while you're gone and let me know what you think of them." Then he strode quickly out of the room. The papers described a plan for a new County Health Department which rejoiced Ruth Taylor's heart and which was promptly put into effect by the Board of Supervisors. After reading how carefully Mr. Ward had worked out every detail of the new Health Department, she realized that he felt deeply about this latest idea of his and that he treated her in such cavalier fashion to conceal his emotion.

Never was Boss Ward content with the *status quo*. No sooner was one idea put into effect than his creative mind began to look for new loopholes in our government. Nor was he thinking merely in terms of his own county. Just as the construction of our beautiful parkways forced New York City to build similar parkways to connect with those of Westchester, so in less tangible ways his activities constantly influenced the thinking of other municipal or county officials. Throughout the thirty-seven years during which he ruled his considerable kingdom — it has a greater population than seven of our states — as the most enlightened of monarchs, he was ever conscious that his example sooner or later was bound to raise the quality of local government throughout the nation.

CHAPTER VIII
Commissioner of Recreation

IN APRIL 1923, two years after I began my political education, Boss Ward telephoned that he would be at my house
in Mount Kisco on a certain day at 3 P.M. I knew that something must be up if the Boss was coming to my house instead of calling me down to headquarters at White Plains.

Mr. Ward arrived with customary promptness. We were
scarcely seated on the porch when, without preliminaries, he
fixed his eagle eyes upon me and announced: "I have appointed a Recreation Commission consisting of five women
and you are the chairman."

"But, Mr. Ward," I exclaimed in alarm, "I don't know a
thing about public recreation."

"Neither does anybody else. You'll have to learn. This is
the first county commission of the kind. I'm sick and tired of
spending such big sums putting people in jail and patching
up the weaklings. We've got to do something to keep people
out of the penitentiary, from landing in lunatic asylums, or
on the relief rolls. If we don't do something to help people
live happy lives in their spare time, our country will soon be
a hospital in which half the people will have to work like
the devil to take care of the other half. Folks don't get into
mischief while they're working. If they raise hell when they
get home from work it's because there's nothing else to do.

Working hours grow shorter every year. That means more time to get into trouble. A recreation program will give them something worth while to do during their leisure hours."

"Where'd you get this idea?" I asked.

"On my visits to Grasslands.* I just said to myself, if we do so much to patch up the weak, why not do something to make the strong still stronger? I made this a women's commission because it's a motherly kind of job. Now let's see what you women can do with a new idea like this. The supervisors still think it's crazy, but they're willing to go along and give the commission $5000 a year to experiment. I've already found a good woman executive for you. Her name is Chester Marsh. She'll be here next week.

"What's more," he continued, without giving me a chance to interrupt, "I've put Ruth Taylor, who is in charge of our child-welfare work, on your board. She's a smart woman ('smart' was the Boss's highest praise for women). She has had a lot of administrative experience and knows her way around. You're pretty young and impetuous, and you'd get into trouble in no time without a steady person like Ruth to sit on you now and then. The necessary office space has already been set aside in temporary quarters."

By the time Mr. Ward had finished painting the picture of the great possibilities in this new job, there was nothing to do but to say "Amen."

Five women who had never set eyes on each other began to work together the following week. One member eventually moved away and was replaced. The rest of us continued to serve the county for eighteen years with deep satisfaction

---

* The county reservation where the county hospital, the penitentiary and the Home for the Aged are located. The prisoners run the farm, dairy and laundry.

to ourselves and with an ever-growing respect for each other. The Boss was quite right about his reasons for appointing Ruth Taylor. That "smart woman," became our County Commissioner of Public Welfare in 1931, and held that position with distinction until her retirement in January 1951. One of the happiest occasions of my life occurred recently when the American Public Welfare Association chose me to confer upon Miss Taylor its highest honor, the Terry Award for Distinguished Service in the Field of Social Welfare for the year 1951.

Even as a young woman Ruth's character and mind were so mature and judicious that, as the Boss prophesied, she "sat on me" over and over again to my great benefit. The other permanent members of our commission were Mrs. Thomas J. Blain, who had earned a reputation as a faithful Red Cross worker in her home town of Port Chester, and Mrs. Paul R. Reynolds, one of the ablest Democratic women in the county. Mrs. John Tyssowski replaced the first Mrs. Noel Macy when she resigned and left the county.

Under Ruth Taylor's wise leadership always spiced with humor, the whole commission would gang up on me when I got impatient with the supervisors, with the staff, with the Civil Service Commission, with the many groups and individuals that obstruct, hamper and delay every public official whoever he may be. I felt exactly like a wild colt that is being broken into harness. If I had not had such a deep affection and respect for the women whom Boss Ward, in his mysterious wisdom, chose as my associates, I would have broken the traces again and again and no doubt made a fool of myself. Public service is a hard grind, but it is also the most profound education that can be obtained anywhere. If I have acquired any capacity for getting on with my fellow citizens in the many public activities in which I have engaged since those early days, it is because Ruth Taylor supplemented Boss Ward's lessons in the arduous task of teaching me to be a public servant. But I confess that one reason why I like Robert Moses, the New York Park Commissioner, is because he blows his top whenever he feels like it; and in spite of my own careful conditioning to the ordeal of co-operative effort, there are still occasions when I forget all about my public manners and let fly at the trimmers and obstructionists and the self-seeking racketeers who try to get in the way of all endeavors for human progress. But the art of timing — when to do this and when not to do it — I learned through eighteen years of service on the Recreation Commission. Over the years my friendship with all the members grew as women's friendships rarely do, because we worked and argued and rejoiced together when gradually we saw our plans flourish and bring zest and happiness, as the Boss predicted, into the lives of thousands of people.

As nobody had ever heard of "recreation" in Westchester, our Recreation Commission had to devote itself first to a selling job. The experience taught me how stubborn the resistance in our country is to new ideas. I had to tour the county, interviewing mayors, supervisors, and the presidents of women's organizations to explain the values of recreation. Children's playgrounds seemed the best bait, but some of the fish wouldn't rise even to this obvious appeal. "Why can't they play in the fields? I did," said the old-timers. "Are there any fields left in your town that aren't private property?" I would ask. "Well, no." Slowly, and after constant repetition, we made a little progress. But patience and persistence are inevitably rewarded even in public work. The mayor of Yonkers must have been in a good mood or perhaps he needed a political talking point, I don't remember which. In any case in one hour flat he committed himself to a budget of $100,000 for the construction and management of recreation centers. It was the kind of break that comes to the weary toiler in the social vineyards when he least expects it. From that time onward the other city and village mayors could not afford to be outdone by Yonkers. In four years the towns and cities in Westchester County had over one hundred children's playgrounds going full tilt under professional leadership.

While persuading the local community leaders of the necessity for constructive leisure time activities, we made it clear that the County Commission would not impose its own ideas upon their communities, but would confine itself to a purely advisory relationship with their own recreation departments.

As our budget increased, we supplied trained specialists to the local communities on such subjects as handicrafts, storytelling, choral singing and other activities, but only after the local officials asked for such assistance. We also established annual training courses for the voluntary and professional recreation workers, to improve the quality of the local leadership. As the number of local directors increased, they formed themselves into a recreation council which met every month to advise the commission as to new trends and needs. In 1940, the last report issued under the original commission, there were fourteen affiliated but independent countywide organizations that managed their own affairs, whether in dramatics, chamber music, trails, arts and crafts, horseback riding, skiing, swimming, hockey and other athletic activities. The fact that all these organizations and programs have continued, with the exception of the big annual music festivals for adults and school children, proves that we built soundly. The effects of these two musical events can still be felt in the number of orchestras that now exist in the county, both among adults and in the public-school system.

Playgrounds and programs of physical education were not new in our country at that time. But our commission felt that the usual track meets, boxing tournaments and other athletic competitions did not reach enough people. In addition we decided to experiment with classes in adult education that would lend greater significance to the recreation movement, and bring new values, new depth to the life of the participants. We felt that freedom from toil should enlarge the opportunity for culture quite as much as for sports.

We found scattered dramatic clubs, orchestras and choral societies in some towns, and encouraged these groups to promote their hobbies in other communities. In a year or two there were enough to hold an annual drama tournament and a music festival. But where to hold the music festival? We needed a place big enough to accommodate the orchestra, the audience, and some four hundred choral members. For three years we set up a large circus tent in White Plains and prayed it wouldn't rain. Two or three thousand patrons sat under canvas on uncomfortable camp chairs to hear classical music while the nearby trains every so often drowned out even the most valiant efforts of the chorus. Walter Damrosch, who saw the value of what we were trying to do, conducted the orchestra under these unsatisfactory conditions with the greatest good humor and with astonishingly good results. Later Albert Stoessel was made county conductor.

These festivals cost the county nothing. The salary of the county conductor, expenditures for the orchestra and the expenses of the tent were covered by the admission fees. Occasionally we made a profit. When we had a deficit, generous county residents helped to meet it, among whom Eugene was always my mainstay. Another person who never lost faith in our activities even when they were financial failures was Felix Warburg. His goodness of heart and staunch friendship helped me over many humiliating defeats. When most people would have reproached me for incurring too many deficits, Felix would tell me that the Recreation Commission was wonderful and that it was a joy to help us out. Such friends give one courage when it is most needed. Nor could we have undertaken such costly experiments without the support of our well-to-do citizens. It gave us the freedom to be creative without straining the confidence of our County Supervisors and the taxpayers in the recreation movement by asking for too big a budget. Only after we had put our more expensive programs on a paying basis, did we include them in the county budget.

After several of our big events attracted nation-wide attention, the Boss stepped in and said the music and drama festivals as well as our numerous athletic tournaments needed a proper building. The supervisors swallowed hard and voted a million dollars for the construction of an auditorium at White Plains to be called the County Center.

This building, whose main hall seated five thousand people, also contained a little theater with a seating capacity of six hundred and a huge basement, equipped with a kitchen, which could be used for a variety of purposes. The County Center was a great help but a greater responsibility. We on the Recreation Commission were determined to make it function to suit the wishes of the people; at the same time we knew that the supervisors expected it to produce as much revenue as possible. We soon made it hum with activity. Like the hub of a wheel it held the many peripheral programs together.

A choral festival opened the new building on May 22, 1930, with twenty-five hundred singers from some thirty different communities on an extended stage. The big hall was jammed to capacity when Ray Lyman Wilbur, then Secretary of the Interior, rose to make the inaugural address.

Soon the dramatic groups increased to a point where the annual drama competition took up a whole week. Sports nights, athletic tournaments, track meets followed each other in succession. The basement became a nightly beehive of people eager to become painters, sculptors, musicians or craftsmen of one sort or another. As our county had among its residents many college professors, we organized classes in anything our citizens wanted to study; the only requirement was to sign up thirty or more people, willing to pay fifty cents a lesson. Our County Center became an unofficial annex of Columbia and New York Universities.

But these popular pursuits did not solve the pressing problem of keeping down our costs. To stimulate the use of the building for concerts, we persuaded the Metropolitan Opera to give performances at the County Center. They were an enormous success, but gave us many a headache. On one occasion when Lily Pons was singing, the opera in the main hall coincided with our annual poultry show in the basement. In the afternoon as I stood on the big stage to check whether all was well with the lights and curtain, I could hear the roosters crowing lustily. I rushed downstairs, ready to choke every rooster with my own bare hands. "What are we going to do?" I gasped to the manager of the poultry show. "If the singers and the audience hear the roosters crowing, we're ruined." "Oh, lady, don't worry," he drawled.

"When your opera begins, all we do is push a piece of cardboard into the cages so the roosters can't get their heads up. Then they can't crow." The opera singers never heard a peep out of the roosters. But during the performance I kept listening for a sudden triumphant crow.

To our Negro fellow citizens the County Center was a real boon, as they had no other dignified place except their church halls for recreational activities. It came to be understood that Thursday evening belonged to them. Many of them were in domestic service and that was their night off. When they had no program of their own, the commission provided a top-flight jazz band for dancing; an art in which the Negro always shows originality. In addition, they were welcomed at all of our other county-wide events. Their own music festival of spirituals, which culminated a whole year's practice among local groups, was one of our most beautiful and popular annual events.

I am greatly encouraged about America's attitude toward its Negro fellow citizens when I remember the great progress made in our country in this respect during the past generation. Thirty years ago the Park Commission was frequently in hot water when they abolished segregation in the many lovely parks, the public swimming pools, picnic grounds, golf links and bathing beaches for which the county also has Boss Ward to thank. Now much of this tension has disappeared. It is no empty boast if I claim that the quiet but effective work of our Recreation Commission in inter-racial activities helped to bring about this improvement in human relations. From the outset we encouraged the Negro population to take part in all of the recreation activities and to use the public playgrounds, the summer camp, the workshops and other facilities. But we let these developments come about as if they were something to be taken for granted. We never boasted about these achievements in the press. We found, as everyone else does who succeeds in mingling the two races in genuinely common interests, that both derive a feeling of exhilaration from normal, natural, co-operative endeavor.

To be sure I, personally, was attacked in the press by a neighbor of mine who was a typically theoretical friend of the Negro, because we had a white and a Negro music festival. He accused me of deliberate segregation. I settled the matter by going straight to the members of our Negro music groups and telling them the reasons for these attacks. They were furious about the whole business. "We don't want to sing with those white folks," they said. "What's more, we don't want the white folks to sing with us because they don't know how to sing spirituals."

If we white people could learn that the Negro is a human being who thinks, feels and reacts exactly the way we do to justice, good will and kindliness, we would become more successful in our endeavors to break down old patterns of segregation. What's more, we would learn that the Negro is far less eager to associate with us socially than a lot of fearful whites can imagine. Most white people are too poor in the milk of human kindness, in spontaneous humor and joyousness to be a treat to the Negro.

It is my conviction that we whites have far more subtle things to learn from the Negro than he has to learn from us, among others, his sense of rhythm, his appreciation of the poetry of life, his deep aversion to regimentation. Let us hope that in the process of integration in our society, which fortunately is now well under way, the Negro will not allow the American steam roller of conformity to destroy his creative gifts. I realize that in adumbrating this subject of the Negro's contributions to our society I am touching superficially on what should be a whole book, a book that can only be written by a Negro who senses the immense potentialities of his race, a book that is not aggressive but objectively perceptive of the profound and mysterious influences the Negro can bring to our culture, particularly to its aesthetic development, if he is encouraged to be himself. The only Negroes who make my heart ache are those who think that they have to make themselves over to conform to the stilted patterns of behavior that we try to impose on them. This is murder, psychically speaking. But the pressure for conformity in our country is powerful. It flattens out most white people; why not the Negro? We can only hope that the Negro's capacity for passive resistance will save his integrity. If that happens, the white man will learn, in time, to call him blessed.

One Saturday morning, Jack Brown, Manager of the County Center, who knew that the commission wanted to give equal privileges to Negroes for the use of the building, called me up and said: "Mrs. Meyer, I have rented the whole building for this Sunday to a man named Father Divine. He paid the usual deposit. But he hasn't paid the balance of the rent. What'll I do?"

Bright and early Sunday morning I met Father Divine, then at the outset of his career. I stated politely that rents had to be paid in advance. "It'll materialize, Mrs. Meyer. Just you wait and see. God always helps those that trust him." In a few minutes he dove into an inside pocket and pulled out fifty dollars. "You see, there it is"—and he handed me the money. "But you owe us $600 more, Father Divine." "It'll materialize if you just give God a chance," he said in mild reproof. The upshot of it was that Jack Brown, Father Divine and I stood there one whole hour while God materialized the entire sum in small amounts from some ten different pockets of Father Divine's black suit.

For a whole day and evening Father Divine's angels had a glorious time. When the mood seized them they would jump out of their seats and perform an ecstatic dance in the aisles, clapping time with their hands and singing hymns with eyes closed in rapture, while "Father" sat quietly on the stage like an impassive Oriental deity. I remained through the luncheon for more than seven thousand people. As I sat on "Father's" right, I had to pass about a hundred heavy turkeys, hams and vegetable dishes, all of which he blessed before giving them to me to hand on to my neighbors. The intellectual Negroes resent Father Divine's power over his followers, but his undeniable influence for good arises out of his understanding of their needs.

The only experiences at the County Center that really distressed me were the boxing matches, which brought in the steadiest revenue. It makes me physically ill to see two grown men beat each other about the head. But I frequently sat through the first match just to be sure that the huge audience was safely installed and all the other regulations for such events carefully observed. The professional wrestling bouts on the other hand seemed to me straight comedy and not very straight in any other respect.

As we were living in Washington during the winter, I was frequently obliged to take the midnight train if my recreation work made it necessary to be in Westchester County the next morning. When I walked from the station at White Plains to our County Office Building, it warmed my heart to be back in an atmosphere where the street cleaner, policeman or passing citizen greeted me by name. In the very same county in which I was so at home as a child I was again at home as an adult. It was the same sense of return to my roots which I had experienced intellectually in my Chinese studies and was now experiencing in action and in my growing devotion to the public welfare. One has to have felt in one's blood and bones this personal involvement with the natural and social environment, to realize what an inspiring, uplifting, regenerative force it is. If I now bring a passionate conviction to my endeavors to break down our vast urban congeries into neighborhood groups where people can be rescued from mass anonymity and feel their divine uniqueness as the greatest good in life, it is because I, too, lost myself in the complexities of contemporary society. But under the influence of local co-operative endeavor with all kinds and conditions of men, I found my way back to simplicity of thought, the love of my fellow beings and the fundamental striving of our American democracy toward universal brotherhood.

On one occasion this rapid-fire change of environment between Washington and Westchester was thoroughly confusing to a beloved European friend, Paderewski. He had played at the Westchester Music Festival in 1931. Now in '33 when all the banks were closed he was to give a second concert in the County Center. I was a member of the Washington Committee which backed his concert in the capital. Two days later he was scheduled to appear at the County Center. I knew that because of the depression we had sold only a few dozen tickets in advance. What a fiasco for our building and for me if the maestro should have to face 5000 empty seats! But despite closed banks the county people dug into their jeans on the last day and filled the hall. After the concert, I gave Paderewski, who could never go to bed right after a performance, a party at my sister-in-law's apartment in New York City. Paderewski played bridge until 4 A.M. As he left he said in puzzled tones: *"Chère amie,* yesterday you organize a concert for me in Washington, today you do the same at White Plains. And then you give me a party in New York City. Where do you really live?" I replied, "Don't tell anybody — I really live on the Congressional Limited."

When it appeared that we could keep the County Center in constant use even during the depression and make enough income to pay for our overhead, the supervisors and the people who had called it a white elephant became convinced of its value to the county. But the hard work which the commission put into the job of making it a quick success — for it had to be done quickly to capture popular good will — proved to us how difficult it is to sell a new concept of public service even in so progressive a county as Westchester. Had we had a single bad accident while handling the huge crowds or transporting thousands of school children to their music festivals or athletic meets, the fault would have been ours and the use of the building badly handicapped. I am grateful to Jack Brown, the Manager, who is still in charge of the County Center, for his humor when things went wrong and for his ability to make things go right.

After the building had been running to capacity for some five years, our commission had its reward. The White Plains paper which had originally denounced the County Center as a white elephant, wrote a eulogy entitled "An Elephant No Longer White." That is the only public recognition the commission ever got for its hard work. That's the way we do things in our democracy. The reader may well ask what kept us going so long at a task for which nobody ever thanked us and for which none of us ever expected gratitude. When

I finally resigned at the beginning of the war, the supervisors uttered no word of recognition. In fact I knew they were glad to get rid of me. Public service, rightly understood, is its own reward in precisely the same way that a poet or painter or novelist or composer is rewarded for his endless pains by the finished product, however insignificant or ununderstandable it may seem to everybody else.

Only Mr. Ward appreciated how arduously the commission had toiled to realize his objectives. No one took more satisfaction in the humming activities at the County Center than the man who had had the vision to foresee how much it would add to the attractiveness of life in Westchester. One day when Ruth Taylor, by this time our Welfare Commissioner, wandered into the building to hear the high-school orchestras practicing, Jack Brown said to her: "The Boss is all alone up in the gallery." Ruth went upstairs and sat down beside him. Mr. Ward was listening to the playing of these youthful musicians as if they were the angels' chorus. He looked up, beamed his happiest smile at Ruth and snorted: "If we have enough of this kind of thing, you will soon be out of a job."

But the County Center was by no means the most vital part of our recreation program. It was important only through the stimulus it gave to the all-year-round activities in the local communities throughout the county. It was the property of the people and was thereby a natural lever in the delicate task of our commission to originate, encourage and guide these local programs without dominating them. This is the whole secret of successful democratic administration, whether in local, state or Federal governments, a secret which our commission learned from Ruth Taylor.

She also taught us to look upon individual initiative as the most powerful force in democracy. Ruth, though a public official all her life, never lost her respect for the contributions which voluntary agencies can make to social progress. She had a gift rare in government administrators of remaining the servant rather than the master of the people. If our new commission made few mistakes in guiding the recreational activities of the county communities while encouraging them to independent action, it was due to her experience in mobilizing both public and private agencies to harmonious co-operative endeavor.

Another fundamental contribution Ruth Taylor made to our education, was the emphasis she placed on the need for justice to all the conflicting elements with which a public servant must deal, especially the religious groups. "Always try to get the view of the other fellow" was her motto. As a result all three main religious divisions, Protestant, Catholic and Jewish, had implicit confidence in her — a major achievement in public life. This reputation paid dividends at a critical moment. Ruth had been appointed Commissioner of Public Welfare in 1931 when the incumbent, George Werner, died. In 1932 she had to run for the office, which had become an elective position.

At the instigation of Governor Roosevelt, then running for the Presidency, the Democrats nominated Frederick C. Howe, a man of ability with a great reputation as a liberal, who had formerly been Commissioner of Immigration in New York, to run against her. It was a strongly Democratic year and I knew we had the toughest kind of a battle on our hands to re-elect her. Suddenly I felt the trend shifting in our direction, without understanding exactly why. Then I discovered that many Catholic priests in the county had received word from Cardinal Hayes to support Miss Taylor. Although the diocese was Democratic in New York City, the Cardinal had such respect for Ruth's impeccable fairness that she received his and other Democratic support. Her majority that year was the highest hitherto obtained by any of our Republican county candidates.

The finest contribution to the welfare of Westchester's dependent children was — and still is — the Recreation Commission's summer camp. As it was the first public camp of the kind we were determined that it should be a model in every respect. This, to be sure, took several years of planning and hard work. The site loaned to us by the Park Commission, which was also responsible for installation and upkeep of equipment, is a spectacularly beautiful wooded point of land that juts far out into the Hudson River at Croton. We took care of 1200 children in all who came for two weeks each, unless there were special reasons why a given child needed a longer vacation. The girls had the wooded point, the boys the cove which sheltered the bathing beach. Instead of huddling the children together we eventually spread the tents around the big acreage in groups and even had one Indian Village in charge of a native Indian who was an excellent craftsman and storyteller.

Day and night the campers were under expert supervision and the food chosen by a dietitian was so good that some of our undernourished youngsters gained twenty pounds during a month's stay. The private agencies paid the actual cost of food and supervision for each of their wards. The Recreation Commission was responsible for the management and the educational program. The total cost to the county was less than $2000 a year and the benefit to the children in physical and mental health was so remarkable that the camp became one of the county's permanent institutions.

The pride we Westchester people took in our county

achievements when Mr. Ward was encouraging us to constant new experimentation in social progress, often got on
the nerves of other community representatives whom we
met in national conventions. We doubtless seemed smug
and self-satisfied to other communities with less financial resources. It became natural for us when rising to make our
reports at these national gatherings, simply to say "Westchester County" instead of following the custom of mentioning the state from which we came. On one occasion
when I did this, the chairman rapped on the table and demanded: "And pray where is Westchester County, Mrs.
Meyer?" The laugh was on me but I replied: "Sir, New
York City is just south of it." After the meeting the chairman came to me and said: "I couldn't resist that little
thrust, Mrs. Meyer. You see I live in Scarsdale." It is one of
Westchester's wealthiest townships.

Our great and good Westchester Boss died in 1933,
mourned by the entire county. So well had he built his Republican organization that it still functions largely under
the old leaders though with impaired efficiency. Those of
us who grew up under his tutelage still talk of him as a
living influence upon us. For he was undoubtedly one of the
most brilliant, generous and practical political leaders this
country ever produced. After his death the Ward Poundridge
Reservation was named after him at a memorial service.
It is an extensive area in the north of the county which he
quietly bought up in order that the large urban population
of Westchester might have some place where they, too, could
enjoy forever the natural beauty of our county hills and
forests. "The time will come, girl," he said to me, "when the
city youngsters in our county will want to know what a cow
looks like." He therefore wanted a working farm to be set
up in this memorial park, an idea with which the County

Supervisors are still struggling. But Boss Ward's most enduring memorial is the gratitude in the hearts of the people, who appreciate his long, efficient and disinterested service to the common welfare and his emphasis on the fundamental importance of local government to the future of democracy. To evoke my own memories of the Boss and his beneficent influence upon me I do well to resort to Mrs. Browning's line: "My whole heart rises up to bless your name."

When the Second World War broke out, our county had to be organized to handle a possible exodus from New York City in case of bombing. It was obvious that the main flood of refugees would not risk escape from the city by the long bridges or tunnels even if these were still usable. The whole county rose at once to its responsibility without prodding from any Washington committees, and co-ordinated all hospitals, health and welfare agencies, police, firemen, et cetera, into a well-knit, smoothly functioning organization. Our County Center, which has a big kitchen, was equipped with all the beds and bedding from our summer camp to take care of transients.

I realized that if any bombs should fall on New York City every county official would be expected to report for duty instantly. Since we were now living in Washington throughout the winter, I resigned as chairman of the Recreation Commission in 1941 after twenty years of political and social service in Westchester County.

As a result of this prolonged discipline, faith in the resources of the human spirit has determined my attitude toward social work. Whether in the field of health, education or welfare, I have put my emphasis on preventive rather than curative programs and tried to influence our elaborate, costly and ill-co-ordinated welfare organizations in that direction. Unfortunately the momentum of social work is still directed toward compensating the victims of our society for its injustices rather than eliminating those injustices. This is less the fault of the social workers than of the trustees of the voluntary welfare organizations. Whoever has attempted to pry a board of trustees away from some outmoded charitable program to some greatly needed preventive work knows what a difficult task it usually is. Nor are the trustees more backward in their concept of strengthening community life than the public. It is easy to get contributions for the lame, the halt and the blind, but not to improve the organization of welfare work, or to adjust our efforts to the changing needs of an industrial society. The lag that has always existed between what even the best-intentioned people do and what they should do was never a greater threat to humanity than in this revolutionary era of accelerated change. As our disorderly, competitive technological society is piling up its victims and constantly developing new problems of maladjustment, we must use our scientific knowledge to determine the cause and prevention of suffering rather than putting all our emphasis on its alleviation, or we shall indeed become the great hospital state which Mr. Ward foresaw.

Thus until the beginning of the Second World War my extramural activities were largely confined to Westchester County. I confess that it takes health, careful planning and often grim determination if married women are to carry two jobs at once, responsibility to husband, home, children and to public service. No matter how proud the family members may be of Mother's outside activities, she must be prepared to accept their fierce and natural jealousy of all energies not devoted to them. A good deal of banter around the Meyer family table was aimed at my recreation work. But nobody laughed more heartily than I when Eugene with great solemnity would say: "You must understand, my dears, that Mother is teaching little children how to play": and the children would echo his mood by shouting in unison: "How about a little recreation in the home?"

Nevertheless my public activities expanded of their own inner momentum, as my children left home for preparatory schools, college and eventually marriage. This momentum was accelerated by the demands made on every American by the Second World War. When I was obliged to resign as Chairman of the Westchester County Recreation Commission, it was like pulling myself up by the roots. Yet the war work that lay ahead of me did not tear up my roots in Westchester; rather it has expanded the love I felt for my county to the whole country. I became enmeshed willy-nilly in the democratic process that surrounds us all and presents us constantly with ever new calls to action, if our ears are attuned to its demands. One of the things I was to learn is that any American who is thoroughly at home in one locality feels at home with the people of any other community throughout our great nation. Henceforth the welfare of the whole country and the country's children were to become what Mr. Ward called my "concern."

CHAPTER IX

Washington

AS A YOUNG MAN, my husband made up his mind that
people ought to change their occupations every twenty
years. He has done just that. The first twenty years of his
adult life were devoted to business and the earning of a safe
competence. When he was forty-one, he went into public
life. Eighteen years later he became owner and publisher of
the *Washington Post*. Now that he has owned the *Washington Post* almost twenty years, the children are wondering
what his next choice will be.

Their childhood happened to fall during the period of
Eugene's public career. His preoccupation with financial and
economic problems never weakened their conviction that
they were his first concern. With the acute insight of children they had an instinctive feeling that he was my first concern. "You really love Daddy more than us," said my second
daughter, Elizabeth, at the age of eight. Her resentment arose
from the fact that in addition to my commuting to Westchester I frequently accompanied Eugene on trips around the
country. So sudden were these departures at times, that the
practical Elizabeth announced:

"We ought to have a blackboard at our front door like the
one at school where notices are posted. Then when we go
out, we could see whether you are going to be home when

we come back from school — or in Texas. It would help a lot," concluded this order-loving child.

It was a strain for our children to grow up amidst the hurly-burly of a household in which both parents were extremely active, but it had its compensations. Washington, at that time, was still a small and provincial city. They could walk to school alone, and in the afternoon they played with hordes of other youngsters from the big apartment house that looked down on our yard in Connecticut Avenue. Friendships with children of all nations and conditions was in itself an education: At the age of ten Bill's best girl was Japanese Ambassador Matsudaira's daughter, who married Prince Chichibu, brother of Emperor Hirohito; and his closest pal among the boys introduced him to the fun of delivering evening papers and selling weekly magazines at street corners. It was a democratic atmosphere.

Our Washington life, as I have said, was prolonged far beyond what Eugene had anticipated. In March 1921 he was reappointed Managing Director of the War Finance Corporation. After that he served as Commissioner of the Federal Farm Loan Board under President Coolidge, and was then moved in 1930 to the Federal Reserve Board, of which he was made Governor by President Hoover. For the first six months of the year 1932 he was also Chairman of the Board of the Reconstruction Finance Corporation, a responsibility which he could not refuse, as he had drawn up the legislation for the creation of that once very valuable organization. These were jobs of a most exacting nature.

It is not for me to discuss my husband's efforts to maintain the solvency of his country. Someday, I hope, he will write his own account of the post World War One period in which he played such an important part. I can say, however, that Eugene's contribution to the history of those times was notable not merely because of his wide knowledge and his administrative gifts, but because his personal integrity inspired confidence among the members of Congress, the Federal officials and the businessmen of the country. For he was a type of statesman rare at any time, but especially today — imbued with a passion for disinterested service and for the highest standards of public morality. A man of incorruptible conscience, as an official he had the same rules of conduct which distinguished his private life. When my mind is occasionally steeped in gloom by a long and close acquaintance with political events, my husband's record as a public servant rescues me from too great a pessimism concerning the frailties of human nature when tempted by ambition.

Throughout the eighteen years that Eugene was in public service, I was his partner in the many subtle ways by which any wife can be of help to her husband. In Washington this partnership also involves practical activities of an exacting nature. I learned that visiting cards could not be thrown into the wastepaper basket, but were a major factor in human, social and political relations. On Mondays we women were obliged to leave cards or pay formal calls on the families of Supreme Court justices, Tuesdays on Congressmen, especially those of importance to one's husband's work, Wednesdays upon the Cabinet, Thursdays upon the Senators, Fridays upon the diplomatic corps. In the evening it was frequently necessary to attend dinner parties when not giving a carefully composed dinner in one's own home. Sometimes large gatherings, luncheons, receptions or dinners had to be organized at short notice for important visiting firemen whether from our own or a foreign country. I had to keep book on my social duties as carefully as a businessman keeps book on his financial transactions lest I should inadvertently offend some politician — or his wife — with whom friendly relations were necessary to Eugene's many-sided activities. It was a heavy chore which had to be carried out as if it were the delight of one's life. It called for attention to endless minute details from ordering a good meal to careful consideration of political affiliations or rivalries among the guests. These functions were more than mere festivities. Often busy officials could talk over their problems over the after-dinner coffee more quietly than during their busy working day. At times the most carefully calculated party could also be disastrous. One diplomat lost his job because at his request I gave a sumptuous dinner for his new prime minister who belonged to a rival political faction. I happened to say to the prime minister that his diplomatic representative was well liked in Washington. That ended the usefulness of this diplomat to his home government. If I had said that my friend was unpopular, it probably would have finished him anyway. Yet I felt guilty of having betrayed him. Such were the pitfalls of social life in the surcharged atmosphere of national and international political intrigue. To be a helpful wife in Washington, to share the children's interests and to live a life of one's own is not as impossible as it sounds, but it calls for a careful disposition of that priceless commodity — time.

But in addition to its serious aspects, social life in Washington, after the First World War until the gloom of the depression years descended upon us, brought many delightful compensations.

There was time for relaxation, for good conversation and for evenings of chamber music. The people who were kindest to me when I first arrived in Washington, a strange, bewildered and disoriented New Yorker, were Eleanor Patterson, future owner of the *Times-Herald,* then known as

Countess Gizycka, and Alice Longworth. Both these women were strong personalities who forgave everything in the people they liked and nothing in people of whom they disapproved. As they had catholic tastes they were remarkable hostesses whose homes at that time were centers of political and social activity. Nick Longworth, for whom I had a real affection, often played the violin for his guests after dinner. On one of these evenings, Fred Hale, a lifelong friend of the Longworths, who had just been elected Senator, arrived late. Alice remained seated as she shook hands with him, "Here, you, get up when you salute a member of the Senate," said Fred as he jerked Alice out of her chair. Enraged by this jocular assault Alice fought back so vigorously that both were soon rolling over the floor until they were brought to a halt under the piano. Other stimulating parties took place at the home of William and Anne Hard, who had a gift for bringing together people of the most diverse political, economic and social points of view. Antoine Bibesco, the Rumanian Minister, and his wife Elizabeth, the daughter of the Asquiths, made their Embassy a center of attraction where one met the famous conductor-violinist Enesco and gifted writers, like their cousin Marthe Bibesco. Elizabeth was famous for her clever sayings but liked too well to hold the center of the stage at social gatherings. On one evening when the guests were a little bored with Elizabeth's solo performance, the blunt Eugene whispered in her ear: "Tonight Elizabeth you are repartedious." But Elizabeth was at heart a generous nature and rather enjoyed it if somebody trumped her aces. Of the scientists, I remember with particular affection the biologist Vernon Kellogg and his gifted wife Charlotte. Mabel Boardman and her sister, Mrs. Frederick Keep, had dignified establishments where one met the Washington "cave dwellers" and such venerable legal lights

as Chief Justices White, Taft and Hughes. Our early friendship with the John Lord O'Brians has grown over the years
and is still a joy to both of us. Everyone appreciates the
play of John's many-faceted intellect and his deep Christianity. But I also remember with gratitude how he could raise
my spirits by an amused glance of appreciation when I entered some ballroom or dinner party, in a gown that pleased
his discriminating taste.

Justice Holmes was a near neighbor of ours when we first
moved to Washington. I tried to convert him to the delights
of Chinese painting, whereas he sought to enlist my enthusiasm for the temporary love of his life, the French savant
Fontenelle. Neither of us was very successful, but we enjoyed our intellectual joustings and became warm friends
because we liked differing with each other. Concerning
Fontenelle I quoted to him the remark of Madame de Ten-
cin, who, placing her hand on her heart, said to her intimate
friend: *"Vous n'avez là que du cerveau—"* a riposte that
registered with the Justice because it was certainly not true
of him. Holmes's interpretation of the law was based not
on abstract logic but on experience, an attitude with which
this pupil of John Dewey's was in full accord. Both of these
great thinkers revolted against the abstract formalism of the
early nineteenth century. Both were creators and exponents
of the sociological movement, Holmes in jurisprudence,
Dewey in philosophy; one an experimentalist in the philosophy of law, the other in the philosophy of living. Both insisted, above all, upon a freedom that was not theoretical but
active and real.

People when speaking of their admiration for Holmes,
are apt to forget how much he owed his brilliant wife. Mrs.
Holmes's conversation was so playful and artful that its in-
cisiveness escaped any but the most careful listeners. And

the relationship between man and wife was of the rarest beauty. I saw them strolling in front of me one day on Connecticut Avenue. So absorbed was this elderly couple in each other that they stopped, oblivious of the passersby, and conversed with the intensity of a young couple under the spell of first love. After Mrs. Holmes's death their famous old house on Eye Street was never quite the same joy to me, though the Justice carried himself after the first shock of deprivation with the stoic fortitude that was characteristic of him. One day, when he was almost ninety, I found him reading Aristotle's *Grammar*. "Why are you wasting time on that dry stuff?" I demanded. "My dear," he replied with twinkling eyes, "I am preparing for my last examination."

A great responsibility and a great joy was the installation of the Freer collection in its beautiful new home on the Mall. Before Mr. Freer died he had made up his mind that John E. Lodge, son of the Massachusetts Senator, and then Curator of the Far Eastern Division of the Boston Museum, should be the head of his museum. As both men were highly sensitive and stubborn personalities, their negotiations had come to an impasse. After Mr. Freer's death in September 1919, it became my solemn duty to persuade Mr. Lodge that he and he alone knew enough about the collection and Mr. Freer's ideals for its proper installation and that he must accept the position which our dead friend wanted him to have. It was a burden off my mind when he finally agreed to carry out what I knew had been the ardent hope of Mr. Freer.

It took several years to transport all of the collections from Detroit, to catalogue them and install some of them in the various galleries and the remainder in storerooms accessible to students. For it had always been Mr. Freer's aim to use Oriental restraint and exhibit only a few objects at a time, giving each painting, bronze or jade ample space to reveal its beauty.

Just before the official opening in May 1923, Mr. Lodge and I examined the final arrangements together. All of these familiar objects which I had enjoyed so often in the informal setting of Mr. Freer's Detroit home or in the New York apartments where he lived during his last years of illness, suddenly took on a curious remoteness as if the artificial museum atmosphere had thrown a veil between us that it was difficult to pierce. I said farewell to these beloved treasures as I had said farewell to the friend who had gathered them together just before he was wrapped in the slumber of death. It is essential to have museums for the products of bygone ages, if only to protect and preserve them for posterity. But the feeling of intimacy with these records of man's spiritual striving is scarcely possible when they are imprisoned in cold and formal settings for which they were never intended.

Nevertheless the Freer Gallery became an oasis for me in Washington, especially as John Lodge and I became warm friends through our common delight in Chinese art and philosophy. As my interest in social problems increased, my desire for personal possessions waned and the impulse to collect ceased altogether. But since Mr. Freer had left a considerable sum for the purchase of new acquisitions, and Mr. Lodge with his thorough scholarship and impeccable taste built up the original collection to a new splendor, I could continue vicariously the pleasure and excitement of discovery which, rather than ownership, is the real joy of collecting.

As new and ever more amazing revelations of China's many-sided culture came to light and were acquired by the Gal-

lery, I often felt pangs of melancholy that Mr. Freer had not
lived to enjoy them. But the expansion of the collections
under John Lodge seemed to keep Mr. Freer's spirit very
close and very alive for me. Not until John Lodge died did
I feel that this creative and vital chapter of my life was
closed forever as far as its human associations were concerned.
My love for the art itself and for the race which created it,
can never change, not even now that the Chinese are in
spiritual bondage.

Curious old chapters from my student days in Europe
kept reopening in Washington from time to time. On one
occasion when I was giving a solemn political dinner party
with Andrew Mellon, Secretary of the Treasury, as guest of
honor, my friend Darius Milhaud, one of Les Six, the most
talented of the ultramodern French composers with whom
I had had many a good time in Paris, arrived in Washington.
I wanted Milhaud to have a concert in the nation's capital,
as this was his first visit to our country. I explained that the
audience he would find assembled was probably the least
musical one he had ever encountered, and with this warning
invited him to play after dinner. Never shall I forget the look
of consternation on the face of Mrs. Marshall Field, our
première dowager, when Milhaud played selections from
"Le Boeuf sur le Toit" and other brilliant or playful com-
positions of his, all of which were then strange fruit to
Americans. Mr. Mellon was characteristically indifferent to
Milhaud's modern harmonies, but Justice Hughes when he
said good night looked sternly disapproving at this affront
to his dignity.

My good friend Léon Bakst also arrived in Washington.
This famous Russian stage designer, who had created the
fabulous settings and most of the costumes with which the
Ballet Russe had first made its sensational appearance in

Paris, was now in serious straits. With the disbanding of the original ballet troupe who would not return to Moscow when the Communists took over, Bakst was a lost soul and without means of support as he had spent his savings with typical generosity on his family and innumerable other White Russian friends. He came to stay for a few days and remained for weeks on end simply because there was no place for him to go. As he found my evening dresses far too conventional, he would frequently embellish them with marvelously contrived turbans and other accessories that he created out of bits of chiffon and other odds and ends that were lying about. He spent some of his time making lovely drawings of the children though they were a little awed by this exotic stranger who roamed about the house like a familiar ghost. When I later heard of his death in Paris, alone, sick and hopeless, the deep melancholy I felt was assuaged only by the thought that the tragedy and suffering of this artist and gentleman of the *ancien régime* had ended.

I have a dangerous habit of selecting friends who put my soul on the rack and stretch it to the limit of its capacities. Usually this has been a matter of deliberate choice on my part. But one of the most beautiful of these passionate friendships — with the Catholic poet Paul Claudel, French Ambassador to our country from 1926 to 1933 — was wholly adventitious. That at any rate is the way I describe it. Claudel maintains it was the will of God.

When we first met at a dinner party in Washington, the sparks flew. I made a frontal attack on Claudel because he had recently referred to Goethe, to my mind the highest representative of Western humanism, as a jackass. I was yet to learn the extravagances of which "Clau," as he signs his letters, was capable when his Catholicism and his irrepres-

sible sense of humor are combined. We hurled arguments
at each other across a cultural abyss, both of us in deadly
earnest; we detested each other and all but said so. Since
Claudel, if he was bored, sank back into an inarticulate gloom
that engulfed any dinner party, my diplomatic friends who
noted his animation that evening, made a habit of inviting
us together and putting me next to him regardless of the
strict protocol as to rank. Almost in spite of ourselves, we
grew into a friendship so enduring that it became one of
the real inspirations of my life.

For years he would visit me at teatime whenever the spirit
moved him. If other guests were present, he would vanish.
In a crowd his spirit departed at once and his body followed
soon thereafter. He would spend weeks at our home in Mount
Kisco, making fun of my social work and urging me to save
my soul not by devoting myself to the welfare of others but
by becoming a Catholic. Never did this ardent shepherd of
lost souls undertake a more hopeless cause. Aside from the
beautiful poems he sent me on my saint's day, he wrote for
me some of his most brilliant religious tracts, several of which
he subsequently published. Nor did I remain untouched,
arrant Protestant that I am, by the poetical exhortations of
one of the few authentic religious geniuses of our spirit-
ually impoverished Western society.

For his message to mankind is joy, the pure joyousness of
the birds who sing their salute to every new dawn. "The
duty of a poet is not to convince, nor to explain anything,"
he said to me. "It is his role to make the human soul eager
for music, anxious to put itself in condition where a general
accord with the whole of Creation is impossible to avoid."
One of his favorite quotations which he used repeatedly as
the mission of the poet, was King Solomon's admonition:
"Ne impedias musicam" — "Do not impede the music"

— the music of the soul conscious of God's grace that should bind us all as brothers one to another.

Of Gide, Claudel spoke frequently with bitterness and scorn, with humor and unconquerable love, although their catastrophic break was then some five years old. What he did not say, but what was clear to me and what is clear in their published correspondence as the undercurrent of the whole tragic encounter, is that Claudel was never more serious while Gide was leading him on, the way a flirtatious woman plays with a new suitor out of sheer curiosity. Gide's part in this religious wooing is to me profanation. One does not play with that which to another human being is the holy of holies. The sacred had meaning for Gide only as something to desecrate. Why be an immoralist if there were no morality?

It horrified me to think that Claudel had poured out his whole soul for this cruel man who was laughing up his sleeve. But this was not the only time that Gide acted the part of anti-Christ. His magnificent style is the proof that literary genius can result from a dominating love of evil, just as Claudel's poetry resulted from a struggle against it.

Throughout these many years Claudel endured the torture of being ignored by the French intellectuals, except a few people of independent judgment like Philippe Berthelot, while Gide exerted an irresistible perverting influence especially upon youth. Never have I been closer to one of my childhood outbursts of uncontrolled rage than at a Parisian tea party in 1932 at the home of my sister-in-law, Madame de Souza-Dantas, when Paul Valéry, then the delight of the fashionable world, threw out his chicken-breast and assured me that Claudel's works were of no importance as they were embalmed in his Catholic orthodoxy. I replied diffidently to this *arbiter elegantiarum* that Claudel's grandeur arises from his absolute trust that there is no greater power in heaven or earth than love. Valéry thereupon gave me a pitying, disdainful smile as one who knew with certainty that there is nothing in the human or natural universe worthy of the love of a *bel esprit* such as his. Valéry is a technician on the high level of the Chinese ivory carvers: his brittle verses appealed to an era lacking in heart and in deep convictions.

There was no break between Claudel and me even when he realized that his heroic efforts at conversion were failing, because I always met his vehement proselytism with the awe it deserved but also with complete honesty. We disputed at times about minor aspects of Catholicism, but never about his flights of poetical interpretation to which no sensitive human being could respond with anything less than a close attention of the inner ear. Inevitably the spiritual exaltation and something like a tremulous sympathy which were called forth in me by the sheer beauty and force of Claudel's love of God, would encourage him to think that his efforts to convert me could not fail. But gradually he accepted me as a spiritual ally who was perhaps closer to him for the very reason that I was not of his faith. One day I said to him that he would be unhappy if I were converted because the whole reason for our friendship would no longer exist. It was said in jest. But we both knew that it was true.

Friendship is based on the giving of oneself. A friendship with Claudel cannot be based on anything but the giving of his religious flame. It is his whole reason for existence, a missionary passion which he expressed in his *"Magnificat"*:

Seigneur, vous avez mis en moi un germe non point de mort,
mais de lumière. . . .
Qu'importe la vie que je reçois si je ne la donne!

Anyone who knows Claudel's violent nature and history, cannot but realize that his life might have ended in disaster had it not been for his conversion to Catholicism. His emotions are of such torrential force that he needed the stern discipline of religious orthodoxy to set limitations for him that he could never have set for himself.

At the time of our friendship in Washington his works were appreciated in Germany but still neglected in France. I gave Claudel what every artist needs, genuine delight in his creative gifts. Among his prose works I have no difficulty in selecting *Connaissance de l'Est* as my favorite, but among the wide range of his poems, my choice is a matter of mood though "*Les Cinq Grandes Odes*" seem to me the heighth of Claudel's genius. Among his plays, I have a weakness for *La Ville,* of which I possess the original manuscript, but *Le Soulier de Satin* is probably the greatest because it expresses the world-wide reach of his Catholic imagination. I have many of Claudel's books inscribed to "*L'amie de mes oeuvres quand tout le monde me méprise.*" His American fellow Catholics still do not realize the importance of the only first-rate poetical talent which the contemporary church has produced.

Claudel came of French peasant stock. He has the solid physique of that hardy race. His square face and strong features are illumined by the vitality of genius. As is so often the case in men of real genius, there is a sharp dualism in his two profiles. One eye is fixed on the infinite and eternal but the other reveals the temptation of sensual reality. His expression is sardonic as if good and evil are in perpetual combat in his personality. This conflict of heaven and earth in Claudel, and in Thomas Mann, is the source of their creative genius, their irony and their mordant sense of humor.

Most people do not know that Claudel has this witty, ironical and devastating gift of humor. A group of his admirers in Washington collected what was called Claudeliana, but his outbursts of fancy were so personal that the idea of printing them was given up. On one occasion when Claudel, who loves music, was our guest at a concert together with a talkative ambassadress who bothered him in the middle of a Beethoven symphony with the question: "Ah, monsieur, is there anything more beautiful than music?" he retorted grimly: *"Oui, madame, le silence."* Another time when Claudel and I were motoring he suddenly grabbed my arm and exclaimed: *"Regardez, regardez! Qu'est-ce que c'est que ça?"* He was pointing at a signboard which read "Sodom." I explained that it was the name of the little village we were entering. *"Alors, arrêtons-nous, je dois absolument envoyer une carte postale à mon ami, Gide."* Unfortunately Sodom was too bucolic to have picture postal cards; so Claudel contented himself by asking a bewildered local character if he knew the road to Gomorrah. But Claudel also had the humor of compassion. My children used to sit around him with eyes bulging as he told them fantastic stories with such realistic details that they could not tell fact from fancy. Invariably these tales, like that of *"le lapin au gilet rouge"* settling down in Noah's Ark, ended with grotesque absurdities that made the children roll over each other with shrieks of uncontrolled mirth.

One of Claudel's humorous games with me was a half-real, half-pretended resentment of my friendship *"avec cet esprit Protestant,"* Thomas Mann. Claudel could pronounce the word Protestant with inimitable contempt. When I sent him my translation of Thomas Mann's magnificent defense of the European humanistic tradition, an anti-Hitler document, to which I gave the title "Standards and Values,"

Claudel thundered back by the next mail: "What is this Christianity without Christ, this religion without dogma, this sauce without a roast? I know but one standard, the Cross. And I know but one value, the blood of Christ." But he was generous in his appraisal of Mann. Claudel is too great an artist to allow his critical appreciation to be smothered by religious prejudice. His gaiety always gained the upper hand when I refused to budge in my loyalty to Mann's achievements. On one occasion when I was leaving Claudel in Paris to see Thomas Mann in Switzerland, Claudel gritted his teeth with feigned wrath, took out of his desk a double sheet of Japanese vellum, and in his clear handwriting that looks like Chinese calligraphy indited for me in red and black ink the following doggerel:

FAREWELL

My dearest Paul, je vous lâche,
L'amour comme les fleurs se fane,
Je m'en vais garder les vaches
Avec le poète Thomas Mann.

June 11, 1937   CLAUDEL

Last year when I was in Paris I traveled six hours by train to visit Claudel in his stately château at Brangues near the Swiss border. We were both nervous about seeing each other again after a lapse of ten years. He in the meantime had traveled nearer to the heaven he has so magically evoked in *Christophe Colomb* and I had become more consecrated to the heaven I should like to see created here on earth. He met me at the Lyons station. We could scarcely see each other. Tears of joy obscured our vision. We knew instantly that our diverse paths had brought us closer together than ever before. Arriving at his château, we walked back and forth under a double row of ancient trees on the parapet of the garden overlooking the Rhône valley and talked of cabbages and kings. We laughed together as heartily as ever. What we felt — what even Claudel's gift for words could not express — meant more to us than anything that was said. The peace which lay over the valley and mountains reigned as well in our minds, moods and hearts. It is the most exceptional and the most mysterious of miracles when the relationship between two human beings creates an emotion so intense, exalted and pure. And the greatest miracle of all is that at a time of such violent hostility between Catholics and Protestants, two such extreme representatives of these cultures could meet in perfect harmony above and beyond all the petty hindrances of dogma.

Claudel at eighty-three looks like a Buddhist lohan. His deep-set gray-green eyes have all the old fire. They become black when he speaks of the spiritual puerility of modern life, just as they become luminous when he speaks of the love of God. For most contemporary French writers he has little respect. "They have no feeling for the language. Their style is achieved by mixing cod-liver oil with gooseberry jam," he says in disgust. He makes an exception of Aragon. He admits that Sartre has talent but adds: "*Violà l'enfer.*" Claudel himself works regularly every morning for two and a half hours after he has heard Mass in the village church and eaten his breakfast. This steady productivity has piled up numerous unpublished works.

Claudel is now the rage of Paris. He has been elected to the Academy at long last, after being rejected many years ago in favor of a nonentity. "They considered me too revolutionary," he explained to me at the time, not without regret. The final gesture of official sanctification took place when President Auriol in October 1951 conferred upon him the Grand Cross of the Legion of Honor. In 1949 he had three plays running simultaneously in Paris to crowded houses, and a year later two others were produced. His new publications are immediately bought up, especially by young people who see in his poetical Catholicism an answer to the equally popular nihilism of Sartre. Nevertheless the printing presses cannot keep pace with Claudel's creative urge which he says overflows as regularly as the breasts of a nursing mother. "There is after all a limit to what the market can absorb even of Claudel," he commented. "People must be allowed to read something else now and then." Most of the belated and uncritical praise now heaped upon him seems to Claudel a new but more agreeable kind of insult.

When I left by plane the next day Claudel arose at six A.M. to take me to the airfield. We were too moved to speak very much for we both knew, as Clau put it, that our next encounter might be in heaven. But he is still well, still active, writing, doing radio interviews on his life and still asking me by letter when I intend to leave "ce no-man's land ou ce no-woman's land" as he recently described my Protestant world of thought.

As to Claudel's certainty of immortality, I cannot do better than to quote a passage from his last letter in which he prophesies that our friendship will reach beyond the grave:

Ce n'est pas l'homme que vous aimez en moi. C'etait ce Dieu en qui vous n'avez jamais cessé de croire et dont vous sentiez que j'avais le coeur rempli. Et moi c'est cette soeur aveugle et enchainée que j'aimais de tout mon coeur. Un jour, quand je serai mort, vous comprendrez tout cela et nous reprendrons nos anciennes conversations. Nous avons encore tant de choses a nous dire!

My encounter with Thomas Mann was as impersonal as that with Claudel was personal. I had inherited from my

North German parents an enthusiasm for *Buddenbrooks,* Mann's first novel, which deals with such themes as the decadence of the German bourgeoisie and the agonies of the sensitive artistic mind in its struggle to survive and remain creative during this gradual social disintegration. I had responded less to the short stories that followed *Buddenbrooks,* including "Tonio Kröger" and "Death in Venice," because my youthful insecurity was disturbed by the death-fixation, the sharp irony and the sense of doom which pervades these works.

But then a curious combination of circumstances, as so often in my life, had cataclysmic results. In 1936 the whole family was on a pack trip in the Wyoming Mountains, just south of the Yellowstone. When Eugene and the children decided to return to the ranch, which was our point of departure, I remained at our last camp, an idyllic spot at an elevation of 9000 feet, for the enjoyment of complete solitude, which is essential every now and then to my well-being. In the afternoon I went on long solitary climbing expeditions. Every morning I lay in a shaded spot beneath giant trees next a meandering trout stream and read in German, Mann's *The Magic Mountain* and his then recently published novel, *Joseph in Egypt,* while squirrels, mink and various birds circled around me, curious as to why I lay so still hour after hour. As when I first beheld Chinese painting, I fell in love — passionately in love — with Thomas Mann's style. I have never wavered in considering him the greatest literary craftsman of our day. In the criticisms I subsequently wrote for the *New York Times Book Review* and the *Washington Post,* I tried to help American readers understand the profound themes, the complicated interplay of German philosophical and literary influences, the symphonic structure and biographical content that make reality in Thomas Mann's novels a translucent picture of Germany's cultural evolution and its eventual catastrophic downfall. But I have never been able to convey in these analyses the deep subconscious cultural affinities that make Mann's writing qua writing irresistible to me. I turned toward his works with as much or as little reason as a plant turns toward the sun.

Goethe, as personality, poet and intellectual genius, as the creator of Germany's cultural traditions and as one of the last literary figures who dared to conceive of himself as embracing the totality of Western civilization, has been the greatest single influence on Thomas Mann. Schopenhauer, Nietzsche and Wagner have been other powerful stimulants in Mann's literary development. But the music of Mann's style also harks back to romanticists like Fritz Reuter, Theodor Storm, Theodor Fontane and other North German novelists, little known to Americans, whose enchanting, joyous yet melancholy cadences had become familiar to me when I listened to their works being read aloud during my earliest childhood. To be sure, Mann's style has a psychological intensity, and a virility of form, revealed in its highest manifestation in the Riemer chapter of *Lotte in Weimar* (*The Beloved Returns*), which these earlier North German authors who lived in less anxious, simpler days, were incapable of achieving. Much as I enjoy Mann's complexity, what holds me captive when I read his prose is a nostalgia for all that was musical and good and essentially Protestant in the cultural sense of that tradition, in short, for a Germany which nourished my aesthetic senses throughout an intensely happy childhood. In a poem called "Lost," by Theodor Storm, which Thomas Mann also loves, this mysterious charm of half-forgotten days which I relive in Mann's works is perfectly conveyed:

Was holdes liegt mir in dem Sinn,
Das ich vor Zeit einmal besessen;
Ich weiss nicht, wo es kommen hin,
Auch was es war, ist mir vergessen. . . .

I did not meet Thomas Mann until he came to America for a lecture tour in 1937. His very appearance was familiar to me as he looks not unlike a sophisticated version of some of my mother's relatives, North German sailors and sea captains, who visited us from time to time when their ships landed near New York. Few Americans can have my sense of identification with Mann, but I do not believe that anybody, myself included, can claim to know him as a human being. I have always been most at home with him through our long correspondence which concerned itself chiefly with his literary productions. I take pride in the fact that Mann on one occasion said he had never exchanged so many letters with any other person and on another that I wrote German better than most Germans.

This correspondence was an enriching influence upon me. It obliged me to define and express the values I found in Mann's works; and in exploring the paths of his genius, I was traveling undiscovered regions of my own mind. I should not forget to say that the American public owes Mrs. Lowe-Porter a debt of gratitude for wrestling with the impossible task of translating Mann's intricacies of language, structure and style. I was nearly ready for the madhouse after translating one of his political essays whose prose is just the A, B, C, of Mann's linguistic pyrotechnics.

Mann rescued for me, as for all humanity, Germany's highest cultural traditions from the shame and the moral collapse of the Nazi period. He reaffirmed our faith that the human spirit can survive the vilest environmental influences if it knows whence it comes and has the strength to continue its individual growth. His roots, planted as they were in the deep soil of German culture, could be transplanted without withering in the American climate to which he emigrated. Was not that the reason why my own parents were able to hand down to me the noble human values which they too brought to this country from their native land? In other words, what happens to the individual is not as important as what he makes of those happenings. Freedom of mind and soul cannot be given to us nor can it be taken away by outward circumstance because it resides eternally in the human breast.

Mann's development has followed closely that of Goethe. As the child of German culture in a state of dissolution, Mann had a more difficult trial by fire than his great prototype, and his victory over self, his refusal to lose himself either in Schopenhauer's philosophy of escape from life, or in Wagner's dionysiac frenzy, is all the nearer and more important to us.

Mann's early work was haunted by a Hamletlike obsession by these two irreconcilable alternatives. The First World War revealed to Mann the dangers to German civilization if the artist remained aloof from life. *The Magic Mountain,* the result of this revolution in his thinking, was the first novel in which the hero, after exploring the temptations of the mountaintops, returns to the flatland of duty. From that time onward Mann struggled with the dangers of the split personality until in his last full-length novel, *Dr. Faustus* (of which his more recent book *The Holy Sinner,* is but an off-shoot), his hero seeks absolute purity and arrives at an aestheticism so abstract that it lacks all human love and common experience. Like Nietzsche, like modern Germany, he finally breaks down and goes insane. In this amazing novel Mann warns his dishonored country and the world that creative art

like creative living can issue only from the interpenetration
of reason and sense, mind and matter, or *Geist* and *Natur,* to
use the German words. Mann's *Faustus* is the apotheosis of
the symbolism of his *Transposed Heads* in which the body
becomes coarsened when separated from mind, and mind
loses its spiritualizing influence when separated from the
body.

Mann's humanism seems to me the most consoling answer yet given to the agonies of our split personalities. For
he helps us to find our way through the turmoil of modern
life toward a new balance of demonic passion and calculated
order, of spontaneity and responsibility, of freedom and
self-discipline.

This humanistic religion will come into being, Mann in-
timates, only after the dangerous search for absolutes is
abandoned and humanity realizes humbly that we make the
world in which we live. Though we have nearly destroyed
our cultural heritage, a new world will be born out of our
despair and the sheer necessity for self-preservation.

Claudel and Mann thus represent the two main trends of
Western civilization between which we must all make our
choice unless we can reconcile them — whether to shut our
eyes with Claudel and accept intuitively an ancient myth of
persuasive beauty or whether with Goethe and Thomas
Mann to use our reason in order to rescue fertile territory
from the mysterious seas with which human existence is en-
compassed. My love for Claudel is profound because he has
breathed new life into the Christian cult, ceremonial and
faith which the clergy have done their best to routinize. But
in the no less religious works of Thomas Mann which tell us
that evil as well as goodness is a creation of the mind and
that their interaction can be controlled through insight, I
see more awareness of our psychological tensions, a deeper

response to the need for a world-embracing sympathy and therefore a greater hope for the universal brotherhood of man here on earth.

If we poor human beings, challenged and tortured as never before, should succeed in saving our souls in this world, how could the good God not be content with such heroism? The covenant with God makes the Deity just as dependent upon man as man is upon Him. The real sin against the Holy Ghost, as we learn in Mann's Joseph series, is failure to recognize when old forms of worship, such as Abraham's willingness to sacrifice his first-born, become outmoded. As Thomas Mann said to me one day when we were discussing the Joseph novels: "God, too, has His biography" — an unending biography to which another chapter is added whenever humanity raises its spiritual stature and elevates its concept of the Divine.

For me there is no sharp antithesis between the positions of these two artists, possibly because I have learned so much from each of them. Both men are concerned with the reinterpretation of myth as a guide to life's deepest wisdom. Both realize that the present is tied to the past with hoops of steel. If Mann's use of the myth seems to me more comprehensive, it is because Claudel has learned to live with himself but Mann has learned to live with all mankind. Seen in this complementary light, they solve what the philosopher Whitehead termed the central problem of the twentieth century, the reconciliation of religion and science.

My husband resigned his public office as Governor of the Federal Reserve Board in May 1933 because he refused to go along with some of President Roosevelt's monetary ideas. For two years he had worked from twelve to eighteen hours a day. He was exhausted and I literally feared for his life. His fatigue was so appalling that he could not walk straight. But his recuperative powers were such that after three weeks' repose on the farm he became restless again. My doubts as to whether he should undertake a new career were dispelled when he came downstairs one morning and, running his finger along a slightly dusty banister, announced: "This house is not properly run." Obviously his energies needed a new outlet.

For many years Eugene had wanted to purchase the *Washington Post* which had long been running downhill under the ownership of Mr. and Mrs. Edward B. McLean. At exactly the right moment, just as he was really beginning to feel better, it was announced that the paper would be put up at public auction on June 1. He sent a lawyer to make the purchase for him and announced a few days later that he was the sole stockholder of the *Washington Post,* and that he would run it as an independent paper devoted to the best interests of the community and the nation. Without the slightest experience in newspaper work, but with his usual self-confidence, he began a new career at the age of fifty-eight that was one of the most difficult of the many difficult tasks he had ever undertaken.

Eugene bought the *Post* for only one reason, because he realized that this Washington newspaper was the most effective means for continuing his public service. The publisher of any paper has two jobs on his hands, its financial solvency and the guidance of its editorial policy. Both tasks were extremely difficult on the *Post*. The building and the presses were wrecks; the staff was a mere skeleton force. All three had to be rebuilt without interruption of daily publication. Guiding the paper's policies was a full-time job in itself for the Roosevelt New Deal was in full swing. Every day there were developments of momentous importance which had to be evaluated with objectivity and courage. In business Eugene had been known as the first man to use statistics to chart economic trends. He had always combined a capacity for analysis of facts with an intuitive grasp for their future significance. His capacity to look ahead — with accuracy — was to serve him well.

Yet when Eugene first bought the *Washington Post,* even his good friends among the publishers assured him that he could not possibly make a success of it. As the paper gradually but steadily gained in prestige, readability and advertising, and as Washington became more and more the news center in the national and international scene, a leading publisher said to him: "Eugene, it's just your luck to buy a paper in a city that has become the Capital of the World." To which Eugene characteristically replied: "Jimmie, it's just like you to think that that was luck."

My contributions to the paper were spasmodic until the outbreak of the Second World War. I wrote the articles on the W.P.A. in Westchester County, which I have already mentioned. And I published an interview with John Dewey on December 19, 1937, just after he had returned from Coyoacán, Mexico, where he had acted as Chairman of the Commission of Enquiry on Leon Trotsky. The headline read: JOHN DEWEY, GREAT AMERICAN LIBERAL, DENOUNCES RUSSIAN DICTATORSHIP. Completely disillusioned of his early hopes concerning the Bolshevik revolution, he warned the American people that Communist authoritarianism was as great an evil and just as serious a menace to the democratic nations as that of Hitler. To American fellow travelers of whom there were many at that time he said:

> I do not think that a confirmed Communist is going to get anywhere by concluding that because he can no longer believe in Stalin he must now pin his faith in Trotsky. The

great lesson for all American radicals and for all sympa-
thizers with the U.S.S.R. is that they must go back and reconsider the whole means of bringing about social changes and
of truly democratic methods of approach to social progress.

And he finished his appeal to the Communist fellow travelers in these words:

> The conclusion, or moral, or whatever you want to call it,
> is that we must depend upon our own community, upon our
> own democratic methods for the working out of our prob-
> lems, both domestic and international.

The day after the interview appeared I met Oumansky,
then in the Russian Embassy, and later Russian Ambassador
to Mexico City, at a tea party. This man, who was killed
in a mysterious plane crash, was one of the most dangerous
because he was one of the cleverest Communists I have ever
met. He was blind with rage over Dewey's attack on the
Stalin regime, a loss of self-control unusual in any Communist, especially in this cold, calculating creature. "I con-
gratulate you on your journalistic enterprise, Mrs. Meyer,"
he said with a vicious, threatening expression. Then unable
to control his anger, he broke out with: "John Dewey will
live to regret this attack."

Finally, I took part in the *Post's* campaign against Nazism
by translating Thomas Mann's essay "The Coming Victory
of Democracy." The translation, as I have said, was a tough
assignment but I like to think that it helped Americans
understand that we were in a battle for the survival of individual freedom, human dignity and the whole structure of
Western civilization.

On Saturday, December 7, 1941 Eugene and I gave a
picnic luncheon for some forty people at a charming little
cabin jutting out over the Potomac River, on the Virginia

side, which we use as an escape from the hectic life of Washington. All sorts of people were there including justices of the Supreme Court, Cabinet members, Senators, and a number of young people who were friends of our children.

Just after lunch as we were sitting around open fires Eugene was called to the telephone by the city editor of the *Washington Post*. He came back and said: "Pearl Harbor has been bombed by the Japanese." A silence fell upon that group which I shall always remember. It seemed to last an eternity. Then one of the young men said very quietly: "Now I know how people behave in a crisis." That broke the spell. Without bothering to say good-by, officials streaked for their cars and rushed back to Washington. A new world had begun for all of us.

CHAPTER X

World War in Britain

IN JULY of '42 our only son, Eugene Meyer III, Bill to all of us in the family, was about to leave for service as a medical officer with the 64th Fighter Wing, and our son-in-law, Philip L. Graham, who enlisted in the army, was departing for Sioux Falls to take his basic training. As Bill had only just completed his first year as an interne at Johns Hopkins Hospital and Phil had been working hard in the Lend Lease Administration, both boys were given a week's furlough, which they spent at our farm in Mount Kisco with their young wives. I need hardly say it was a touching family reunion.

Every morning I closeted myself in the Chinese room, as my hide-out under the eaves of our house is called, to continue the writing of a philosophical essay on the works of Tolstoi, Dostoevski and Thomas Mann, a theme which seemed to me relevant to the tense social, ideological and spiritual conflicts which had precipitated the war.

The day before both boys were scheduled for departure, Bill said that he and Phil would like to have a talk with me in the library. When we had closed the door, Bill opened the discussion with characteristic candor. "I know how important your book is, Mother, but to us there's just one thing that is more important today than anything else. That's beating Hitler. While Phil and I are away we'd like to feel that you are doing your special kind of job here at home."

Thereupon Phil joined in: "You know your way around Washington," he argued, "and you know the grass roots. It will take a lot of doing to keep the Federal government in touch with local problems. Many of them are bound to be a headache. Bill and I think that's where you come in and where you can be most useful." Thus Bill and Phil summoned me to action.

Destiny has a curious way of taking hold of us if we do not try to force the issue but respond to the call when it comes. One of my friends in Washington was Craig McGeachy (now Mrs. Erwin Schuller), Minister of Welfare in the British Embassy. When we returned to Washington after the boys had gone, she aroused my curiosity by describing how efficiently the British were managing the social aspects of the war effort with a view to conserving every ounce of human energy for production. She urged me to make a tour of Britain's war centers and report in detail how the machinery for production and for protection against bombing was organized. When I sought permission from the State Department, I also asked that my old friend, Ruth Taylor, should be allowed to accompany me. Together, on September 2, 1942, we flew across the Atlantic on a plane so heavily overloaded that it raised itself slowly, arduously from the waters of the East River. When we entered Foynes Harbor, the plane skipped over a choppy bright blue sea under two perfect rainbows that reached from one brilliant green shore to the other.

In London the magnitude of our task soon became apparent. We had to get the permission of five different ministries, Information, Food, Health, Labor and the Home Office, to see all that we wanted to see and to co-ordinate in each city the mass of projects which each of the various ministers thought it necessary for us to understand. Fortunately Craig McGeachy had told us to consult George Haynes, National Secretary of the National Council of Social Service, if we got into trouble. This highly efficient Secretary of the National Council of Social Service, and now also President of the International Organization of Social Work, immediately took over the responsibility of organizing our whole journey beginning in Edinburgh through Glasgow, Clydeside, Newcastle, Tyneside, Bristol, Cardiff and the southern mining valleys of Wales. As a result we lost not a minute of time. When we arrived at Edinburgh, we were met at 7:30 A.M. at the railroad station by A. M. Struthers, head of the Scottish Council of Social Agencies, and his assistant, Grace Drysdale, with three long typewritten pages that listed all of our appointments filling every hour from morning until late at night during the three days we spent in or near the Scottish capital. This routine was followed in each successive city.

The first protracted bombings caught the British nation ill-prepared. The London County Council had provided extensive hospital facilities, beautiful morgues, and vast numbers of coffins. But they had failed to anticipate that the death rate would be comparatively low, and the number of homeless, hungry and destitute people enormous. The country at first paid a high price for this lack of foresight; but if lack of imagination is a weakness of the British, their gift for co-operation and their ability to learn by experience constitute the national genius. The result was that the local communities themselves evolved much of the machinery which when I saw it after three years of war was certainly highly efficient. Every town or city of any size had worked out its own mobilized defense units, which could be rushed at a moment's notice on motorcycles or specially fitted trucks to any other community that had been hit by "Jerry." We should consult the experienced British on what they are now doing to improve their methods of defense against possible attacks by atomic bombs. It is high time we realized that many of our own plans for civil defense units manned by amateurs are inexcusably silly, and economically wasteful.

The co-operative local effort to protect their homes and lives from air attack constituted the most intensive education which a whole population has ever received, in the latent powers of democracy. I experienced several alerts and one attack on London which was taken so calmly and expertly that it created in me a sense of exaltation rather than fear. When I expressed admiration for the morale of the people at a meeting of the Coventry defense unit, one of the members replied: "Oh, we're not much now. You should have been here at the time of the heavy bombing. That's when our spirit was really grand."

Before leaving London for Scotland, I had had a salutary but distressing experience. A high British civil servant whom I had met in Washington asked me to dine with him and his family. They lived in a large house in one of the fashionable sections of London. All the housework including cooking was now done by the hostess and her two daughters, ten and fourteen years of age. The spare rooms including those formerly occupied by servants had been requisitioned by the government for six Wrens or women naval volunteers. These billetees, as they were called, had to have their own sitting room and three meals a day, a hot one at noon, which my hostess provided on a small government allowance. Often these billetees had different hours of work which, of course, meant different hours for meals. But this was a typical situation in the homes of the well-to-do. Every inch of living space throughout the British Isles had to be utilized for military personnel and transferred war workers, and I'm not sure that those matrons who became maids of all work "for the duration" have received the credit they deserved. One British officer said to me: "We military men live a comparatively sheltered life, but my wife works around the clock."

In addition to her endless household chores, my hostess had raised three ducks in her garden and they were cherished in this time of the meat shortage. One of the precious animals was sacrificed in my honor. When the duck was passed I took as small a piece as I could, realizing that one duck will not go far for five persons. But when the remains of the duck were passed a second time I was deep in conversation with my host and absent-mindedly I took a second helping. The silent dismay which I immediately felt in the children gave me an overwhelming sense of guilt, so appalling that I could scarcely endure it. While talking glibly along to cover my embarrassment I weighed the problem of whether to leave that morsel of duck on my plate or not. Was it more heinous to take what I did or to leave what I had taken? In any case I ate it. The humiliation of this experience has never faded. It became to me a symbol of American insensitivity to the living conditions of other people.

Our first day in Edinburgh revealed how heavily the impact of total war falls upon the whole population, especially the women. Near Edinburgh we saw a steel plant run almost wholly by womanpower, from the direction of the great crane with its dangerous load of molten metal to the lifting of heavy cores weighing more than a hundred pounds. Fifty-three per cent of these young women had become anemic under the strain, yet they stuck to their tasks.

In the rural areas the Woman's Land Army was felling trees, clearing ground and doing other heavy manual labor under the bad weather conditions which had already set in during September. It was so cold and damp that Ruth and I succumbed to "woollies," a thing we had never done at home in the severest winters. Many women rose in the dark at six A.M., prepared breakfast, got the children ready for school, left their shopping basket at the butcher's, took a bus trip of an hour or more to a factory and after eight hours' work, returned in darkness to the butcher's for their allotment of food and the preparation of the evening meal. On Sundays these mothers had to clean house, do the family wash and the week's mending. As the sun rises late and sets early for six months, these women never saw the light of day during the week except through a factory window.

The British government did everything possible to make life more livable for the housewife. "What I try to do," said Lord Woolton, then Minister of Food, "is to treat the people justly. The rich get less to eat, the poor get more. Therefore, I am doing a service to both." As the British people have a profound sense of justice, anyone who is "fair" — the adjective they all used for Lord Woolton — always wins their respect and confidence.

I was curious to see this popular official. The man who was official housekeeper for the British nation began life as Frederic James Marquis, a settlement worker in the Liverpool dock district before he became one of England's most successful business executives. Tall, gray-haired, affable, his gentle, easygoing manner belies the energy which his good-humored, steel-gray eyes reveal. The same contradiction exists in his character. It mingles humanity and efficiency, charm and firmness, kindness and first-rate intelligence. "We started food rationing from the very beginning," said Lord Woolton, "not with the negative idea of tightening belts but with the positive aim of keeping the British people fighting fit."

Lord Woolton's first concern was for pregnant women and infants to ensure the future of the nation. His next concern was for children under three. All the available supply of milk and eggs was reserved for children and pregnant women. At school a hot midday meal with milk was introduced to ensure a basic food supply to older children. In many schools the children could get breakfast and on Fridays they could take food home. But the greatest help to the whole population were the British Restaurants, as the communal feeding stations were called. An excellent meal of meat and two vegetables cost fifteen cents. Strong soup and sweets cost five cents each. Tea was a penny. These meals, and we ate them all over the country, were tastier and more nourishing than the food at the expensive hotels. It was possible to supply them at such low rates because communal cooking saved three items, the value of which in Britain during the war were beyond price: labor, food and fuel.

These British Restaurant meals did not come out of the ration cards. They were "extra." The importance of communal feeding as an adjunct to the war effort was not foreseen by the Ministry of Food or anyone else. Like most of Britain's revolutionary war measures, they were the result of bitter experience. They were forced upon the government by the blitz, which left many thousands of people homeless, hungry and destitute. As a by-product mobile canteens and kitchens, canteens for factory workers in all industries employing more than 250 people, and strategic storing of food supplies were also evolved. Lord Woolton saw food rationing as a preliminary step toward the realization of a permanent basic health diet which would be within the reach of the lowest incomes. Our American conservatives would condemn him as a Socialist for such ideas. The importance of food rationing was summed up for me by a Tyneside doctor. "Lord Woolton has done more for the health of the British people than the whole medical profession put together."

Never have I seen a nation work as hard as the British worked during the war. Everybody — men, women, and children as young as fourteen years — was at work. Our war tempo was far less exacting. We had more manpower to do the job; we had an ampler food supply; we were spared the menace and destruction of the blitz as well as the depressing effect of the blackout. In Britain more than two thirds of the population between fourteen and sixty-five were wholly employed in the war effort. Registration was compulsory under the Manpower Act for all men under fifty-one and women under forty-five, except those with children under fourteen, and wives of men in the military services. In the factories production was not interrupted even by the air alert. Only when the klaxon sounded, which meant a German plane was three minutes away, did the workers dash for the air shelters. When they got home, at night, the civilians had voluntary duties connected with defense mobilization which kept many of them on duty sometimes the night through. Never did I hear anyone grumble. "Oh, we've been knocked about a bit but it's not too bad. The only thing we want is to get on with it," was a frequent response to our sympathy.

While going through a Tyneside shipyard with the works manager, we passed an elderly man wiping the sweat off his face and completely exhausted as he came off the shift. "What's the matter, Jim?" asked the manager. "It's them women," replied Jim. He had been relining a furnace with bricks which three women in relays were tossing up to his scaffold. They passed the bricks to him so rapidly that he had to work furiously to keep up with them. "I wasn't going to let them beat me," he panted, "but they nearly killed me."

The constant shifting of labor entailed great hardship. In "the battle of the bodies," as the British termed it, labor had become just as mobile as the armed forces. I met one married woman with five small children in South Wales who had been evacuated from London to Folkstone and then after the fall of France to the countryside near Cardiff. Her husband, a skilled worker, had been bombed out of his first job, moved to a second, and finally sent to a munitions factory near Cardiff. The family was overjoyed to be united again after two years of separation.

This was not an exceptional case. Many families were scattered far and wide. One fourth of the laborers were living away from home. Most of these families were not reunited until the war was over. With parents away from home, delinquency was rising among the older boys and girls. The British were worried about the disintegrating effects of war work upon home life. If their family life did retain its loyalties it was chiefly because the organization of the British war effort was more orderly and more humane than ours. But the British are now just as worried as we are over a rising divorce rate.

The most delicate job the Ministry of Labor had to handle was the revolutionary policy of conscripting young girls for factory work. To assist him with such problems, Mr. Bevin,

the Minister of Labor, appointed a Factory and Welfare
Board that co-ordinated two welfare services, the old Department of Inspection, which functioned within the factory,
and a new organization of trained social workers, which controlled the welfare programs outside the factory. I saw the
convoy officers of this board handle the most obstreperous
conscripts, the Scottish girls who came from as far away as
the Hebrides and had never before left their homes and
native surroundings. With two weeks' warning, these naïve
youngsters were torn from their families and "sent to
slavery," as their friends called it, in royal ordnance factories employing from 5000 to 18,000 women in various
parts of England. The Scottish parents, good members of
the Kirk, felt at first that their daughters were being sent
straight to hell when they were suddenly whisked off to great
industrial centers like Brimingham or Liverpool. Yet this
explosive situation was handled with such tact and efficiency
that over 10,000 of these girls were moved to factory hostels
or billeted in private homes without arousing lasting complaint. In a huge powder plant I interviewed a large group
of them, who had just come off the night shift, the most un-
propitious moment. They said firmly, "Home is best" but
"we wouldn't be anywhere else for the duration."

The administration of the Manpower Act in Great Britain was efficient because the Ministry of Labor, while shifting men and women about the country, never forgot that it
was dealing not with numbers but with human beings. The
government realized that it incurred a social responsibility
toward workers when it transferred them from their homes
to a strange environment and a new occupation. It foresaw
that a discontented worker cannot make his maximum effort.
For moral and practical reasons it dignified labor as it has
always dignified military service.

The war effort also caused Britain to evolve an exceptional plan for the care of children, especially those under five. At all ages, they were better nourished and therefore healthier than they ever had been. This was especially noticeable in the slums of London. In one of the most depressed areas I carefully watched five hundred boys and girls file out of school. I never saw a huskier group. This is a record of which Britain can be proud. It is hypocritical of the defenders of nationalized medicine to claim that the improvement in the nation's health is due to free medical care. It is due chiefly to the excellent war program for the conservation of the energy of the whole population.

The problem of child care in a nation exposed to bombing was extremely difficult. Thousands of children were evacuated from dangerous areas or because their homes had been destroyed by the blitz. Some were moved with their mothers. Others saw them only on occasional visits. In September 1942 some three to four hundred thousand children were evacuees, mostly in foster homes. The foster mothers were patience itself. Often the country women could not even understand the language of the city children.

About 12,000 infants lived in 380 residential nurseries, many of them beautiful country houses taken over by the government. These were children whose mothers had been killed or who had to remain at home to look after other members of the family. Older children were placed in hostels or boarding schools, of which there were over 600, including 200 for "difficult" boys and girls. The close family solidarity in Britain inevitably complicated the care of children, whether "difficult" or not, who were separated from their parents for the first time. This extensive child-welfare program was also handicapped by lack of adequately trained manpower, but British officials and volunteers bent their backs to do the best possible job. The social workers and volunteers in charge of the institutions for evacuated children repeatedly assured me: "The evacuation problem has convinced us of one thing — any home, even the poorest, is better for a child than none."

The importance of Great Britain's local government and of its voluntary organizations was demonstrated by the sensitive and expert handling of evacuated families. No effort was spared by the local communities to make these strangers feel welcome and to furnish them not only with the necessities of life including medical care, but with recreation and clubs of various kinds. I remember one seaport, Weston super Mare, whose normal population was 34,000, where the mayor, his town clerk and billeting officer placed 17,000 evacuees in four days. When we visited Weston it still had over 3000 evacuees, including a huge and strange assortment of pets. One woman showed me her canary and vowed he had been blown out of the house by one blast and in again by another. "He sulked for a while," she declared in answer to my look of incredulity, "but now he's beginnin' to sing again." The evacuees took their experiences as cheerfully as this canary.

As we visited several large and beautiful homes for old men evacuees I asked why we had not been shown any such homes for old women. "There aren't any," replied one official. "The old women are all doing their bit in factories or in homes. Grandpa is only a nuisance but Grandma is one of our greatest assets."

"What keeps England going," said one woman with whom I conversed on a train, "is a profound sense of duty." This sense of duty has been developed in the British to a far deeper extent than in Americans. They have, to be sure, the advantage over us of being a homogeneous people who have worked at the problem of human freedom for almost a thousand years. They are not as brilliant, imaginative and spontaneous as our American workers, nor are they on the average as well educated. But they have a rocklike stability and self-confidence combined with an uncanny awareness of others. Because they are so tenaciously individualistic, they are intuitive and secure in co-operative endeavor.

This is a point we Americans must understand in evaluating the future development of British Socialism. During the war, for example, Britain was severely regimented, yet through sheer self-discipline, the people became stronger and more democratic in the fire of that ordeal.

How did they do it?

There is one fundamental difference between the British system of government and ours. We carry out government policies exclusively through governmental agencies; they frequently put government policies into effect through a close partnership between the state and the voluntary groups, both local and national. Their centralized nation-wide program for meeting the requirements of total war depended almost entirely on local administration and upon innumerable voluntary groups that worked together intuitively, but with a smoothness and efficiency that remained baffling and mysterious to anyone not accustomed to the British way of doing things.

There existed hard and fast official regulations, especially for such crises as a blitz; but these regulations acquired flexibility when carried out by so many heterogeneous groups who never interpreted their duties narrowly.

In our country we hold meeting after meeting — we are doing it now on the subject of civil defense — at which we pass innumerable resolutions which people forget the minute they leave. In Britain we attended crucial meetings on defense at which not a single measure was formally adopted. When, somewhat baffled, I asked the chairman whether the people present understood what they were to do, he replied: "Of course. They got 'the sense of the meeting,' a phrase we have borrowed from the Quakers. They will carry out the regulations according to their own way of doing things, but with a clear understanding of the results to be achieved." This, it seemed to me, was an illustration of responsible, active and truly intelligent democratic procedure at its best.

To me the most arresting fact in the British adjustment to total war was that the unavoidable growth of central authority was accompanied by a parallel growth of voluntary action and local initiative. Curtailment of freedom in some respects only stimulated the British to find new areas for its expression. Their whole war effort was an exhilarating demonstration that a genuinely democratic people can always work out a new balance between state regulation, local government and individual initiative. Having seen this British reaction to centralized authority, I feel justified in believing that they will never be placed permanently in the strait jacket of an absolute Socialist government.

One of the most useful by-products of the British war effort which we would do well to study are the Citizens' Advice Bureaus of which there were twelve hundred in 1942. They were not unlike our Veterans' Service Centers except that they served the civilian population as well. They were organized as information centers to save people from running around aimlessly after a blitz; their purpose was to help the civilian find food, clothes, new ration cards or other necessities without loss of time. From this point of departure, these Citizens' Advice Bureaus became one of the most useful supplements to democratic government. At present there are approximately five hundred such bureaus. They are manned by some five thousand workers of whom about one third are paid full-time employees; the remainder are volunteers. A large proportion of these bureaus have a panel of advisers, probation officers, welfare and other social workers upon whom they can call for guidance. In addition the majority of bureaus have some arrangements for free legal advice and all work in close relationship with the new State Legal Aid Scheme which provides for litigation in high court matters, largely divorce. The central committee of the C.A.B. is a department of the National Council of Social Services.

The general inquiries are now about one million annually. The number of family and personal problems that are brought to the bureaus is increasing steadily; a recent circular attempts to give bureaus some guidance about "home-making advice." The questions being brought to bureaus are in many cases extremely complicated and it is vital that this large band of paid and voluntary workers is hand-picked, adequately trained and kept thoroughly up to date with new legislation, new regulations, and new services.

Inquiries come from all walks of life, although the family and personal problems and matrimonial inquiries come largely from the poorer classes; that is, from the kind of people who have no access to legal or other professional advisers. These C.A.B.'s are needed because the average citizen does not yet trust the Welfare State. On paper it looks as if it carried people in its arms from birth to death, but in reality it still creates something akin to fear in the ordinary man and woman for whom its ministrations are intended. Moreover, it is so complicated that the individual

confronted with a sudden difficulty is often ignorant of how
to get the assistance to which he is entitled. "You can't get
anywhere with those people (meaning public officials),"
they tell the C.A.B. staffs, "unless you know the ropes."
And even when these timid souls are directed to the right
office and have filled out all the endless forms correctly, they
suffer a sense of outrage when the almighty state says "No"
and they are convinced it should have said "Yes."

At the local C.A.B. these frustrated citizens feel that they
get a more sympathetic hearing and go away more reconciled, even when their problems cannot be solved. The
bureau often takes over an old shop on the local main street.
Over the front is a blue sign that says CITIZENS' ADVICE
BUREAU in nice friendly letters. The room is Spartan, but
bright posters hang round the walls and there is a pleasantly
informal feeling. At separate tables sit a woman and a man,
giving ear to two customers in full spate. There is no disagreeable sensation of waiting on the headmaster, or even
the bank manager. The customer on the left is a weather-
beaten cottager with three bulging shopping bags and the
kind of personal drama that hinges mainly on "I says to
him, she says to me." Hers is an ancient burden, trouble
with the landlord. On the other side of the table the expert,
who has heard the same story hundreds of times, listens
quietly until at last, seizing a moment when the orator is
seriously out of breath, she tells her exactly where she stands
and counsels moderation. The old lady gets up, radiantly
happy, collects her bits and pieces, and departs. She has
been allowed to let off steam. Someone who really knows is
interested, and will act.

The next customer is a girl, evidently in graver trouble.
"Well, it's family," she murmurs tearfully, and is led into
the private room beyond. In the meantime the other expert

(a retired judge) has told a youth how to get to Canada
without stowing away, has made clear the ingenious conditions governing the surrender of bacon coupons by amateur
pig-keepers, and has put through an effective telephone call
about the lapsed pension of a worried ex-serviceman.

To answer all these questions takes patience and a sense
of humor. But the C.A.B. volunteers declare that the
tragi-comic pageant of humanity that passes their tables
and the obvious satisfaction and release from anxiety they
feel in their clients is a rich reward for their services. In
the wordy miasma of officialdom exuded by the Welfare State
the bureaus are a guiding beacon. They tell people what
they want to know, and tell it tactfully and efficiently. Once
the beautiful simplicity of their function is grasped it's hard
to imagine how Britain ever did without them.

Individual bureaus are supported where necessary by grant
from local authorities and have not been seriously affected
so far by Britain's financial crises. The work at headquarters, which is vital to the bureaus' service since it provides,
among other things, the whole of the background information for their work, is seriously affected by the recent
cessation of the Ministry of Health grant of 10,000 pounds a
year. This has thrown a great burden on the National Council of Social Service general voluntary funds. Drastic cuts in
personnel at headquarters and in the field have had to be
made. The C.A.B. Committee is deeply concerned about
the possible effect of these cuts on the quality of work.

I give these details of the organization and services of
the Citizens' Advice Bureaus as they may be useful to our
local communities. But they also make it clear with what
tenacity the British continue to develop voluntary work
under a Socialistic, or more accurately, semi-Socialistic pattern of life.

It is this ardent faith in the importance of voluntary service that will prevent Britain from succumbing to the tyranny of an overcentralized planned state. For example, we
take for granted in the United States that the National
Health Service Act, passed by Parliament in 1946, is wholly
administered by government officials. This is not so. The
administration of the state hospitals is carried out by a
partnership of the public and private agencies. It is a blend
of central direction with decentralized voluntary administration. Under the terms of the Act, hospital service was nationalized. But its administration in the field has been entrusted
to voluntary committees, Regional Hospital Boards and
Hospital Management Committees, each of which is given
by the Act statutory responsibilities and corporate status. It
is the first example in Britain of a public service which is
financed almost entirely from public funds being operated
by a government department and voluntary service in partnership.

The concept of such a partnership is not new to the British as it has been a long-standing informal arrangement
which proved of great value during the war. The private
health and welfare agencies carried out expanded programs
with public funds but without public control of the expenditure of these funds. The National Council of Social Services
has received grants from different government departments
for the past twenty years. Americans who fear that the British will lose their freedom under the "Welfare State" will
do well to ponder the statement made in the House of Lords
on behalf of the government on June 22, 1949, by Lord
Pakenham:

> We consider that the voluntary spirit is the very life-blood
> of democracy. We consider that the individual volunteer, the
> man who is proud to serve the community for nothing, is he

whose personal sense of mission inspires and elevates the whole democratic process of official government effort. We are convinced that voluntary associations have rendered, are rendering, and must be encouraged to continue to render, great and indispensable service to the community. . . . I want to make it plain, beyond any shadow of misunderstanding, that, in the view of the government, democracy without voluntary exertion and voluntary idealism loses its soul.

In describing the profound faith of the British that freedom can be maintained through voluntary effort, I am not making a plea for Socialism nor for nationalized medicine for that country nor for ours where my record of opposition to compulsory health insurance has been clearly established. I am making a plea for patience on the part of those Americans who resist co-operation with the British on the theory that Britain's postwar acceptance of Socialism marks the end of that nation's devotion to democracy as we understand it.

On the contrary, we must realize that the war effort of the British masses set a revolution in motion and made Socialism inevitable. Even in 1942 the people were well aware that their efforts were winning the war and they knew what they wanted when at last peace came. "We know exactly what we want and we are going to get it," they said to me again and again. "We want better health, better education, better housing and no more unemployment." They were disappointed that no government leader was voicing their demands during the war and hoped the new social planning would not be postponed until the war's end. They were demanding immediate recognition of the sacrifices they were making because in their hearts lurked the fear of the dole. Now, they said, when the nation feels united through shared insecurity is the time to push reform bills through Parliament.

Nor was it surprising that their first demand was for better health protection. For the health of the British people had been neglected for generations. The very stature of the British people had suffered from long years of overwork and undernutrition. I shall never forget one terrible experience which revealed to me how shamefully the welfare of the British masses had been ignored. I was surrounded early one morning by hundreds of young girls from the slums of London as they came off the night shift in a Royal Munitions Plant. Their physical condition was horrifying even to one who had seen the most impoverished Americans. When these youngsters tried to talk to me, I could scarcely understand them, so misshapen were their teeth and so numerous were cleft palates and other facial disfigurements. Their bodies were pathetic, their bone structure warped, their skin discolored. But there was nothing wrong with their minds. They were as rebellious as a mob in the French Revolution. Their wild energy after eight hours of dangerous night work seemed to prove the law of the survival of the fittest. No wonder Britain had to compensate its people after the war for long-standing economic and social injustices. For these indignant children of the slums were but an extreme example of revolt against Britain's dual-class system whereby the leisure of the rich had rested upon the exploitation and poverty of the masses.

It is to be regretted that the postwar government did not have the courage to shatter Britain's antiquated dualistic educational system as thoroughly as was demanded by the report of the trades unions. The education of the people in Britain, as distinct from the education of the elite, has been a charitable enterprise of the established church. No government schools existed until 1870. The McNair Committee in 1944 reported, "We have not yet emancipated ourselves from the tradition of educating our children on the cheap." The worst schools are the church schools, whether Anglican or Roman Catholic, especially in the heart of London. Yet when I saw R. A. Butler, then Minister of Education, and now Chancellor of the Exchequer, he told me that grants to these deficient institutions would have to be continued because it was impossible to build enough new schools although the trades unions vigorously opposed grants to denominational schools. Out of 54 schools in the three central boroughs of London, 37 are still church schools. "No historian of state education in England," said one prominent woman, "can ignore the fact that the battle of the sectarian leaders did as much to hinder the growth of education as any class or economy campaign." Let that be a warning to Americans who are now being besieged by the same type of sectarian leaders for state support of church schools.

Britain had a school problem far more serious than ours because they lost hundreds of school buildings in the blitz and because they, like us, have an expanding birth rate. In London alone, out of 600 schools, 73 were totally destroyed and 143 seriously damaged. The national school population has risen by 30 per cent since 1945. The London County Council has opened 27 new primary schools and provided 40,000 extra places through war damage repair. Yet the overcrowding of the new and the antiquated schools is horrible and getting steadily worse as the postwar babies come of school age. The most fortunate cities are those like Coventry, which was so thoroughly bombed that it received the highest proportion of new housing and new schools. Nine modern primary schools have been completed and plans have been made to build ten secondary schools within the next ten years. Herefordshire has built no fewer than 45 primary schools since the end of the war.

There are other areas that have made good progress. But the "regulation levels" which prescribe classes of forty in the primary schools, cannot be achieved unless England constructs about 11,000 new classrooms and trains as many more teachers. In the face of such a critical situation the conservative government has cut the educational budget. Finally the content of British primary education is on the whole antiquated. This makes it difficult for the children to pass the intelligence tests which at the age of eleven open the way to the secondary schools.

To decide at that age whether a boy is to be "factory-fodder," or continue his education is the sheerest injustice. This drastic policy affects not only the working classes but cultivated families with small incomes who cannot afford to pay the secondary school and university fees. The intelligence test which was to eliminate cramming for scholarships has resulted in a threat far more serious to genuine education as the children are now coached for a year or more in the tricks of passing intelligence tests. Thus despite some improvement in the government schools, Britain's educational system is still undemocratic. The opportunities offered children of working-class parents or other impecunious families for acquiring a higher education are too few and too difficult to obtain.

In spending so much for free health provisions and so little for free education, Britain may have put the cart before the horse. Much poor health is the result of ignorance on the subjects of hygiene, nutrition and child guidance. But the churches and their allies, the people of wealth, are so entrenched in Britain's educational system that even the Labor Government did not dare to challenge them by establishing a unified state system of education equal in merit to that afforded by the expensive private schools.

The British masses have not by any means won their battle for equal rights. But they have a sense of democracy so mature, deep-seated, stable and tenacious that victory in every area of inequality is assured, if we preserve our faith in them and are not misled into withdrawing our sympathy and our financial aid by their experimentation with Socialism. With their innate love of liberty, their profound individualism and their faith in voluntary effort, the British given half a chance are sure to achieve a modified type of Socialism that will strike a new balance between security and freedom and add another great chapter to Britain's long struggle for the liberation of man.

Nor must we be deterred from seeing in that great nation the most reliable of allies, because of the momentary anti-Americanism of the left-wing labor leaders, and some of the most influential newspapers. Ruth Taylor and I were deeply moved by the gratitude to America which was expressed daily by the working people. They thanked us for the food they ate in the British Restaurants, for the clothing they distributed after a blitz, for the medical supplies which were such a boon to the sick and wounded, for the orange juice and toys which fortified the bodies and the hearts of their children. "We pray God will bless America," said the mothers with tears in their eyes.

But gratitude is not a healthy emotion in the long run. The fact that we came to Britain's assistance after the war with wheat, food parcels and Marshall Aid necessarily hurt the pride of a people who only recently preserved peace throughout the world and maintained the balance of power through their command of the seas. We, too, once lived a sheltered life because of British naval might. Now, suddenly, we take

Britain's place as the most powerful nation in the world. We must not be surprised if we inherit with this position of leadership the animosity which was Britain's lot when that country determined world history. It is only human nature that the British themselves should resent this, especially when we make the mistakes of policy and tact that are inevitable while we are learning the hard lessons of international amenities and co-operation. "Trade not aid" is now the cry of all the foreign nations, particularly the British. They are tired of subventions which we ourselves can no longer afford. Under our new administration we have an opportunity to create a more wholesome relationship with the British. But if misunderstandings continue, we fortunate Americans must see ourselves through their eyes, and discount the bitter utterances of their press knowing that some of them are just a matter of political policy with the left-wing Bevanite Socialists who are bound to hate the ever growing success of our capitalistic system, and that other criticisms are the result of exhaustion after years of terrible hardships and the short tempers which are its natural result. If tensions between us should ever become acute, let us remember that the U.S.S.R. would like nothing better than friction between the Americans and the British, for the British are and always will be our staunchest ally if the unfortunate day should arrive when human freedom can only be preserved by warfare.

When I returned from England I locked myself up in a New York hotel with my copious notes and poured out six articles in six days for the Associated Press. When they were published, Craig McGeachy was kind enough to say that they gave the best description of Britain's social mobilization that had as yet been printed in the United States.

Edward R. Murrow took the trouble to write me from London that I had done "a better job than most of the visiting firemen." This was balm to a troubled heart. For I, who am not given to neurotic pangs of conscience, was tortured by a sense of failure, frustration and guilt. I felt vaguely that, in my daily contacts with the British people, I had been exposed to a great and transforming experience and had not been equal to it.

CHAPTER XI

America's Home Front

WASHINGTON even in normal times is remote from the grass roots. With the war program speeded up throughout the country by the simultaneous mobilization of our military and industrial forces, the nation's capital seemed to me more and more aloof from the scene of action. After our 1942 Christmas celebration with a reduced family circle I made preparations for a swing around the country.

With the help of Katharine Lenroot, Director of the Children's Bureau, and her staff, I developed a technique for reporting of this kind. About ten days before arriving in a city, I wrote to the officials, the mayor, and the leading social workers, public and private, Federal and local, that I should like to meet with them to discuss and report to the *Washington Post* their most serious problems. The fact that I came from Washington was a great advantage; for the local officials were getting the usual runaround when they traveled to the nation's capital to consult a multitude of different Federal departments. About twice as many people as I had invited appeared at these preliminary conferences. As soon as I posed the question, "What's on your mind?" the floodgates of harassment and indignation were opened. As the local agencies were no better co-ordinated than the Federal departments, these conferences brought out the latent conflicts of divided authority. From talking to me, the local representatives would soon pass to quarreling with each other. All I had to do was to sit back and listen to discover what problem to tackle in that particular community and what individuals would be of most use as guides and mentors.

The pace of the work, the travel, and the writing of one, two or three articles a week that had to be absolutely accurate was so back-breaking that I often wonder when I look back on this formative experience whether I would have had the courage to undertake it had I known what lay before me. On my first trip, which lasted three and a half months, from the beginning of February until the end of May, I worked from twelve to eighteen hours a day including Sunday. Most of the time was spent in factories, shipyards, overcrowded tenements, schools, hospitals, clinics, day care and recreation centers, new housing projects, or just walking the streets day and night, talking to every kind of person from top to bottom of the social scale. I filled notebooks and I wrote when I could. But the reports on each city had to be finished before I encountered the quite different conditions that prevailed in the next. I was fifty-five years old and I was strong. But I had never worked so hard so continuously at any time of my life. After a month I feared that I was going to break down.

My exhaustion was due not merely to the physical strain but to exposure, day in and day out, to the weaknesses of our democratic structure, its inability to adjust quickly to new conditions and the ruthlessness, the lack of self-discipline, and the fierce competitiveness which our American people revealed when the social controls which habit or the community imposed upon them broke down. Daily I had to witness human suffering and degradation which could have been avoided had we not plunged so swiftly into a nation-wide production program without sufficient concern for its effect upon the individual worker, the family, and the welfare of the nation as a whole.

War, especially total war, is a disintegrating influence. But the mass disintegration that took place among our people was too appalling to be dismissed as inevitable. The results would never have been so catastrophic nor so widespread, if deep-seated social weaknesses had not already existed in our society before the strain of war was imposed upon it. Our educational, health and welfare officials worked at cross-purposes and their facilities bogged down under the impact of mass in-migration of war workers in even the best-organized cities. Yet the Federal government at first left the war centers to their own devices much the way it did remote outposts of civilization in the frontier days. Like the early pioneers the local citizens often brought what mutual help they could to alleviate the worst situations. But there was also present an atmosphere of crass indifference, of devil-take-the-hindmost and the weakest, which implied a deterioration of character in the American people since frontier days that had to be seen to be believed.

So cruel was the neglect of children by their parents and even grandparents who could not resist the temptation to earn bonanza salaries, and so awful were the results upon the children that I postponed writing about the misdeeds and the unhappiness of these unfortunate youngsters for several weeks, always hoping that my early experiences were not typical. Family life was turned upside down by night work. Housing conditions were so bad that people slept in shifts, in the same bed. Their children often witnessed drunkenness and sexual promiscuity. When they came to school from such homes, they were so tired that they put their heads on their desks and went to sleep.

Traveling conditions were bad. Never could I be sure that trains would leave on time or arrive on schedule. Added to the physical and moral strain of my daily routine was my apprehension that the lengthy detailed reporting I was doing could not possibly interest newspaper readers. I was haunted by the conviction that the *Washington Post* staff was probably embarrassed by column after column of factual, analytical stories. When my husband telephoned me in Detroit that my descriptions of our social chaos were the talk of Washington, I was so discouraged that I did not believe him. "I'm tired, Eugene, but not as tired as that," I replied. He was exaggerating the value of my reports, I thought, because he was sorry for me—such is the insecurity of an amateur who undertakes highly professional work.

"I am at the end of my rope," I said to myself late one night as I walked into a filthy Kansas City hotel room where the only table was littered with the empty whisky bottles and glasses of the previous inhabitants. Suddenly I saw myself at the end of a physical rope fighting my way up precipitous mountains — the conditions under which I had often felt the same desperation after grueling hours of climbing. And always the transforming moment had arrived when my exhausted body experienced the miracle of second wind. "It will happen again," I said to myself; then fell into bed and slept like a child. When I awoke I laughed aloud at my abominable surroundings and the sleet rattling against the grimy window, for I was reborn and knew once more that the body can carry out what the spirit demands of it.

My itinerary began in Buffalo. My first week there, after the comparative calm of Washington, made me feel as if I had been thrown into the churning caldron of Niagara Falls which I was seeing for the first time. In comparison with the orderly British scene, Buffalo felt like a madhouse. The crowds surging through the streets, the wild excitement everywhere, in the factories, the schools, the hotels, gave the impression of a mining town that had just struck gold. We were supposed to have manpower controls. In essential industry labor had been frozen. Yet the turnover in the Buffalo airplane factories in February 1942 was about 78 per cent per annum. Employers, the Manpower Commission, the War Production Board and the United States Employment Service were helpless.

What did the workers have to say about this game of peek-a-boo they were playing with the authorities? Most of them laughed when I mentioned freezing.

"We just take a couple of weeks off and get a release or we go into nonessential industry for a while and then go to any defense plant and get a new job. You can't blame us for shopping around for the highest pay."

There were, to be sure, thousands of serious, patriotic workers on the assembly lines. But too many others were joy riding from plant to plant and city to city. The youngsters who were earning big money for the first time wanted leisure to spend it. Many of the new workers just off relief proved irresponsible while others were spending all they earned in order to be eligible for relief again when the boom days were over.

What complicated the manpower problem in every tight labor market like Buffalo was the unregulated competition for recruits between the military and the industrialists. No sooner had the factories trained a working force than they lost them to the army. A large percentage of the irreplaceable, highly trained technicians were drafted and then placed in unskilled jobs by the military. In the face of this situation draft quotas for Buffalo were increased, thereby imperiling the whole production schedule at a time when every Buffalo plant was being hounded by the government to accelerate the production rate. Desperate managers made repeated representations to the Manpower Commission. But the army, at this stage, made no attempt to co-operate in a crisis which threatened its own interests and ultimate striking power.

This turmoil in the war-manpower situation never wholly subsided. As late as 1945 I found much the same confusion. This was the penalty we paid for lack of a co-ordinated war-production program, specifically for the fact that the War Labor Board and the War Manpower Commission, from top to bottom, never knew what the other was doing.

When the War Labor Board froze wages, there was an immediate country-wide exodus from the heavy industries making the forgings and castings that were the foundation of the whole war-production program. It was useless to try a patriotic appeal to workers to accept these disagreeable, heavy jobs at 77½ cents an hour when they could be equally patriotic sweeping the floor in a sunny factory at 90 cents an hour. As the wage rates for similar work was different in different cities, Cleveland, for example, in 1944 lost most of its irreplaceable tool and die makers to Detroit where gauge makers could get 50 cents more per hour.

The U.S.E.S. and the draft boards also worked at cross-purposes and both were inefficient often through no fault of the local officials. The industrialists and labor leaders alike condemned the Federal office of the War Manpower Commission as the source of the whole mess. It issued restrictive orders that could not be enforced, told of wonderful results one day and announced a month later that conditions were worse. Failure was followed by worse failure throughout the war, creating friction between management and labor, confusing and discouraging the war workers, generating bad feeling against the home front among our troops and impeding rather than increasing the production records. The effect upon the morale of permanent and temporary labor— the emotional strain, the cynicism, the widespread feeling that the Federal government was hopelessly insincere — could be seen in great and ever-mounting numbers of people who broke down from war psychoses, both physical and mental.

What are we going to do to conquer this manpower problem if war should come again? One British labor expert told me after traveling all over our country that we probably wasted more man-hours than it took to turn out Britain's total war production. But quite apart from the fact that we cannot afford such industrial handicaps in the future, the results upon the war workers' family life, their children and upon our society as a whole were disastrous. When the War Manpower Commission called upon the civilians to go to work, they responded in droves from every section of the country. Villages, farms, whole areas in the Middle West were deserted and the population fanned out toward the great industrial areas in the coast regions of the West, the South and the East. Whole families got into their jalopies and migrated aimlessly from city to city looking for higher and higher wages without a thought of the effect upon themselves or upon the production effort. When the war ended, the demobilization period was just as tangled, just as aimless and just as destructive of human values. And yet we wonder today why we suffer from increased delinquency, crime, divorce, and other symptoms of social disintegration.

That some of the disorder in our war-production centers was the fault of the local communities was demonstrated by cities such as Cleveland, which did an outstanding defense job. A long tradition of good government and independence was continued by Frank Lausche, now the Governor of Ohio, then the Mayor of Cleveland. While the bickerings of Washington were crowding the war news off the front pages, the citizens of Cleveland, with their strong tradition of civic pride behind them, were intent upon fighting the war instead of fighting each other. This could readily be seen in every aspect of war activity, whether in industrial achievement, labor relations, city management, educational facilities, public health or child care services for working mothers.

Instead of waiting, as did most other cities, for Washington to come to the rescue, Cleveland avoided the creation of new agencies whenever possible and handled most of its difficulties by the co-ordination of the permanent public bureaus and all of the private organizations. For Cleveland recognized from the outset that the average American city has enough public and private agencies to cope not only with its usual problems but with any social crisis if only they act in unison rather than in competition. So effective was the cooperation between the Cleveland Council of Civilian Defense and the Welfare Federation that the work I saw in that city for the protection of children, for the employment of the handicapped in war industries, for the care of war workers, especially women, made me proud of my country and conscious of the magnificent society we Americans could achieve throughout the nation, if good will, devotion to the public good, and intelligent use of our scientific and technological knowledge are allowed to prevail. Cleveland taught me what all my subsequent observations confirmed, that the problems arising out of the impact of total war were not new but were our usual American social problems aggravated, intensified, and multiplied by war conditions.

My itinerary circled the periphery of the country with in-

tensive studies in seventeen very different communities, the
northern cities to Seattle, down the West coast, then Texas
through the South to Florida and up the East coast to our
home in Washington. Here I hoped to rest. But the coal strike
had started in Pennsylvania. I was touched by telephone mes-
sages from strangers saying: "We want you to go to the
mines and tell us the truth about the strike." My work had
gained me public confidence. In two days I was off again.
For one reason or another I lived the life of a fireman until the conflagrations of war died down.

The proof that local communities can make or break
the war effort was brought home to me when I visited Camp
Polk, headquarters of the 3rd Armored Division, whose
nearest town is Leesville, Louisiana. I was met at the nearest
railroad station, Alexandria, sixty-five miles away, by the
publicity agent of Leesville and an army officer who had just
been discharged by General Crittenberger, the commanding officer, for I knew not what reasons. These men were
oversolicitous about my plans and I smelled trouble so deep
that I was at once on my guard. General Crittenberger
kindly put me up on the army post as there were no decent
hotel accommodations in Leesville. When I set out the next
morning under military auspices we saw perfect military in-
stallations within Camp Polk and at airfields in the neighborhood. But coming back into Leesville I saw evil-looking
shacks. "Houses of prostitution," said my driver in matter-
of-fact tone. From one of them, as we passed, issued a female
in flamboyant negligee, who reminded me of Sadie Thomp-
son in *Rain*. Next we motored through filthy streets, past
numerous saloons, to a formal luncheon given me by the
Leesville Chamber of Commerce which began with prayer.
I sat through praise of me, of Leesville, of the American

Army, while my nervous apprehensions grew more acute every minute. When I was asked to speak, I thanked the audience for their warm reception and broke up the luncheon abruptly with the announcement that I had come to Leesville not to talk but to work.

Then the miracle of human good will drawing people together happened again. Out of that sinister, hostile gathering two people edged their way to my side, a social worker and a captain of the State Police who offered to guide me, as he well knew that I would need protection. Together we saw the worst hellhole of prostitution, rent-gouging, beer-racketeering, abominable housing and universal corruption that it has ever been my fate to inspect. And all this evil was due to the fact that some of the townspeople in co-operation with a few venal military men were profiteering from the degradation of our troops. This situation was no fault of the commanding officer. General Crittenberger either had to invoke the May Act and declare Leesville out of bounds — which army policy discouraged — or engage in a knockdown fight with the corrupt politicians of Leesville.

I wrote the *Washington Post* a piece about that abominable experience which cleaned up Leesville — for three weeks. After that the rats in the town structure emerged again. But then the incredible happened. Six Leesville clergymen got the local Congressman to publish an attack on me in the Congressional Record — the only attack in my four years of war work — stating that I was a liar, a woman with a "poisonous pen" who had blackened the reputation of their pure and patriotic community. Actually what I had written was an understatement. So I took pencil in hand once more and told the whole truth about Leesville, including the fact that its venereal disease rate was then four and one half times higher than that of the national average. My own Congressman saw to it that my rejoinder was also published in the Congressional Record. I heard no more from these clergymen.

What made my whole soul revolt against this frightful situation in Leesville was less the predicament of the troops who are, after all, adults, but that of the children who lived in the midst of this corruption, and the babies who were dying like flies because the town was indifferent to the quality of the milk supply. Either we must not allow the wives of the soldiers to follow them during a mobilization program, or we must see to it that these poor women do not have to live in chicken coops at exorbitant rents and that they can take proper care of their children's education, recreation and health. If we are fighting to preserve democracy, we must have a democratic society that is worth preserving.

If we see to it that the schools are numerous and large enough in these critical war areas, and that the school superintendents are flexible administrators who know how to cope with community problems, nine tenths of the battle to protect the soldier's family will be won. Wherever there was a semblance of order during World War Two in overcrowded military or industrial communities, wherever the war workers' children received loving care, it was due to the organizing genius of the school authorities.

By dint of pulling all the public and private health and welfare agencies, the churches, management, labor unions, P.T.A.'s, boy and girl scouts, and other organizations into an integrated program, many of our heroic educators reduced the incidence of delinquency and crime and introduced the most recalcitrant families to the amenities of civilized living.

But some communities were dilatory about improving educational facilities because the wealthy and powerful local elements were indifferent to public education. When I arrived in Mobile, Alabama, a city whose population had

jumped from 85,000 to 200,000, I found a situation that
was completely out of hand. Over two thousand children
roamed the streets day and night because there was no room
for them in the schools. Those who could attend schools,
were demoralized by the crowded classrooms and the loose
atmosphere that prevailed throughout the city. They played
hooky by the thousands whenever they pleased. Crime of a
major kind, arson, rape and theft were rampant among
youth. Sex offenses by very young girls were particularly
shocking and grave. "We are fostering and encouraging a
future race of gangsters," said the Catholic bishop of Mobile.

How did this moral chaos come about? The school facilities of this important city had been shamefully inadequate
for the normal prewar population. Teachers' salaries ranged
from $800 to $1300 a year in the elementary schools. Most
of the teachers left when the shipyards began recruiting
workers, to earn a living wage. The social organization of
the city was a farce even as to police protection. For two
years the school authorities had asked, without much vigor,
for Federal assistance under the Lanham Act. But the Federal officials were loath to help a city that had so flagrantly
neglected its educational system. Yet thousands of American
children were paying a heavy price for this atrocious example
of local and Federal indifference to human welfare. The
wealthy inhabitants withdrew into their spacious homes as if
they had no responsibility for the shocking conditions that
were demoralizing the permanent as well as the new population.

I wrote a description of this fantastic situation which
forced the Federal Government to come to the rescue with
Lanham Act Funds for new schools within two months. Since
that time, Miss Bessie, at that time, Mobile's one-woman so-

cial welfare department, has kept me in touch with the city's progress on the social front. But the problem remains — what are we going to do with other communities where, as in Mobile during the war, the dominant politicians are too indifferent to public education because the well-to-do people send their own children to expensive private schools? The nation as a whole suffers from this selfish point of view.

The question of local responsibility is complicated by the fact that no community which suddenly doubles and trebles its population in a war emergency can possibly afford to build all the additional facilities which the inhabitants need to lead a decent life. In such cases the Federal government has a clear responsibility to come to the assistance of the local government.

Fortunately, the Eighty-first Congress realized this and passed two bills, one for construction, the other for the general support of schools in our critical war areas. Moreover, the Defense Production Authority has been quick to realize the importance of good schools to the mobilization and production effort and allocated the needed steel as quickly as possible. The moneys appropriated by Congress are still insufficient and must be increased. What we need in these crowded communities are school buildings with all the recreational facilities required to draw the parents as well as the children into their orbit. We need as well teachers trained in community leadership, social workers to tie the community and schools together, and psychologists who can help adjust these uprooted families and their children to their new mode of life. Such a program will be costly but cheaper than the vast sums we are now spending on remedial efforts that have resulted from the crass neglect of a migratory population during the last war. If I have devoted all my time and effort since World War Two to the strengthening of community life, especially through the extension and improvement of public education, it is because I saw with my own eyes for weeks on end the frightful disintegration of family life and individual character that were the penalty of a disorderly environment and disorderly living during the war.

Nothing has encouraged me more in this battle for the reorganization of community services than the contribution which our industrial leaders are making in ever greater numbers to improve social conditions in their own factory towns. It is of special importance to point out that during the last war, I found many of our biggest corporations to be also the most efficient in handling new factories, difficult labor situations and challenging social problems. Furthermore, I often saw the big corporations working under precisely the same handicaps as the new organizations that were supported frequently with enormous capital furnished by the Federal government. In almost every case the established industries did a better job.

Is there any reason why I should not mention some of them? I encountered the humane efficiency of United States Steel in remote mining towns of Pennsylvania and Kentucky, of the DuPonts in a brand-new powder plant in the sticks thirty miles out of Louisville, the Sherwin-Williams Paint Company running an enormous ordinance plant at Crab Orchard Lake, one hundred miles southeast of St. Louis, the nearest large city. I inspected the General Motors Cadillac Company from the top management to the assembly line because it was selected for me by the heads of the UAW-CIO union themselves as an example not only of efficiency but of excellent labor relations. The Grumman Aircraft Corporation, whose fighter planes were famous over the world-wide battle front, was a favorite company of mine because the social protection of its workers was so intelligently organized. Though Henry Kaiser's shipyards got most of the publicity, I found that the Newport News Shipbuilding and Dry Dock Corporation was beating the Kaiser production record in a huge new plant at Wilmington, North Carolina, without considering this achievement worth mentioning to the press. The Bath (Maine) Iron Works Corporation surpassed all of the nation's shipyards, in delivery of 2100-ton destroyers, because Pete Newell took good care of the housewives, farmers, and fishermen who worked for him.

An amusing personal experience illustrates the speed with which young Edgar Kaiser got things done at his father's Portland, Oregon, shipyards. I had been invited weeks in advance to christen the *Belva Lockwood,* the 147th Liberty Ship, which was to be ready on March twelfth during the stay I had planned for Portland, Oregon. In Kansas City I got a telegram saying the ship would be ready on March eleventh. I arrived in Portland on the ninth with the usual tight schedule fixed in advance. When I checked my first appointment by telephone, I was told that the papers had announced I would christen the *Belva Lockwood* in an hour. I dashed into clean clothes, motored to the shipyard, was rushed up a high scaffolding, shoved in front of a mike and with no warning ordered to address some 15,000 workers who were eating lunch in the yards. Fortunately I could fall back on my British experiences where we had all rushed for cover in one of Tyneside shipyards when the klaxon sounded. "You have troubles of many kinds," I said cheerfully, "but you don't have to dodge the bombs."

It was no sinecure to christen a ship. The Kaiser officials went through the routine about three times a week. But at the final moment, distrust of the female got the better of them. They became more and more nervous until I caught their tenseness. For a curse hangs on the ship, so heavy that it is hard to get a crew, if the sponsor fails to smash the bottle.

As the welders began to burn the last plates that hold the ship, they shouted, "number 1 is burned; number 2; number 3." When they shouted, "number 4," I felt the ship tremble under my hand. I struck, underestimated the resistance of a bottle wrapped in red, white and blue bunting — and missed. With a second swing I reached out and hit the ship's nose with a crash, just as she slipped down the ways like an express train. No sooner had the *Belva Lockwood* hit the water than a mass of workers rushed into the space that had just been vacated, to lay the keel of her successor.

In the Portland shipyards I intervened successfully in a violent battle between the A.F. of L. and the C.I.O. After much interviewing of the workers it appeared that Tom Ray, the leader of the A.F. of L. International Boiler Makers, was conducting a first-rate racket. But nobody had been able to pin it on him. He refused to show his books even to his own Union President and hid from all newspaper people in a large marble palace which he had had built for himself out of the $50 initiation fee he exacted from every new applicant before he or she could get a job, plus $2.50 per month in dues. The C.I.O. at that stage had appealed in vain to the Labor Relations Board to hold an election and allow the workers to choose their own union affiliation. Women and Negroes had to pay the A.F. of L. fees without the privilege of union membership.

I got my interview with the A.F. of L. racketeer through shameless female strategy. I could scarcely believe my ears when Tom Ray put his head in my noose. I extracted from him by telephone the figures on his membership and the admission that the turnover was three to five thousand workers a month, a situation to which he was completely indifferent as he got his initiation fee and dues before they left. These were the figures we needed to put an end to victimization of the shipyard workers. As a result of these and other revelations, too complicated to mention, a Congressional investigation terminated the tyrannical reign of this union racketeer.

The worst of all the union tyrants whose high-handed actions I exposed was Tom De Lorenzo (so-called), who together with a succession of inefficient managers had brought the production of airplanes almost to a standstill at the Brewster Company in Long Island City and at Johnsville, Pennsylvania. Never did I expect to see in America such a picture of managerial chaos, such a complete breakdown of worker morale, as these factories presented. It was the extreme example of what can happen to production if poor labor-management relations are allowed to go from bad to worse. De Lorenzo, whom I interviewed at the Long Island plant, took it into his head to show off what a big bad wolf he could be. "If I had brothers at the front who needed the ten or twelve planes we sacrificed in our last strike," he said to me, "I'd let them die, if necessary, to preserve our union rights. What's more, if I were in their place, I'd expect them to do the same thing. I'd expect them to let me die." I urged him not to make this statement but he insisted. When it was released in the *Washington Post,* the C.I.O.-U.A.W. Union, of which De Lorenzo's Local 365 was a subsidiary, called him on the carpet as his loose talk was bad public relations for labor. He was also summoned before Congress. The hearing ended his career as a labor leader. When I discussed this situation later with Walter Reuther, who has, I believe, a statesmanlike concept of his function as a labor leader, he said to me: "The time has come when labor leaders must modify their aggressive techniques and learn to co-operate with management if private industry is to survive in America."

In Oregon, I discovered that the manpower situation in agriculture was handled by the Federal government with even less competence, if possible, than in the factories and shipyards. My chapter on the Oregon Plan for Agriculture begins with the questions: "Will anything make the Washington war lords realize what their quarrels, their indecision, and their arbitrary behavior are doing to this country? 'Where are we going?' is the unanswered question that haunts the minds of the American people."

These desperate queries were the result of a typical conflict between a state that was competently handling its difficult agricultural problems and the Federal government which was just about to throw everything into confusion. Under Oregon's Agricultural Advisory Committee all local government agencies, the Department of Education, and hundreds of voluntary agencies had perfected a plan used the year before which enlisted thousands of volunteers and saved the state's entire huge vegetable, fruit and sugar-beet crops. They were set to start the machinery going again when I arrived on March 21, 1943. Just at this moment the Federal government angered the farmers to the point of fury by sending out a different release every day stating that this or that new bureaucratic setup would be formed to take charge of Oregon's agricultural manpower needs.

But the Oregon people are not only capable; they are courageous and independent. The State Agricultural Advisory Committee settled the matter with an official resolution that firmly told the Federal government to mind its own business. After several brutally frank "whereases" the Committee members stated flatly that they would do as they had done before and that they refused "to waste public moneys by duplication of effort and expansion of unnecessary personnel." If more states, localities, industrialists and farmers had had similar courage we would have had a more productive and orderly war effort.

Before I left Seattle by train for San Francisco I received a telegram inviting me to address the Commonwealth Club of California. This was a tough assignment as I had three long articles to write on the food and medical problems in the Puget Sound area where the army, navy and industrial personnel were going hungry because the O.P.A. had bungled meat rationing, but where the U.S. Public Health Service had done a superb job in co-operation with the army to control venereal disease. I sat up most of the night to finish these articles, and then before I went to bed wrote a speech which was boiling inside me, comparing the British home front with ours. I finished the speech just as the train pulled into San Francisco. I wish I had space to reproduce this address in full. A few paragraphs will give its gist:

In Britain the whole weight of the war rests upon the people. Here it is carried by the government. There the government is used as a mere tool to make the people effective and to conserve every ounce of raw material and food and human energy. Here the government is entranced with its own powers and thinks of the people as a helpless lot of sheep that need constant watching, with the result that our resources and human energies are restricted by one group of bureaucrats, and wasted by the others.

The greatest shock to anyone returning from what is practically the British battle front to this country is the difference in the tempo in the life of the people as a whole. For of what total war means, we have not as yet learned even the first lessons. It means that the home front is not merely an aid and encouragement to the army in the field, but the foundation upon which the whole weight of the war rests. . . . Great Britain is convinced that if democracy is worth fighting for, it is worth fighting with.

In my travels through the United States, I have found that our government through overcentralization is depriving the people of the opportunity to make their full contribution to the war effort.

Whether it be management or labor or businessman or farmer, everyone has told me the same story of distress concerning their relations with Washington.

Our leaders, both before and since our entrance into the war, have proclaimed the nation's faith in democracy with moving eloquence and deep conviction. We all stand firm in that belief. What our administration lacks is an equally firm conviction that democratic procedures and a decentralized organization must be utilized if, in the United States, we are ever going to learn to wage a people's war. What the administration needs, when all is said and done, is more faith in the American people. It is autocratic and tries to tie everybody up with paper work and senseless regulations, because it underestimates the good will, the superb capacities, and the patriotism of this nation.

If you had seen, as I have, day after day, the energy, the skill, and the brains of our people forging our vast resources into weapons, you would know that nothing on earth can beat us unless we defeat ourselves. If we learn to improve the co-ordination of our active and potential war effort, we shall become not only the most powerful nation in the world, but the nation that can promise the best kind of life to the common man.

This war may be won by our armies on the field of battle and yet lost on the home front. Great social changes, national and international, are already underway; greater ones are impending. If we are to find a solution of the international problem, the only sound foundation is the solution of our administrative problems here at home.

Administration is still as much a nation-wide weakness of our democracy as it was during the war, even if we ignore the corruption which has recently been revealed. Unless we realize this and train an army of capable civil servants who understand how to lead a democratic people with persuasion rather than force, we shall never be able to govern our country effectively whether in peace or in war, much less lead the world in democratic thinking, democratic procedures, and democratic progress of a political, economic and social nature. Let us hope that the new administration, which is just about to take over the management of our present defense production and mobilization, will study the mistakes we made during World War Two, and save the nation from further social disintegration.

CHAPTER XII
The Revival of Community Initiative

Throughout the war I had said to myself again and again, that if only our son and our two sons-in-law, all of whom were commissioned in the air force, returned safe and sound, I would never again worry about anything. My son's return was especially dramatic. Late one night in August 1944 I was reading in my bedroom at the Mount Kisco farm. Eugene was in Washington. When the telephone rang at 11:30 P.M. I wondered who could be calling me so late. When I heard Bill's warm voice saying "Hello, Ma," I discovered that intense joy and intense pain are indistinguishable. He had received sudden orders to return home to study psychiatry as the need in the air service for this branch of medicine was increasing. Now he was at Grand Central Station en route to Boston to see his wife and his son, who was born after his departure. With Bill's return a heavy burden of anxiety was lifted and it grew lighter after the other boys came back the following year.

But they had been home only a short time when my anxieties eclipsed my reasons for happiness. As long as I was working to improve living conditions in our war centers, the sense of accomplishment—the housing, schools and other facilities my articles helped to secure for various communities—drowned out the anguished cries of conscience concerning social conditions in our country. But now that that was over, they rose out of my subconscious and made me sick at heart.

One solution of my melancholy state of mind was obvious. I knew that in many local communities, successful experiments were being carried out to cope with the postwar chaos and the problems it was creating. What more salutary than to describe them in the *Washington Post* to remind the country that democracy is still dynamic and capable of solving even the most serious social challenge to its stability and progress? I had been a Cassandra throughout the war years because I wanted to arouse the Federal administration to its responsibilities toward the great mass of mobilized war workers. But I was tired of bringing bad news and reminding the nation of its weaknesses. The self-critical spirit of Americans is one of our sources of strength. But too much emphasis upon our shortcomings causes the world at large to get a one-sided and false impression of our society. For example, I was disturbed during the war to hear from an American in the Argentine that the Japanese were translating my reports on local conditions in our war centers verbatim as the best anti-American propaganda. To counteract the depressing effect of my war articles, which had just appeared in book form under the title *Journey Through Chaos,* I left Washington during the postwar years whenever I could to report on local activities which replaced the wartime chaos with a new, strong, healthy and happy community life.

My first exodus in the spring of '45 was built around speeches I had promised to make, and one of the most important projects I was to describe came my way by the sheer good luck which always reminded me of Emerson's disclosure: "I am constrained every moment to acknowledge a higher origin for events than the will I call my own."

While speaking at the Springfield [Massachusetts] Forum, on my own program for community reorganization, I suggested that either a civic center or the public schools be used as a focus or clearinghouse for our tangle of local public and private agencies, to co-ordinate our available resources, review overlapping and omissions, and develop new agencies to fill new needs. I could scarcely believe it, when a member of the audience told me that a Dr. Randall B. Hamrick was carrying out these ideas at the nearby Bridgeport Community Service Center. I went directly to Bridgeport and what I experienced during the week I studied his work was the joy of vicarious achievement. I came away saying to myself, "If only we had more Hamricks in America, how we could make democracy hum!" This description of the center brings its work beyond that first report to 1952.

It was the businessmen of Bridgeport who saw the need for co-operative action to transfer the returning veterans and war workers to peacetime pursuits. Experience after the last war had taught them that in spite of all Federal and state agencies, this could only be done successfully through the intelligent and humane efforts of each local community where people in need are a reality to their neighbors and not a matter of statistics.

Thereupon they engaged Dr. Hamrick, a psychologist trained at the Yale Graduate School, to set up the Bridgeport Community Center as a visible hub for all public and private agencies available to the veteran, and for the local representatives of Federal and state agencies. It was a small frame house where people could go for help of any description and where the wealth of resources possessed by any big city could be brought to bear on the individual without loss of time or energy. Bridgeport was thinking of the future and used its responsibility to the returning veteran as a unique opportunity to strengthen the grass roots through the revival of community initiative in intergovernmental relationships.

The center was a clearinghouse for every kind of human problem during the postwar years. But its chief task was vocational counseling for veterans, civilian adults and high-school students, with a view to fitting men not only to a job but the right job, and to prevent the ten or twelve costly years of job-jumping which is the fate of many young high-school and college graduates before they settle down. Now that the center is eight years old, it is still as useful as it was just after the war in guiding both veterans and non-veterans. Over 250,000 people have come to the center for help, and 25,000 have received intensive educational and vocational counseling.

When the G.I. Bill of Rights expired in August 1951, the nature of the demands upon the center changed. It had never cost the community more than forty cents per capita for seven years of service. But for the past two years it has become an independent professional enterprise maintained by nominal service payments from businesses, industries, parents of youthful clients, and individuals. If people are too poor to pay a fee, they are served free of charge. The annual budget is now $25,000 but not a cent of it comes from taxation.

Today the center concerns itself with one of the nation's major problems—the development of latent talent to meet the heavy demand of trained personnel in our expanding economy.

Dr. Hamrick has a democratic philosophy that a happy and adjusted people make for a strong community. "Put the right man in the right job," he maintains, "and you make a friend, for he will become a happy as well as a productive worker. Basic security depends upon the sense of achievement and many persons never find this precious ingredient in their work."

Dr. Hamrick estimates that 50 per cent of our potential human talent is going down the drain for lack of proper training. "This power potential must be tapped throughout the nation," he says, "if America is to succeed in the mammoth tasks it has undertaken." Guidance, he claims, is the art of education. Yet only 6 per cent of our high schools have any kind of guidance program and most of these are handicapped by lack of trained personnel. Where can our young people get the necessary guidance if not in their home community? The Federal Employment Services are not equipped to make a long-term evaluation of individual capacities.

Hamrick and his four assistants have demonstrated by actual results that expert guidance can discover great sources of hidden capabilities. They have made a high-grade engineer out of a truck driver, a first-class scientific researcher out of a second-class upholsterer, an M.I.T. honor student out of a carpenter's son with no aptitude for his father's tools, an automobile-company executive out of a department-store clerk. They have helped thousands of high-school students and college undergraduates find the right job or training course.

Several big industrial concerns have excellent personnel divisions, but the many smaller companies cannot afford the expense of a first-rate guidance service. Nor can each public high school establish its own services for the present. Hamrick's example therefore suggests that the smaller businesses should team up with others facing a manpower shortage and establish a centralized community service center, such as the one at Bridgeport, which could help high-school students find the right training and industries find the trained workers. The program can be prorated among the industries and made self-supporting by nominal fees. I know of no plan for community co-ordination that has done more to assuage management-labor relations, to bring social order out of our postwar chaos, and to give the whole community a sense of direction and progress than the Bridgeport Service Center.

"A nation is no more than the sum of all of its communities," said Carl A. Gray, a manufacturer and former State Chairman of the Connecticut Re-employment Commission. "If we in our communities solve our local problems, there will be fewer national problems. People hunger for leadership. If we businessmen don't give it to them, then we have no legitimate ground for complaint because the sophisticrats offer them their particular brand. The phenomena of government interference and burdensome taxation to promote its so-called programs has resulted from a few simple basic causes. The Federal government has moved into the vacuum created by local inactivity and is doing at extravagant cost what we as proud and self-reliant communities should be doing for ourselves."

He is right. Most industrial communities like Bridgeport can handle their own problems especially when they have a brilliant community organizer and leader like Randall Hamrick as their trouble shooter. But Mr. Gray forgets that wide areas of our country have little or no industry, no first-rate schools or health services, and no enterprising businessmen and professional psychologists to furnish leadership.

From Bridgeport I flew to Chicago to study another community project that pulsated with the will of our masses to manage their own affairs. "We, the people, will work out our own destiny" — that I found was the slogan of 120,000 people in Chicago's Packingtown who had formed themselves into the Back of the Yards Neighborhood Council under the able leadership of Saul Alinsky, a young criminologist who prefers to do the kind of work that keeps people out of jail. The momentum behind the nation-wide revolution of which the Back of the Yards movement is but one illustration arises from the fact that our millions of "forgotten men" are becoming conscious of the fact that they count. They are determined to escape from the horrible anonymity of the slums and the spiritual poverty of our neglected rural areas.

"We are sick of the social worker approach," a council member said to me. "The battle against slum conditions and slum areas is really a fight against all those economic forces that create the human cesspool called the slum and all the powerful elements that profit from its existence."

"Ours is a neighborhood movement," I was told at a luncheon gathering composed of local Catholic priests of six different nationalities, one German Lutheran pastor, Jewish and Catholic businessmen and a Polish representative of the U.P.W.A.-C.I.O. "That means constant exchange of ideas between representatives of business, labor, nationalities, religions and all other groups. Out of the warm human relationships and mutual understanding which resulted, we have formed a people's organization whose character leaves no room for religious bigotry, hatred and violence, but on the contrary, has created a strong basis for calm, orderly, intelligent progress."

Nowhere was such a co-ordinating council more needed than in this overcrowded area of antagonistic nationalities, rival churches, and all-pervasive poverty. Though all these

people worked side by side in the packing houses, they ignored each other in the streets when not engaged in open
feuds. The priests had not been on speaking terms and
passed each other without salutations. Language barriers increased the tensions. The Lithuanians were anti-Polish, the
Slovaks were anti-Bohemian. The Germans were suspected
by all four nationalities. The Jews were everybody's scape-
goat and the Irish called everyone else a "furriner." No Negro was safe in Packingtown. When the Mexicans invaded
this cheap-labor market, they were treated worse than the
Negroes.

Back in 1940 Saul Alinsky walked into this hotbed of
animosities with an invincible fulcrum — a disinterested
passion for democracy. His only supporters at that time
were men of similar convictions: Bishop Bernard J. Sheil,
founder of the Catholic Youth Organization; G. Howland
Shaw, well-known Catholic sociologist whom Alinsky
had met in his prison work; and Joe Meegan, a native of
Back of the Yards who became executive secretary of the
council.

"The study of crime," Alinsky explained, "opened up before me a whole vista of social disorganization. Unemployment, malnutrition, disease, bad physical environment, are
all mixed together in the etiology of crime. They are not
isolated but interdependent phenomena. The typical council of social agencies makes the mistake of attacking them
separately, notably the problem of youthful delinquency.
Such councils, moreover, do not attack the basic forces in
the community and in the nation that create the slums and
their evil by-products. They come to the people of the slums
not to help them rebel and fight their way out of the muck.
Most social work does not even reach the submerged masses.
Social work is largely a middle-class activity and limited by

a middle-class psychology. In the rare instances where it reaches the slum dwellers it seeks to get them adjusted to the environment so that they will live in hell and like it. A higher form of social treason would be difficult to conceive. Because it cannot and will not get down to the roots of our economic and social evils, the conventional community council retreats into a sphere of superficial amelioration and a static, segmental kind of thinking. Is it any wonder that the slum dweller despises this attitude and snarls: 'Damn your charity! We want jobs!'

"As I looked into the vast chasm that divides the mass of the people and our middle-class attempts at charity," continued Alinsky, "I realized that the only way out is a democratically informed, active, participating people who have confidence in themselves and their fellow men, a People's Organization, whose program is limited only by the horizon of humanity itself.

"That, it seemed to me, was the only 'plan' worth fighting for," concluded Saul Alinsky. "The professional 'planners' have no faith in the people. They want to do everything for them. It is a fascistic mentality. All they do is shove a pill down the people's throats."

The council was formed with the greatest difficulty. "The picture of doing a job for ourselves was what hooked us," explained one of the local merchants I visited who had lived in Packingtown all his life. "At first the churches balked because they thought the C.I.O. meant Communism. We told the priests not to be afraid of a few Communists but to show them that democracy works.

"Of course we had to keep on working, brushing shoulders and getting to know each other. One experience doesn't change people. But when people really get to be friendly, anything can happen. The motivating forces behind our council are rugged individualism, enlightened self-interest and common work."

What really held the council together were the amazing results which it achieved. Their first concern was for children. Infant mortality was high, 10 per cent. Malnutrition and T.B. were appalling. Ninety-seven per cent of the children had bad teeth or mouth diseases.

An Infant Welfare station transformed the scene with educational and preventive work, hot lunches were introduced in all schools, free milk on the playgrounds, an important program as 85 per cent of these mothers are employed. Orange juice was preached on Sundays from the pulpits as a "must" for children.

The Back of the Yards movement deserves careful study, if only because of the transformation it has brought about in the hearts, minds and bodies of Chicago's children. Some five hundred Lithuanian boys and girls filed past me on Mother's Day. They were well dressed, healthy, and radiant with life.

The council reduced the high rate of crime and delinquency among adolescents by a co-operative approach to the problem. When the teen agers were out of work, the council got them jobs. It organized gangs into athletic clubs, rented store fronts as recreation centers and gave the boys and girls responsibilities as regular members of the council.

As vandalism among our youth is now a nation-wide program, let's listen to Lou Cohen, local clothing merchant, tell about the council's program for combating it. "The older boys used to smash our windows for the fun of it and shoplifting was a plague to all the merchants. Vandalism of all kinds subsided like other types of delinquency when the youngsters were made self-governing members of the council, with representation on the council's Juvenile Court. None of the boys and girls are anxious to face a court consisting of their own neighbors, priests and close friends."

What hasn't the council done? It has established a Credit Union to lure borrowers away from the loan sharks, where the members are educated in family budgeting. The council acts as a referral for public and private welfare agencies. It has established new playgrounds and parks and a variety of recreational activities. But its greatest contribution lies in the creative vitalizing effect upon the people themselves, the broadening of their horizons and the sense they have gained of belonging to their neighborhood and their country. "It's dramatic," said one worker, while describing the effects of the council. "It's exciting. It's building the future. And the fun of doing it is just as exciting as the amazing achievements." It is a practical demonstration that genuine democracy has the leverage to transform and exalt the human spirit.

After I had met with priests, merchants, labor-union leaders for five days of constant interviewing, Alinsky said to me: "Now you're ready to meet Bishop Sheil. I've made a luncheon date for tomorrow."

I had worked hard for several months on end before I arrived in Chicago. Feeling weary I replied disrespectfully: "I've been wading around knee-deep in Catholic priests for almost a week. I've had all I can take. I'm catching the night train."

"No you're not," insisted Alinsky. "You can't write this story without talking to the Bishop." "Why not?" I demanded. "Because there wouldn't be a Back of the Yards without Bishop Sheil." That decided it. I never leave a stone unturned when I'm working on a story. But I consented much against my will.

At one P.M. the next day Alinsky and I awaited His Excellency in a minute private cubicle in a restaurant beneath the Catholic Youth Organization headquarters at 32 East Congress Street. Bishop Sheil entered with the light step of an athlete in perfect training. I rose to shake hands and had a sensation akin to fear. Like most Americans I had never met a Catholic bishop. I realized instantly that this personality was not the strange representative of a strange religion I had expected, but an old friend whom I was meeting for the first time. Was the Bishop right when he said weeks later that we were at home with each other because we both love God above everything else? I think this may be the true explanation of our instantaneous sympathy even though the Bishop's concept of God is very different from mine.

My article described our meeting thus:

> Bishop Sheil's personality was for me a challenging experience. I weighed the reasons carefully while we were conversing and realized that for similar reasons truly democratic clergymen like truly democratic school administrators or business executives are few and far between. Powerful but not tall of stature he is a robust saint with the integrity, compassion and joyousness of a person who has the courage to live his Christianity. His spirituality presents no barriers to a non-Catholic because it is not worn like a mask but permeates his whole being. Like that of a great poet, it has been forged by the role of mediator between heaven and earth.

The Bishop had shown the mettle of which he is made when the C.I.O. came into Packingtown to organize the non-union workers. He was determined that the Church should support the union movement as it was so obviously for the benefit of the people. When the mass meeting was called at the Coliseum to decide whether a strike should be called, the Bishop accepted the workers' invitation to give the invocation and address them. Every pressure was brought to bear on him to stay away including threats against his life and one attempt to shoot him. He was determined to go as he thought it absolutely necessary to prevent a strike which would have torn the city to pieces. It was largely due to his influence and courage that a settlement was negotiated.

"America is such an amazing thing," the Bishop exclaimed. "The people are all that counts. They will never become Communists if they have a fair chance to participate in the advantages of democracy and feel that the government is theirs. Communism, wherever it appears, is the result of a frustrated sense of justice.

"We now have the greatest chance in the world to create a broader justice in America and we must not fail. The Catholic Church must make its contribution to that evolution. Above all, it must remove the odor of Fascism if it is to fulfill its real destiny in American life. It must free itself from any association with Fascism, abroad and at home, and all similar forces that make for reaction. Unless we root out Fascism in America, we betray the kids who have died in this war.

"We Catholics are never going to get anywhere with a state-of-siege mentality. That is why a democratic movement like Back of the Yards, where a majority of those participating are Catholics, is so important. There is something so fine, so gracious down there. The priests have grown with their people. This new type of leadership takes on a character of great generosity and accomplishes much more by the force of example than by the word."

During one Back of the Yards parade, while banners recording the latest accomplishments were flying over the heads of the multitude, voices could be heard murmuring excitedly: "Look, there's the Bishop walking with all the people." That is why Bishop Sheil is beloved in Back of the Yards, because he walks not only with his own flock but with all the people toward an America in which they can live together in peace regardless of economic status, national origin, race, color or creed.

For me this interview was the beginning, as I had antici- pated, of a friendship that has grown over the years. Only last year my husband was thrown and seriously hurt when the Chicago express whipped around a curve. There was no doctor on the train. But the conductor got a telegram through to the Bishop, whose telephone often rings at night with appeals for help of one sort or another. When we arrived early in the morning there was the Bishop with a wheel chair, a doctor, an automobile and more doctors waiting at Augustana Hospital where all was ready to take the best care of Eugene. No wonder Bishop Sheil is the best-loved clerical figure in our country by all kinds and conditions of men, the bad as well as the good, the rich and the poor, non- Catholics as well as Catholics.

The Chicago Back of the Yards movement has spread to many other areas in the past years. It has one other branch in West Kenwood, Chicago, a Negro section. It has some 40,000 members in South Omaha and 16,000 in South St. Paul. But its most successful new movement has taken place among the Spanish-American population of Los Angeles where it has a membership of over 100,000. Among its achievements as of 1952 in the last-named city are:

1. Raising the number of registered voters in this area from 4000 to 40,000, of whom 85 per cent went to the polls at the last election.

2. Election to the City Council of the first Spanish-Amer- ican member.

3. Improved safety conditions by the installation of new street lights, crosswalks and traffic signals.

4. A guidance bureau for Mexican-born Americans who, because of language difficulties, have heretofore lacked vocational outlets and an educational committee which helps students hampered by racial prejudice to find the best schooling.

5. A twenty-four-hour telephone service at the disposal of any person needing help regardless of the problem.

This disadvantaged Spanish-speaking population, hitherto socially and politically neglected, is developing a new sense of dignity and of belonging to the American scene. When I think back to the brutal treatment meted out to these people by the police of Los Angeles, which I described in my wartime articles on the zoot-suit riots, it makes me happy that a wholly new atmosphere of mutual understanding has been developed between these Spanish-Americans and the Los Angeles authorities.

The Industrial Areas Foundation is now embarking on a nation-wide organizing campaign in eight more cities. It is a significant movement for the encouragement of genuine democracy among our impoverished millions who live all too often in a climate of cynicism, fear and incipient revolt.

Early in 1946 I was urged by some Extension Service officials in the Department of Agriculture to study the problems of migratory labor and the experiments being made by that department to alleviate the hard fate of these unfortunate people. I spent four months on the road, following the trail of migrant labor, from February to May. It was a beautiful trip, most of it done by automobile. It took me from the southern mountains of New Mexico, through the oceanlike plains of Texas, up the Mississippi Valley to Missouri and then over to the Tennessee Valley dams and the mining fields of East Kentucky.

My recollections of the Spanish-speaking population of Taos County, New Mexico, still bring tears to my eyes. From seventy to one hundred miles from the nearest railroad, these Spanish-speaking people, isolated, impoverished and maltreated, have lived on the same little unproductive plots of land for generations. They were systematically exploited by a handful of Anglos (people of English descent) when the state of New Mexico was annexed by us in 1848. The ancient Spanish and Mexican land grants to the various villages were gradually purchased at low prices or stolen by "Yankee" speculators whose operations were subsequently legalized by the state legislature. These Spanish people became American citizens only in a political sense, with no attempt to condition them socially, educationally or economically for this new responsibility.

Since then the economic spiral has been steadily downward. A number of mercantile companies, whose local representative is called the "patron," own or control the land surrounding the native villages, own the general store, and the herds of sheep which the villagers take care of under conditions that reduce them to the most abject peonage. Two thirds of the families around the Taos area grossed a maximum income of $250 a year in 1946 when I was there.

It is abject poverty such as this — not only in New Mexico but throughout the South as far north as Kentucky — which forces millions of families, mostly Negroes and Spanish-Americans, to leave their homes and to take to the road to harvest the varied crops of California, the beet fields of Colorado, the Middle Atlantic wheat fields, and the beans, tomatoes and potatoes along the East coast.

The Negro migrants who trek up and down the East coast lead a hard life. But the Spanish-American migrant workers are the most pathetic of all. When they go out of their villages they are in a strange world whose language they often do not speak. As every community rejects them, education of the children has been neglected. Their health has been undermined by working at stooped labor at a tender age. Before the Federal government intervened to improve health conditions, one third of the children in the Taos area died before the age of eighteen, the infants mostly of enteritis. The infant mortality rate was twice that of the national average. Almost 70 per cent of the babies in this area died without medical care. New Mexico also has the second highest tuberculosis death rate in the country.

In Taos County I saw what the Agricultural Extension Service had achieved in transforming the health of the mothers and children through excellent clinics established under the local supervision of the Taos County Co-operative Health Association. It was hard work to break down the superstitions and resistance of these suspicious villagers to modern medical care. It was accomplished by the use of Spanish-speaking doctors, dentists and public health nurses who persuaded them to experiment with the services of the clinics. When diet improved the children's health, when the maternity and infant death rate was reduced at the hospital, and the babies throve under instructions given the mothers in feeding and cleanliness, a new hope was born in the hearts of these people and a new sense of the meaning of democracy. The adaptation of this medical program to the peculiar mores and geographical conditions of the area gave me my first inkling that practical health programs of a state or national scope must grow from the grass roots upward and cannot be imposed on a rigid whole-sale plan from above.

In Texas a real improvement in the well-being of the migrants was achieved by the establishment of labor camps at various crossroads of the migratory route by the Department of Agriculture. Even the farmers forgot to be indignant at this "socialistic" coddling of the migrants when they found that it meant a steady supply of reliable workers if the farmer in turn could be persuaded by the agricultural officials to deal honestly with the laborers. Although the health record in some of these Texas counties was still bad, the U.S. Public Health Service was co-operating with the Department of Agriculture in fly control and other methods to eliminate intestinal diseases.

As a result of many trips such as this one I developed an affection for the Spanish-Americans and gained a respect for them that surprised me because previously my impression of their characters was derived from their American employers to whom they show their most unreliable and disagreeable traits. This mutual dislike is the usual business of hostility begetting more hostility.

My most vivid impression of these people I gained surreptitiously. I wanted to see how the wetbacks lived who came over the Rio Grande illegally. An official of the Department of Agriculture who knew their hide-outs led me after much scrambling through low shrubbery over canal banks to a small concealed village made up of canvas tents. The whole place was deserted as the men were all at work. The tent flaps were confidingly open. When we entered, I expected to see confusion and filth. All the more was I surprised to find that these workingmen had left their pathetic domiciles in immaculate order; every pot and pan shone, the beds were neatly made, the earthern floor swept clean, partly covered with a piece of carpet. Each man's Sunday suit hung neatly on the tent pole. What made me feel like an intruder was the holy picture, a madonna in bright colors, placed opposite the entrance in every tent, as if each little home were a chapel in her honor. The silence in that little tent village, the neatness, the fact that each man had set up an impromptu altar in his temporary abode, gave me a better idea of the hearts of these people than all my interviews.

But the children moved me even more deeply than the adults. Many a time I disrupted their arduous discipline by strolling out amongst them, as they carried heavy onion bags down the endless furrows of the Texas fields. They came rushing toward me as if they welcomed anybody who would break the dusty routine of their common days. If I wanted to snap a photograph of them at work I had to move quickly or they would drop their heavy burdens and show their desire to please by standing in stilted rows so that "the lady could get a nice picture." Often we could only communicate by sign language, but this did not hinder our rapport in the least. In repose, the faces of these little adults are sad with the wisdom of the ages. When they smile their slow reluctant smiles, it is even more heart-warming. Instead of the sudden bright, sunny smiles of happy American children, theirs have the poignant quality of a moon emerging slowly from behind clouds. But they are resolute little souls with all the professional pride of their parents and grandparents. When I stopped a four-year-old boy bending under a load that weighed more than he did, with the question: "What are you going to do when you grow up?" He dropped his onionbag, drew himself up to his diminutive height and declared proudly: "I'm going to be an onion cutter like my father."

Whatever was done for these people before the First World War was due to the Catholic charities. Since then the courageous leadership of Archbishop Robert E. Lucey, of San Antonio, has stimulated national awareness of our responsibilities to these defenseless Spanish-speaking American families.

In New Mexico the Presbyterian Home Mission has also done effective work and contributed, among other beneficial programs, an excellent, modern hospital at Ambudo which exerts a salutary influence throughout a wide periphery among these ignorant mothers and their all-too-numerous progeny.

When I sent my first reports to the *Washington Post* on the problems of the impoverished New Mexican population, the articles were not published. "Who the hell in Washington cares about a lot of Mexicans," said the then managing editor of our paper. As the publisher's wife I could not remonstrate with the paper's management. It reflected the indifference of the average American for whom the problems of the migrant workers, and the economic forces that produce them, are very remote. When I filed my Texas stories the managing editor finally relented sufficiently to try them out on the Washington public. The *Post* readers responded with so many enthusiastic letters and telephone calls that the paper thereafter printed the New Mexico series, and all the subsequent stories from Texas. I am grateful for the support I have received from the reading public and from papers like the *Christian Science Monitor* and the *St. Louis Post-Dispatch* who frequently picked up my articles and commented favorably on my work. They helped to establish me with the *Washington Post* as something more than just the boss's wife.

Since I wrote those reports on the problems of the Spanish and later on the Negro migrants that harvest our Eastern crops, the public has become more aroused to the hardships these people endure. Last year President Truman appointed a National Commission to inquire into the social, economic, health and educational problems among migratory workers and to make recommendations for their solution. The report is heartbreaking in its descriptions of life among these people. Will it touch the sympathy of the American people and the Congress sufficiently to bring about reforms? The whole sad story has been told so often without result that I am skeptical. Identical recommendations have been made before. Better means must be found to house the migrants, better health provisions must be established, child-labor laws must be enforced and the children must have a chance to go to school. There must be Federal aid to the states to carry out these programs. All of these obvious necessities are difficult to meet, when families are the victims of crew leaders who move them wherever there is work to be found. The migrant belongs nowhere and no interstate or Federal department has exclusive responsibility for his needs.

Nothing of a constructive nature will happen unless the Congress carries out, what to me seems the most important suggestion of President Truman's commission, the appointment of a permanent Federal Committee to fight for the rights of the migrants. The committee would consist of three public members and one member from each of the departments, Agriculture, Labor, State, Immigration and Federal Security. Without such a group to prod the Federal and state agencies into co-ordinated action, the fate of these stepchildren of democracy will continue to be one of deprivation and hardship.

The President's Committee on Migrant Labor, when it is appointed, could learn much by studying the War Emergency Program for farm labor placement of the Extension Service of the Department of Agriculture. The Extension Service had the courage to formulate a philosophy that protection of our human resources, in this case migrant and local farm labor, was the surest method of increasing agricultural production. Their program proved in dollars and cents that what is sound humanly speaking is also sound financially. Their program was based on educating the farmer to treat his worker like a human being instead of a commodity and upon educating the worker to the moral responsibility of giving a fair day's work for a fair day's wage, plus fair treatment as to housing, living and working conditions. To achieve these purposes, the Extension Service leaders saw that flexible administration keyed to local necessity and the mobilizing of local co-operation were essential. Everywhere they enlisted the latent power of public and private community organizations to meet such problems as health, child care, housing, or the construction of reception centers where migrant families could rest, wash and sleep instead of being driven like animals from pillar to post for weeks on end. The program rotated around the county agent, an office that is one of our most successful examples of democratic Federal-state-local co-operation. Another significant result of this decentralized administrative procedure is that it made for self-reliance in the staff and produced from top to bottom a remarkable group of spontaneous leaders, combining professional skill with the ability to apply it with practical and humane consideration for the people they served.

A certain momentum was lost when the broad educational aspects of the Extension Service program were discontinued. Its great benefits to the migrant workers can be regained if the recommendations of the President's Commission on Migratory Labor are carried out, and the activities of all the Federal and state agencies concerned with migratory labor are co-ordinated by the proposed Federal Committee.

During this agricultural trip a kindly fate decreed that I should write three stories whose humane results are a compensation for many failures. I went to Memphis (Tennessee) because it is a great crossroads for the migrant trek. So deeply was I engrossed in agricultural economics that I never thought about Boss Crump and his political machine until I began to bump into the tyrannical impact of this man in every interview. Whether I was talking to leaders of the Farm Labor Union and the C.I.O., to employers, newspapermen or local officials, up loomed the sinister power of Crump in every conversation. The pay off came when I was invited to a secret meeting of Negro citizens — clergymen, teachers, college professors, businessmen and social workers — who wanted to give me a picture of their enslavement by Crump and knew they could trust me not to reveal their names. Despair, indignation, anger sizzled in these people, but sheer terror was the permeating, dominating note. Especially tragic was their feeling of utter helplessness. "We are much too cowed to fight," they admitted dejectedly. "If the white man in this city is too afraid to open his mouth, what can we do? Besides a lot of our people have been bought by Crump. Some of our leading businessmen who have the ear of his machine, betray their own race. He has spies among us as among the white people. For all we know there may be one in this room this very minute."

At these words I felt creeping over me a sensation I had experienced only once before — a despair over the utter degradation of human dignity that I felt in the Germany of Hitler in August 1939.

I was incensed that "it could happen here." I dropped agriculture and interviewed some fifty key people in two days. Then I wrote a series of articles in which I allowed my passionate indignation to speak through accurate facts.

For the first time Crump was attacked not as a politician but as a corrupter of human nature whose power must be destroyed. I was told that when Crump read these reports, he had difficulty removing the arrows of my criticism from his thick hide. Crump wrote me a letter full of Biblical quotations, inviting me to come back to Memphis to learn the truth as the "truth would make me free." I never answered this hypocritical appeal. It is a characteristic of our era that the devils quote Scripture more frequently than anyone else. Estes Kefauver spread my Crump articles all over the state when he ran for the Senate and thanked me for invaluable assistance in breaking Crump's political power.

The second series of articles dropped into my lap in the same fortuitous manner. While in Memphis I was told that no press account of the Columbia riots in which two Negroes had been killed, twenty-three arrested and most of the Negro business district destroyed, had ever given a full, unprejudiced version of what really happened. "Yet the fate of those twenty-three young Negroes hangs upon the true facts of the case," said the Memphis lawyer with whom I was talking. "There's no use trying to get the story," he replied sadly when I offered my services. "The sheriff, Jim Underwood, has been told by high officials that he mustn't talk." With no hope of success as the story was three months old, I nevertheless took a taxi for the long ride to Columbia. I went straight to the jail and was told the sheriff was in the Courthouse Square. I can still see that square under a soft, sleepy spring sun with little groups of idlers sitting or lounging about as if time had stopped. Out of one eye I could see the courthouse window from which a rope had hung as a warning to the Negro population for three weeks after the last Columbia lynching, which took place on December 15, 1933.

Having identified the sheriff, I walked up to him and said nonchalantly, "Hello, Sheriff." "Who are you?" he asked suspiciously. "I'm a newspaper reporter from Washington, Sheriff. I want to talk to you about your recent difficulties." A shutter closed over his face. "I'm not talking," he said truculently. "Too bad," I said casually. "I came all the way from Memphis to talk things over with you." Then I turned my back on him and walked slowly away. My heart missed a beat when I heard the sheriff's voice. "Say, wait a minute," he called. "I hate reporters. They've lied about everything that happened here. But — you know" — his words issued slowly, reluctantly from his mouth — "I — think — you — look — honest." I looked him square in the face as his eyes searched mine. "Sheriff, I am honest." "By God, I think you are. Come over to the jail with me. I caught a wonderful bass this morning. We'll have a fish dinner together and I'll try once more to get the truth into those darn newspapers."

We ate a delicious lunch waited on by a "trusty," a huge good-natured Negro prisoner, while the sheriff gave me a play by play account of the events. I put down every word in my notebook as he spoke. I knew the sheriff was freeing those Negro prisoners with every word. So did the "trusty." I caught his eye while he stood behind the sheriff's back. He gave me one quick smile of appreciation as between fellow conspirators. After lunch the sheriff took me to the room where the two Negro prisoners were shot and gave a damning account of the brutality of the State Guardsmen and the even greater brutality of the State Patrol when they march into Mink Slide, the Negro business street.

I filled in the sheriff's story with corroboratory material

gathered from local clergy, the Negro leadership, the Negroes still suffering from the beatings they got, Magistrate Denton, who issued warrants for Negro arrests right and left without evidence, and capped it all with an interview with Governor McCord who sent the State Patrol and State Guard into the fray.

All this factual material was given me like a present from heaven just two weeks before the trial of those twenty-three Negroes took place. The most famous reporters went to the trial including my British friend, Rebecca West. I remained in Washington. I couldn't face the moment I knew was coming when the sheriff would be confronted with his own testimony. When my interview was introduced by the defense, conducted by an able Washington lawyer, Leon A. Ransom, the sheriff was asked: "Did you make these statements?" "I reckon I did," he answered, showing he, too, was honest. Twenty-one of the Negroes were freed at once. Only two served light sentences. I hope the sheriff took pride in the verdict.

Soon after Mr. Ransom returned to Washington, the Negroes of Washington gave him a public dinner to which I was invited as a guest of honor. Mr. Ransom thanked me for my services to his race. A touching experience happened six months later. In a sleet storm I got off the last car beyond the shed in the Washington railroad station. With a dozen other passengers, I stood shivering. No redcap. My bags were too heavy for me to carry. Then one Negro porter appeared, but without a truck. He looked over the passengers, walked up to me, picked up my bags and said: "Follow me." While we walked the long platform I asked, somewhat conscience-stricken, about the other passengers: "Look here, why did you pick me?" "I know you, Mrs. Meyer," he replied. "I know what you did for the Columbia boys. I wasn't going to leave you out there in that snow. Why wouldn't I be glad to help you? You don't know how many friends you have in this country." That tribute came from the heart. It means as much to me as the public dinner, the Doctor of Letters from Howard University, or the award of the National Association for the Advancement of Colored People, however much I appreciate those honors.

The third story was even more a matter of chance. I arrived at Asheville on a Sunday evening to study the effects of the T.V.A. on the farming communities it serves and heard that the eventful coal strike of 1946 had just been called. I had only three days' leeway as my schedule was fixed. I knew I could not get a total picture of the coal situation in three days without help. As I had met John L. Lewis after reporting the 1943 strike in the Pennsylvania coal mines, I called him at his house in Arlington and by great good luck found him at home. My long-distance call for help confused Lewis at first. "Where are you anyway?" "Don't you read the *Washington Post?*" I countered. "Oh, of course, you're on the road again. Well, I'll get in touch with the boys tomorrow." "Tomorrow is too late, Mr. Lewis. Please tell your U.M.W. representatives at Middlesboro, Kentucky, tonight that I shall be at their headquarters at 9:30 A.M. tomorrow morning." Then I explained: "I want to report to the *Washington Post* just exactly what this strike is all about. But I only have three days and the boys have to understand that my story must be unbiased, accurate and balanced if it is going to be of any real use."

The two union organizers who motored me through the Kentucky bituminous coal region bent over backward not to exaggerate their case. They understood that I was responsible not only to the miners, but to the operators and the public. They revealed to me in graphic terms the whole economic, social and legislative background of the strike as well as the differences existing at that time between the high standards of management of the Northern operators and the reactionary policies of the Southern Coal Operators Association.

The miners were in an ugly mood. These shy, fearful and suspicious mountain folk would not have felt free to talk to me, had I not been accompanied by two of their own leaders. In comparison with the abominable housing, the lack of elementary safety measures, and the general wretchedness of life I saw in East Kentucky, conditions in the Pennsylvania coal fields seemed a veritable heaven. Again it was my problem not to let my outraged feelings betray me into a single factual error. In those three days of complete concentration, I managed to outline the relationship of an impoverished agricultural region to the mining industry, the slavery to which these mountain people were condemned because the politicians were controlled by the operators, the manner in which pressure of population in these large impoverished families kept feeding an ever fresh supply of victims into the maw of unsafe mines, and the bloody machine-gun battles that took place before the U.M.W. organizers could gain a permanent foothold in these isolated mining towns.

No wonder these miners love John Lewis. He is the only person who has ever helped them. Public justice and private charity alike failed to come to their rescue. But now John Lewis has established an ever firmer strangle hold upon the mine workers than the operators ever had. "What these dispirited, oppressed and exploited people need most," said my articles, "is an opportunity to escape both company and union domination, to live in an incorporated township (instead of company-owned housing) and to learn slowly what it means to belong to a self-respecting, self-governing, free American community."

When the hearings took place in Washington to iron out the strike settlement, my articles were introduced and read aloud by the U.M.W.'s attorney. The operators were then asked whether they objected to any of the facts presented. There was complete silence in the room. After John Lewis had gained his chief objective, the welfare fund, he called me up to thank me for my contribution to the victory. "The miners, their children, and their children's children will be forever grateful to you," was the way he put it.

I have not had time to go back and find out at first hand what impact has been made on the lives of these neglected Americans by the welfare fund. But I know that the medical program under the able direction of Dr. Warren F. Draper now reaches over 200,000 beneficiaries, that the maternal and infant mortality rates have been lowered through hospitalized deliveries, and that hospitalization and rehabilitation measures are now promptly provided for the totally and severely disabled miners. Only someone who has seen some of these broken and helpless men lying about in their shacks without professional attention can imagine the immeasurable saving in human suffering which this program provides. The whole medical program will be improved and expanded as soon as the ten new hospitals are completed in the isolated mountain areas of Kentucky, West Virginia and Virginia where they are most needed.

I have at times been critical of John Lewis because he, like many another labor leader, has too much power over his membership. But I have a real affection for him — and I forgive him whatever shortcomings he may have — because he has achieved a great and enduring service for the most underprivileged people in our country.

CHAPTER XIII
The Mills of Democracy

IN MY CHILDHOOD DAYS we absorbed our democratic traditions from everyday life in a simple society. Today we have to teach them in school. But when the children graduate into our modern complex society, they find it difficult if not impossible to apply the experiences in co-operative action they learned through the happy associations with their fellow pupils in a controlled environment. This creates a deep feeling of frustration which explains why some of our finest young people turned toward Communism in the course of the depression.

It is high time we realized that the havoc wrought in human life and ideals by a technological revolution and too long ignored has caught up with us. The American people are aware that appalling weaknesses exist in our social structure. But they are not sure how the most serious failures have come about nor what we can do to correct them. There is an uneasiness in people's minds, a sense of guilt, and a passionate desire to overcome our social ineptitude.

This thought tortured me as I saw in war center after war center how indifferent we had become to human welfare. Had this not been the case we would never have broadcast a summons to the nation to man the war industries with so little provision in Washington for the protection of the human beings who responded to the call. The price we paid for this uncivilized behavior was appalling. We are still suffering the consequences in broken families, divorce, mental instability and crime. The children are always the chief victims of social chaos.

We Americans are supposed to be overly concerned about the child. But actually the intelligent care of children in our society is balanced by a crass indifference to the helplessness of infancy and youth. Cruelty to children has become more widespread but less noticed in the general unrest, the constant migration, the family disintegration, and the other manifestations of a civilization that has been torn away from its original moorings.

The hostility between the well-to-do settled populations and our transients proves to what an extent many Americans are still dominated by a selfish individualism, an outmoded laissez-faire psychology that still worships the bitch-goddess success. During the war many communities let the war workers' children wallow aimlessly in the mud that surrounded their emergency housing rather than admit these poor youngsters to the expensive suburban schools. To this very day the children of migrant agricultural workers are similarly rejected by the communities whose economic prosperity depends on the services of these migrant families. We Americans must find new and broader social patterns for a more generous and vital liberalism that recognizes the mass problems of our postwar world.

Our failure to keep pace with changing social conditions is attributed by foreigners and many home-grown "intellectuals" to our lack of "spirituality." We should not be apologetic about our so-called materialism. Unlike Europe, we had a continent to explore, to tame, and to develop. Among the effects of our frontier days are a devotion to individual achievement, hard work, and economic progress — all traits with profound moral values. Thus our high per capita productivity has deeper roots than the mere desire for more and more possessions. But to the extent that this development has encouraged materialism, John Dewey has this to say in his essay on "Renascent Liberalism":

> I do not see how it would have been possible to avoid an epoch having this character. Its termination cannot be effected by preaching to individuals that they should place spiritual ends above material means. It can be brought about by organized social reconstruction that puts the results of the mechanism of abundance at the free disposal of individuals — Democracy has been a fighting faith. When its ideals are re-enforced by those of scientific method and experimental intelligence, it cannot be that it is incapable of evolving discipline, ardor and organization.

The renewal of a democratic ardor in America and an evolving discipline as a result of better organization of our tangled governmental machinery became my postwar obsession.

The average American who is not concerned with government can scarcely picture the organizational chaos to be found in almost every large community. A study of Blue Earth County, Minnesota, was made shortly after the war, because this county was considered typical. The investigation revealed that the local government had 155 district units, the state was represented by 100 agencies either regularly or intermittently and the Federal government by 36 resident agencies, not counting those that came and went. The conscience of the people has been aroused by this plethora of public agencies, but they no longer feel able to control the army of experts in charge of them.

The average citizen has not the time, the knowledge, nor

the self-confidence to cope with this situation. He literally does not know where to take hold. For the fundamental difficulty which he faces is that our government system has become so complex, so specialized, and so varied that it is slowly but surely being taken over by the trained specialist and the professional civil servant who are just as apt to obstruct progress as to further it. The private organizations and their trustees are often more recalcitrant than the public agencies. Every charitable group starts its own agency. Every new scientific discovery, whether sound or not, results in new professional or lay organizations. If we add to this appalling conglomeration of agencies and organizations, the fact that most of them are staffed with experts and administrators, jealous of their professional status and the control of their budgets, then you have a situation that is bound to intimidate any sensible person who would like to serve his community. He feels utterly unfit to compete with so many specialized authorities, few of whom are ready to co-operate with each other, and none of whom have the power to take over the responsibility of constructive local leadership. For these experts, also, have had the spontaneity of leadership trained out of them by the need to fit into the particular niche they may occupy. They console themselves with innumerable national conferences where they take in each other's intellectual washing and talk a jargon that is often ridiculous because it is devoid of life.

During both the wars and the depression, the Federal government reached into every important local function and created more confusion. Moreover people began to lean on Federal aid and allowed the central government to do their thinking. For years Federal agencies have expanded and taken over more and more local responsibility. For years

Washington has become the source of the greatest accumulation of tax funds and therefore of powers of decision. As a result, the local community now suffers from an inferiority complex concerning its ability to deal with its own problems. It also acquired doubt as to the state's ability to deal with these problems together with an exaggerated confidence in the ability of the Federal government not only to solve every problem but to pay for the solution.

With such a vacuum in community leadership, it is only natural that national leadership should try to fill the void. Furthermore, there are many acute problems on whose solution Federal officials must take the lead. They cannot possibly wait until each local community awakens to the need for the control of veneral disease, malaria, or T.B. Neither the officials nor Congress can afford to ignore the inequalities of education, social security, health protection and housing throughout the nation. They are obliged to furnish leadership for the solution of such nation-wide problems.

The Federal grants in aid to state and local governments in social security, health, education and welfare now amount to nearly two billion dollars. In addition there are other grants to the tune of nine hundred millions. They are the result of haphazard social and political thinking which was criticized by the Council of state governments in these words:

> These systems in the various fields of public services have developed separately and independently without relation to each other, with the result that there is a different policy, different program, and different administrative procedure with respect to almost every activity. The net result has been and is over-lapping, duplication, and confusion which not only result in waste of public funds but also make it extremely difficult for the States to establish and maintain a constructive and economical over-all budget.

The wisest of our Congressmen and Federal officials are aware of the danger to democracy which this trend toward Federal grants and centralized administration brings with it. While grants in aid will always be necessary, they should be kept at the lowest minimum consistent with the national interest and many of them should be varied according to a state's per capita income. The feeling is growing that each level of government should function as far as possible upon its own revenues.

President Eisenhower has appointed a commission to reconsider the whole problem of Federal-state-local relationships, and to study the unequal tax resources of the states versus the Federal government. But unless the Congress gives President Eisenhower the power to implement the findings of his commission, the Federal bureaucracies will run up on the Hill as they always do and kill any bills that lessen the authority of their departments. That is what happened to many of the sensible recommendations which were made only five years ago by the similar Hoover Commission appointed by President Truman.

Why do our Federal departments resist changes that are in the interest of the nation? The nonfraternization between Federal, state, and local agencies now so commonplace is due to false departmental pride, acute interagency rivalries, and competition for power. Since these multiple agencies are with us to stay, they must learn to work together. Otherwise this mandarin mentality is one of the greatest obstacles to social progress, especially in an era of rapid change to which an inelastic, overcentralized government service cannot possibly adjust itself with sufficient speed.

Max Weber, the famous German sociologist, pointed out as far back as 1907 that our American democracy must oppose an overroutinized civil service as having a tendency to produce a caste of mandarins, removed from the co-operative and competitive, formative democratic processes through tenure of office. Democracy depends on a balance of power between the executive, legislative and judiciary, and the limitations of these powers by short-term tenure. But civil servants go on forever, and their sense of prestige and power grows with length of service. The only answer, therefore, to the tendency of every bureau to become static, self-satisfied and overprofessionalized, is to introduce into its organization, the co-operative and competitive, formative processes which are the essence of democracy. For if these large, ever increasing Federal-state structures are not kept in touch with and responsive to the will of the people, they may eventually lead democracy into a new kind of serfdom by establishing the dictatorship of the expert official. With a tendency on the part of democratic government to become ever more scientific and rationalized, the onward march of a professional bureaucracy is the most recent but also the most dangerous contemporary element in the structure of domination.

To counteract this tendency to Federal centralization of power, I helped enlist a movement to raise the Federal Security to Cabinet status and to have the bill for this purpose specify that the new Secretary of Welfare should give leadership to state and local education, health and welfare departments without domination of their programs. A committee of experts met for a year and a half to draw up a report called "The Road to Community Reorganization," which spelled out in detail what was needed at the local and state levels to improve community services and especially what was necessary at the Federal level to bring together scattered agencies concerned with the same responsibilities.

The recommendations we made to the local communities and the states are just as necessary today as they were then:

In local communities:

The organization for every community of co-ordinating bodies of representative citizens designed to study, analyze, strengthen and extend community services in education, health, recreation and welfare as needed.

The establishment for every community of Community Service Centers or of Information and Referral Centers to aid in the co-ordination of services and to provide readily accessible information, advice and service to individual citizens and families.

The recruiting and selection of both volunteer and professional personnel, properly, efficiently and humanely to administer community services.

Improved financing of community services in co-operation with state and Federal agencies, both public and private.

A reawakening of the citizen to his rights, obligations and opportunities to contribute to his own development and the welfare of all the people of his community.

In the states:

The organization of a state council or interdepartmental committee designed to co-ordinate and when feasible integrate the functions of education, health, recreation and welfare.

The extension and substantial improvement of education, health, recreation and welfare functions.

Close co-operation with local communities in providing leadership, building adequate standards of service and furnishing financial aid.

Clarification of the vital and unique role of the state in relation to local communities and the Federal government.

The philosophy underlying this report was: "The welfare of all the people is the concern of all the people." The report ended by recommending the establishment of an inclusive Federal department of health, welfare and social insurance.

The importance of this last recommendation can scarcely be overemphasized. Cabinet leadership in the guidance of health, education and welfare is necessary to repair the frightful damage inflicted upon the environment throughout the war and postwar years. But we also need the prestige of this cabinet position to interpret the meaning of democracy, its new orientation and its growing idealism at the meetings of Unesco, the International Conference of Social Workers, and the World Health Organization.

The members of our committee worked three years drawing up legislation for this new cabinet position, under the bipartisan leadership of Senators Taft and Fulbright. This process was time consuming as it involved numerous preliminary discussions with the major groups — political, economic, religious, labor, etcetera — whose interests are involved in such legislation and whose support must be gained, if the project is not to be defeated in Congress. In May 1950 President Truman sent his own bill to the Senate which followed the provisions of the Taft-Fulbright bill for a Secretary of Welfare. But I knew the cause was hopeless as Oscar Ewing, the Federal Security Administrator, would become the first incumbent of the position if the bill passed, and he had become anathema to both Democrats and Republicans because of his violent espousal of compulsory health insurance. The measure was defeated in the House by a huge majority.

President Eisenhower's bill to establish the Secretaryship has passed the Congress with overwhelming approval. Yet the President would have had difficulty with this proposal, had it not become a bipartisan measure, long accepted in principle by the Senate, by the public welfare groups, the labor unions and numerous other national organizations.

A typical problem of reorganization in the Federal Security Administration that has not been solved is the status of the Children's Bureau in our Federal-state-local relationships.

In May 1946 President Truman sent to Congress his Reorganization Plan II which, among other things, transferred the Children's Bureau from the Department of Labor to the Social Security Administration. With the usual recalcitrance of Federal agencies the bureau opposed the Reorganization Plan with all of its considerable political power in the Senate and throughout the country. In the Senate hearings it was brought out that the State Welfare Commissioners were tired of the confusion and the waste of time and money created by the separate administrative functions of the Children's Bureau. They claim that the child should not be considered as separate from its family, and that two systems of health and welfare, one for the child and one for the family, are a fantastic waste of money, time and energy. As an administrative agency the bureau has no clear-cut position and can never have a clear-cut position in the Federal-state-local machinery because it has no counterpart in the state governments.

The Act establishing the Children's Bureau authorized it merely "to investigate and report on the welfare of children among all classes of people." Thus the Children's Bureau has a great role to play in our national life. To arouse the public to the needs of childhood as a whole, to lift our concept of responsibility toward children, to lead the states in formulating protective legislation, to improve the lamentable care of delinquent and dependent children in state institutions, to focus all our education, health and welfare facilities toward the well-being of the child — these are some of the all-important functions of the bureau. But its aims should be the welfare of children, not the expansion of the executive authority of the Children's Bureau. Only if it is above the battle and holds aloft the highest objectives for all children, can it keep its role in our national life constructive.

After the Children's Bureau was transferred to the Social Security Administration in July 1946 a single set of policies, procedures and reports was worked out in joint meetings between the Children's Bureau and the departments of health and welfare, to the partial relief of the state officials. But they still feel that the Children's Bureau as an executive rather than a standard-setting agency is a fifth wheel in our administrative structure.

In all but the most backward areas we have enough public and private agencies and good will to turn a community into a paradise, but at present most of these organizations still run in parallel lines that never meet, thereby wasting untold sums of money and energy. Nobody is responsible for the total community need, nor for the contribution of each public or private welfare agency to the total need.

One of the greatest obstacles to social efficiency on the local level is the conservative, self-satisfied mentality that affects too many of our private welfare agencies and dominates some of them.

If voluntary welfare work is to remain voluntary, reform must come from within. One of the prime requisites of these groups is courageous, alert and informed leadership that will recognize the impasse created by the inherited limitations of private welfare work, and face the fact that the usual slow tempo of social progress is dangerous in a revolutionary era. This leadership must see its responsibility as a public trust, rather than a private avocation, and use the same methods of close supervision, the insistence upon efficiency in fellow trustees and employees, the same financial controls that are required of any good businessman.

Every city might well set up a central group of five or more of its ablest citizens, men and women, with critical judgment who are able to get the facts and evaluate them. Let them engage professional advice if they need it. Power must be conferred upon this committee to act not only on reorganization but to initiate methods by which all serious gaps in the local welfare program could be filled. The Councils of Social Agencies should invite industry and labor, the Chambers of Commerce, and professional leaders to join their boards, so that every group will realize to what an extent its own interests are at stake.

Much has been done by private welfare groups on the local level to fill the gaps of voluntary effort and to achieve better co-operation with the public agencies. But this movement would be greatly accelerated if the numerous and powerful national voluntary organizations for health, education, welfare, housing, et cetera would set up a joint council with headquarters in Washington to give leadership to their local branches and to confer with the new Secretary of Welfare on all their many common problems. The present National Social Welfare Assembly has always been handicapped in its aims because its headquarters are in New York City, but chiefly because it admitted the public agencies to membership, thereby undermining the independence of the voluntary organizations.

To keep the local communities in touch with all Federal legislation in the broad field of social legislation and with the Federal departments, some fifty of the major national voluntary groups formed an agency called Social Legislation Information Service, with offices in Washington. This service is important because it is the chief link between Congress and the vast number of local welfare agencies, both public and private, who have no other means of keeping in close touch with Congressional action and Congressional hearings in the fields of their immediate interests, and with the important new regulations and reports of the Federal departments in the same areas.

The chief problems in community reorganization are the improvement of public education and the organization of a health program which will give a feeling of security to the average citizen in these two fundamental fields. As these measures call for detailed analysis, they must be considered in the following chapters. The emphasis in these chapters is not on the separate development of these functions but on their relationship to a total community situation so clear-cut that the individual can readily obtain his rights and carry out his obligations as a responsible citizen.

This, it seems to me, is the only way by which we can revive a new passion for democratic solidarity. For example, we deplore the disruptive effects of war, migration, and social chaos upon the family. The weakening of religious, moral and social traditions make the family our most important focus of cultural continuity. But mere preaching concerning its value will have little effect. The family can only be stabilized in a stable society.

Furthermore, racial and religious intolerance is becoming more acute every day. The causes are not far to seek. Fear of impending change, sharper competition for power and general unrest make us all insecure and intensify antipathies that had been softened during days of peace and prosperity. We Americans, in spite of all the injustices we have committed, were the world leaders in generous treatment of minorities. We are still a generous people; but when conditions become unsettled we revert easily to the primitive frontiersman's fear of the stranger. If we regain our former security through social solidarity and participation in a meaningful world, our fears, jealousies, and hatred will again be brought under conscious control, and our creative forces will be released.

We have made great social progress ever since the establishment of the Social Security Administration. But this partial cure of the wounds dealt our society by fifty years of technological transformations is not enough. More drastic remedies must be found to counteract the crime records, the divorce rate and a general cultural deterioration. If we think of the enormous program now needed to liberate the latent forces inherent in the American people, it becomes clear that reforms of such dimensions cannot be handled by the local communities alone, nor yet by the states, least of all by the Federal government acting as a dictator, but only by the united and streamlined efforts of all three pulling together. Yet from the harmonious interaction of all these gigantic forces, there could arise a new America, a new moral and spiritual power commensurate with the physical grandeur of our vast country.

We have no time to lose if we are going to fortify our nation for the enormous responsibilities that lie ahead of us. The whole world looks to us for assistance and leadership. We will not fail in that sacred mission if we begin at once to strengthen our country by correlating our social and economic objectives. Let us preserve a tenacious faith in the value of individual endeavor and rely, as democracy has always relied, upon the power of organized human efforts. In short, let us have faith in ourselves.

The world is not merely *the* world. It is our world. It is not merely an industrial world. It is, above all things, a human world. And, however powerful the outward circumstances may be, they will yield to the still greater power of a free people determined to preserve their freedom.

CHAPTER XIV

The Battle to Improve Public Education

THE LABORIOUS EFFORTS to improve community organization was work I enjoyed — in spite of little genuine result — because I was trying to make a dream come true — a vision of what life could be in America if only we aim at quality as well as quantity and develop the will to build a more cultivated society in a more wholesome environment. A people that can build beautiful, efficient, productive industrial plants, I told myself, can also clean up the intolerable social mess by which these plants are often surrounded. They can build equally beautiful communities that will be productive — not only of material goods but of human happiness. The sociologists excuse their failure to get practical results with the explanation that mechanical science is easier to apply than the social sciences. The explanation of our defective social structure is that we have thought long and hard about scientific problems, whereas we have only begun to think — and not very profoundly at that — about our human problems. So far the best brains of this and other countries have gone into pure science and its practical application. Where is the Einstein, or for that matter the Madame Curie, of the social sciences? The exploration of the use of science to transform daily living has only just begun.

When I faced the long accumulation of our serious social defects, Boss Ward's admonition to keep my mind simple led me to one obvious conclusion. Basic to our national vigor, whether in war or in peaceful pursuits, is the vast reservoir of educated people produced by our public-school system. Basic to our failures — the millions of young men, for example, who were rejected by the army for illiteracy, poor health, emotional instability — was lack of sound education. Now that we need more and more highly trained personnel to man the ramparts of civilization and to run our complex industrial society, more and better schools have become an obvious necessity — schools which will give all children, and especially our talented boys and girls, a chance to rise to their highest possible development.

This growing conviction that our common schools have made America strong and can make it stronger, was reinforced by other influences. What, after all, would have become of me, I asked myself, without this priceless opportunity for an excellent free education? Was it not my duty to see to it that no child should be denied a privilege that had been such a boon to me? Could I forget the lesson of the war centers that the public school is the greatest single social force in American life to bind together its diverse races and creeds, the old American elements and the recent immigrants, to keep our society orderly yet fluid, to encourage the love of individual freedom, and to reinvigorate our tradition of liberty and justice for all? Such were the thoughts, experiences and ideals that have given to all the work I have done in recent years for the public-school system an intense emotional drive and, I confess, an impatience with its detractors that is no less vehement. Honest criticism I welcome, as does any other friend of public education. In fact my campaign began with severe criticisms of my own. But the groups who attack our public schools for selfish ideological or sectarian religious reasons I despise, and it is difficult to conceal this contempt in my counterattacks.

Woven in and out of every chapter of *Journey through Chaos* and emphasized in the summary was one theme song, the central importance of the public-school system to all of our democratic aspirations and responsibilities. The administrators of public education, the teachers and their state organizations decided that they had found in me a new friend. Moreover, they were in a mood to look for support among the laity. After the depletion of their ranks through the war effort, they were tired of bearing the burden of protecting and advancing the cause of public education by themselves. They needed reassurance as to the importance of their work as much as they needed allies for the solution of their numerous postwar problems. As a result I found myself with more invitations to speak at state and national educational conventions than I could accept.

In a nation-wide lecture tour I tried to arouse sympathy for the public schools among the American people, and to assure the teachers that laymen like myself were interested in their problems. But I also used these teachers' conventions to reach a wider audience through the newspapers, as these meetings are well covered by the national press associations. From Maine to Texas, from coast to coast, I fitted into my itineraries as many speeches as possible, keeping in touch with local school conditions wherever I spoke. If anything, I worked harder after than during the war. Often I comforted myself by reading the history of education in America. For it shows that our unique system of public schools has progressed steadily in the face of popular indifference and the outright hostility of the various private-school interests.

I came home from my war journeys through the South with the firm conviction that these states must receive Federal aid to education before they could give their children even minimum standards of education, especially in the rural areas. I am sure every American who has spent his life in a comfortable prosperous environment would have shared my astonishment when I first beheld in row after row of tents, or other impoverished housing, thousands of human beings so neglected as to education, health and ordinary mannerliness that I was ashamed to think these were Americans — Americans not of recent immigration but of old native stock. Let us not deceive ourselves into thinking we have no proletariat in America. We have a vast proletariat of the illiterate, the untrained and the physically blighted that our past injustices have created. "Are these Americans?" I asked myself incredulously. And lest the reader think I exaggerate their numbers, let me remind him that the 1940 census listed 10,000,000 Americans as having so little schooling that they were unfit to meet the ordinary demands of life. As of April 1953, we still have 2,500,000 people who are illiterates and six million who have not gone beyond the fourth grade.

What are proletarians? They are citizens who have been so totally deprived of self-development that they are a burden rather than an asset to the state. They are the first people to go on relief when economic recession begins. They are well-nigh useless as producers, and the young men are unfit for military service. But we have an inescapable responsibility toward these people as Americans. If we refuse to accept the responsibility for purely humane reasons, common sense should teach us that we cannot afford to carry this economic burden. The wealth of a nation depends upon the proportion of the productive to its nonproductive citizens. The war simply highlighted the fact that we must in self-defense pull up these ignorant millions or they will pull the rest of the nation down.

Why are we inaugurating a Communist witch hunt at this very moment? Why are we afraid of the Communists in the Federal government, in the labor unions, in the colleges and elsewhere? Largely because certain Congressmen and related Tory factions have whipped up this hysteria for purposes of their own. But these dubious elements could not have shaken our self-confidence if we had had a clear conscience as to the social justice of our democratic society. We have been weakened in our resistance to the professional anti-Communists because we know in our hearts that our so-called democracy has excluded millions of citizens from a normal life and the normal American privileges of health, housing and education. We cannot defeat Communism by driving it underground. We can only defeat it by promoting community and family stability, by keeping all lines of communication open between all classes and conditions of men, by making democracy a reality not for the favored citizens who were born in the upper half of the economic level or in the right geographical area but for all the people everywhere. It is a heavy responsibility, but it is a responsibility that cannot be ignored unless we want to see Communism flourish in this country like the noxious weed it is.

When our nation is threatened by the Communist promises of greater equality among people, however specious such promises may be, it is defeatism to say that we cannot afford to give every American child a fair start in life. Money is flowing like the Mississippi now that the military might of Russia threatens us with another war. Well, education is also a war, a war against poverty, ignorance and despair. It is the only constructive war any nation can wage. I do not care how large the military budget is or what the budget-minded people say. The cost of education is not money lost. It is money invested in the safest possible way — in our human resources. If we help the public schools develop more skilled workers, the productivity and the buying power of every community will be increased. Gradually these less prosperous states could take over their own educational expenditures. Thus economizing on public education is economic suicide. The question is not whether we can afford so much education but whether we can afford so little. Twice two certainly makes four as our budgeteers remind us. But when we begin to economize on education, it can also make catastrophe.

With feelings raised to a compelling intensity by my wartime memories, I threw myself into the battle for Federal aid to education, especially for our less prosperous areas.

In 1947 six different bills were introduced into Congress for Federal aid to education. As the postwar interest in education had become intense, over sixty people testified, representing most of the great national organizations of education, labor and religion, the women's clubs, the service clubs, the United States Chamber of Commerce, Negro groups, and outstanding educators, such as Dr. James B. Conant, of Harvard, and Dr. John K. Norton, of Teachers College. Never were more irrefutable facts and figures assembled to prove that Federal aid, especially to the less productive Southern states, was essential to the well-being and progress of our nation as a whole.

I testified first at the Senate hearings and again at the hearings in the House of Representatives. Like most of the other witnesses I was in favor of Senator Taft's bill S. 472. It was drawn up with the Senator's usual legislative skill to protect the independence of the state departments of education, to restrict Federal aid to the areas of need, to encourage the states to increase their own financial efforts, to protect the interest of the Negro in the segregated schools of the South, and to put a modest base of $50 under the expenditures per child in every state of the nation. Article 6B permitted those states which give some assistance to nonprofit or parochial schools to use a fraction of their Federal aid for the same purposes.

In my testimony I avoided statistical and financial evidence for the need of Federal aid to the less prosperous states, as Dr. Norton had made a brilliant and comprehensive presentation of the economic arguments. I told the committee that I would fill in Dr. Norton's arguments by describing the tragic realities behind his figures as I knew that several members of the committee, who like myself came from prosperous states, could not imagine the havoc wrought in our proud land when human beings are denied the elementary rights of every American citizen to self-development.

At the end of my testimony I based my appeal on the need to strengthen democracy for its coming test of endurance with Communism:

> The outcome of the international ideological warfare between democracy and communism will ultimately decide the future of world development.
> The conflict is largely centered on this problem: Which does more for the people, democracy or communism?
> The claim of democracy that it and it alone affords the

good life to all people is by no means accepted in other countries. It has to be demonstrated in clear, unanswerable terms. We must prove it with all the means at our disposal.

As long as our educational system is deficient, uneven, and almost nonexistent in large areas, we are on the defensive in our campaign for a democratic world.

The fight against both communism and fascism cannot be carried on by a segment of our people. There must be unity of purpose on foreign policy among all our people. This unity of purpose can only be brought about through equalized opportunity for the basic rights of an American citizen.

If we succeed in the adaptation of our educational system to the needs of all our citizens, it is safe to say that this will be one of the factors that may help to save civilization.

In the Senate hearings I favored the provisions of Article 6B in Senator Taft's bill giving a small fraction of Federal aid to parochial schools in such states, and only such states, as granted these schools transportation or other public services. I was one of the few people who agreed to this provision. I was in fact amazed at the violence of the opposition to giving any Federal aid to parochial schools for any purposes whatsoever. Only the A.F. of L. supported the Catholic hierarchy in its efforts to secure Federal aid for its parochial schools. When I asked some of the other witnesses why the attacks upon Catholics and Catholicism were so vehement, I heard for the first time that the Catholic hierarchy had defeated every bill for Federal aid to education that had been introduced in the Congress for the past thirty years. It was a revelation that made me very unhappy. Indeed many witnesses reproached me severely for supporting article 6B on the theory that it would be an opening wedge for ever greater demands on the part of the hierarchy for Federal moneys.

As I was worn out by May after a winter of constant

traveling, speaking and writing, I withdrew to Saratoga Springs for two weeks of rest. One day I was surprised by a long-distance telephone call from a Catholic Monsignor in Washington with whom I was on friendly terms as we had worked together on some national commissions. He asked me if I would go more fully into my reasons for supporting 6B of the Senate bill when I testified before the House committee the following week. I agreed to do this but suggested that my advocacy of 6B would be useless unless some of the leading Catholic prelates gave the nation some assurance that the Catholic Church in America would respect the first amendment, as reflected in our state constitutions, and confine its demands for transportation, health, and school lunches to states whose constitutions permit such services.

When I testified in the House, I stated that no public tax moneys should aid parochial schools as such since the first amendment as recently interpreted by the Supreme Court in the Everson case forbade it, but that local public service should be given all children alike, and that the Federal aid granted by H.R. 2953, as S. 472 was called in the House, was restricted to these categories in states where such assistance to parochial schools was customary.

I was shocked when I later read the statement filed by Father McManus, trouble shooter for the National Catholic Welfare Conference on educational matters, in the printed Congressional Hearings on Federal Aid for 1947. He demanded Federal funds not only in states that grant bus transportation and other facilities to parochial schools; he urged that the state constitutions which forbid any use of tax funds for parochial schools be circumvented by direct grants in such states from the Federal Security Administrator to the parochial schools. This legislative device, for which the faulty school lunch bill is the precedent, would ultimately undermine every state constitution.

"The Catholic position," said Father McManus, "is endorsement of a bill for Federal aid to both public and nonpublic schools." This, he claimed, would be wholly consistent "with the Federal government's traditional policy of equity in its educational legislation"! But then, he added a threat to the Congress and the American people. "It will also reflect a keen political sagacity because it is a fact for the record that the educational bills which have passed Congress are those which provided for funds for *the direct or indirect* aid of both public and private educational institutions, and the bills which died, Congress after Congress, are those which were *discriminatory* and *unjust* in their failure to count the children in nonpublic schools among the beneficiaries of the Federal government's assistance." This ultimatum to Congress meant in so many words: "Accept the dictates of the Catholic Church or suffer the consequences."

The Senate passed S. 472 including Article 6B, which granted Federal aid to parochial schools only in states which permitted them public services, with a vote of 58 to 22. The National Catholic Welfare Conference, the Catholic lobby, defeated the bill in the House where the Church concentrates its power to control the Committee on Education and Labor, as it did not satisfy the new demands of the Church for Federal aid in every state. It was a lesson to me. I was disappointed by the defeat of Federal aid. I was horrified by the insight this legislative battle gave me into Catholic policy and strategy. But I learned the salutary lesson that the more one makes concessions to the Catholic hierarchy, the more they demand. And from that time onward I became one of the numerous Americans who are forced by the militancy of the Catholic hierarchy to refuse any form of public aid to parochial schools except health protection including school lunches.

When the Catholic bishops issued their official statement of 1948, "The Christian in Action," which stated that the first amendment never was intended to establish absolute separation of Church and State, and does not forbid the support of religious institutions provided all religions are treated alike, I made speeches and wrote articles for the *Atlantic Monthly* refuting this misinterpretation of our traditions with ample historical proof. As one of their principal arguments that the first amendment meant "cooperation" and not separation, the leading Catholic bishops and their adherents have repeatedly quoted a clause in the Northwest Ordinance of 1787 which reads: "Religion, morality and knowledge, being necessary to good citizenship and the happiness of mankind, shall forever be encouraged." But the Catholic bishops fail to mention that a similiar clause in the Ordinance of 1785 was struck out by the Congress and provision made only for the establishment of public schools. In all but the Ohio land grant this became the rule. Moreover, these land grants to public and only to public education were a great influence in the secularization of our public schools.

When Madison heard that the Congress of 1785 had refused to support religion, he expressed his relief in a letter to James Monroe*: "How a regulation so unjust in itself, so foreign to the Authority of Congs, so hurtful to the sale of public land, and smelling so strongly of an antiquated bigotry, could have received the countenance of a Comtee is truly a matter of astonishment." That is the response of Madison, one of our Founding Fathers, and together with

---

* *Writings of James Madison,* Guillard Hunt, Volume II, page 145.

Jefferson, the framer of the Bill of Rights, to the clause upon which the Catholic bishops base their claim for support of their parochial schools.

In the opinion of many Americans the freedom of our country is at stake in this effort of the Catholic hierarchy to destroy the traditional meaning of the first amendment. Since 1947 the hostility of our people toward the Catholic Church has grown to a dangerous intensity, not solely but chiefly because of the campaign of the leading Catholic bishops to force our Federal and State governments to support their institutions. If this use of Catholic political power continues, equally powerful reprisals are inevitable. It is to prevent such an outburst of religious warfare that I and other Americans who hope to avoid increasing bitterness have thrown ourselves into the fray. It has been an unavoidable and distasteful responsibility which this controversy has placed upon us. My articles on this complex issue have hurt some of my devout Catholic friends who do not understand that the intimate friend of Paul Claudel is not losing her respect for their religion because of this battle over tax funds. There are, in fact, millions of Catholic laymen who share my point of view that public money should be reserved for public schools, but the discipline of their church is such that they are not free to express their opinions. They realize as clearly as any non-Catholic that the first amendment must be kept inviolate as the chief bulwark of American liberty. For the separation of church and state means separation — absolute and eternal — or it means nothing. "Complete separation of church and state," say four contemporary historians, "ranks as one of the most notable American contributions to the modern world." *

* *An American History,* by Curti, Shryock, Cochran and Harrington, Harper and Bros., 1950, page 165.

During the Eighty-first Congress we went through the same battle all over again. In May 1949 the Senate again passed a bill by 58 votes to 15, for Federal aid to education containing the same clause for the use of Federal funds to provide free textbooks and transportation for children attending parochial schools in states whose constitutions permitted the expenditure of tax funds for such purposes. Congressman Barden rejected the Senate bill and persuaded the House Education Subcommittee by a vote of 10 to 3 to substitute a bill confining Federal aid to the public schools. The full committee headed by the late Catholic Representative Lesinski became deadlocked over aid to parochial schools. The mutual recriminations in the committee meetings were the talk of Washington. This time the conflict between the Catholics and their opponents was highlighted by Cardinal Spellman's famous letter attacking Mrs. Roosevelt personally because she supported the Barden bill in her column "My Day." The nation-wide reaction in support of Mrs. Roosevelt revealed the distaste of Americans for such authoritarian tactics.

Nevertheless we managed to pass through the Eighty-first Congress a bill to provide Federal grants to school districts severely overburdened by Federal activities connected with the military and the rearmament program. Congress appropriated a total of $195,000,000 for school construction and $51,750,000 for maintenance and operation of public schools. In the fiscal year 1952-1953 the school districts affected by the defense effort received $315,702,680.

It was my good fortune to be of help in creating sentiment for these bills. After I had completed a year's careful research on school conditions in the Maryland and Virginia counties adjacent to the District of Columbia for the *Washington Post,* citizens of these counties formed a joint committee for the public schools of which I became honorary chairman and Reed K. Pond, a Federal official living in Arlington, chairman. As these counties were eligible for Federal aid under critical areas bills, we held a mass meeting in Washington at the Western High School to which we invited representatives of other similarly overburdened communities from all parts of the country, some delegates from as far as Alaska. We invited the Congressmen from these districts to sit on the platform while the delegates rose one after the other to give figures on their swollen populations and their school shortages. The novelty of the idea together with the alarming statistics to which the Congressmen had to listen resulted in speedy action.

No serious consideration was given by the Eighty-second Congress to bills proposing a general program of Federal aid to education. But the great increase in the birth rate and the shortage of classrooms and teachers which prevail in every part of the country are sure to bring the question to the fore in the coming year.

Our public-school system is America's unique contribution to Western civilization; it is our nation's center of gravity, a vast treasury of knowledge, aspirations and values; and at the same time it is a comparatively new instrument for revitalizing the ideal of a vigorous, free society whose possibilities we have only begun to explore.

Next to our free political institutions, our free public-school system ranks as the greatest achievement of democratic life in America; it is the glory of our culture and our civilization. Nothing comparable to it has ever existed anywhere else in the world. I feel very strongly that our public schools are the necessary condition for the continuation of our democracy and its further development and that both depend on active community participation with the school system.

Politically, socially and economically, American life is unstratified. We have no fixed classes and ranks. We have endless opportunities for individual development and individual progress. Therefore our school systems should not determine for children at an early age whether they are to have a vocational or academic education. For the adolescent this hard and fast classification should not exist. In speaking to a national meeting of school administrators, I said: "Refuse to admit that the academic cannot be vocational and that the vocational cannot be cultural. Keep your guidance experts in check with their tendency to restrict freedom by deciding for young children arbitrarily what specialized program is good for them. Refuse to believe in educational predestination. Believe rather that for all American children there is the possibility of continued growth and that for every adolescent there is a future that has promise." In such exhortations, largely aimed at stimulating zest for teaching as a noble profession, for experimentation with new ideas, and for the expansion of freedom in our society, I poured out my soul week after week for months on end.

At first I felt very lonely as I battled up and down the country on behalf of the public schools, especially when the sinister attacks upon the system, upon the loyalty of teachers and the content of textbooks began to multiply. I took heart when President Truman in December 1947 appointed his Commission on Higher Education, since equal opportunity for college and university training could not be discussed without facing the source of these inequalities in our uneven public-school system. The Commission outlined all the barriers to college entrance that arise from inadequate preparation in the lower echelons of our public schools and demanded "free and universal access to education in terms of the interest, ability, and need of the student."

Of special importance to the public-school system was the recommendation of the commission that two more years of schooling in community colleges be made available, tuition free, to all Americans able and willing to receive it regardless of race, creed, color, sex, or economic condition, and social status. Some of the inferior colleges, of which we have several hundred, fear the spread of the community college as it is apt to put them out of business. But the advantage of what will in effect be two-year terminal colleges for many students will be of great benefit to the four-year colleges and the universities that maintain high standards. For they will siphon off the students who are not suitable material for higher learning and the professional schools.

The President's commission recommended that Federal aid for current expenditures and capital outlay should be provided by the Federal government not only for the public-school system but also for institutions of higher education that are publicly controlled.

Then came another unexpected lift to the battle for public education whose importance can scarcely be properly gauged at this time. I frequently met Dr. James B. Conant, President of Harvard University, on my speaking tours when by accident we spoke on the same program. I marveled that this busy university president who is also a leader in the development of atomic energy, should be so interested in public education as to devote a great part of his crowded life to its advancement. Dr. Conant has been called our Number One Educator in one of the popular magazines. Since John Dewey's death he is that in the fullest sense of the word. For he has a clear vision of the function of public education in a democracy — an understanding of the contributions it has made to our country and the infinitely greater contributions it will make in the future. His very personality is reassuring. It is unmistakably American. No other country could have produced this combination of austerity and friendliness, scientific intellect and deep feeling, scholarly attainments and devotion to the welfare of mankind. His courage, his determination, his belief in the possibility of human betterment are an inspiration to the whole educational world.

I was especially grateful for Dr. Conant's leadership in moments of despair such as I felt when Federal aid to education was repeatedly defeated. And when I emerge battered but defiant from some of my battles against the encrusted habits of established authorities, my sense of humor is restored by Dr. Conant's motto: "Behold the turtle! He makes progress only when he sticks his neck out."

Therefore my hopes for an acceleration of interest in the public schools soared when a group of leading educators and laymen were invited at Dr. Conant's instigation to meet at Rye, New York, to discuss the formation of a National Citizens Commission for the promotion of the public-school system. This, I felt at once, was the best means of putting steam behind a cause second to none in importance to the future of our democracy.

It was decided at the very first meeting that the commission should consist only of laymen and that various educators should be invited from time to time to act as consultants. But it took a whole year of meetings before we were clear in our minds that we must go forward with the idea, and just what we could do and could not do to give leadership to the states and communities in developing their school systems without infringing upon the independence of the local boards of education and the school superintendents. Mindful of the dangers of overcentralization in any democratic field of endeavor, we knew that we must first reassure the educators of the country that our purpose was to help and not to dictate.

Early in the year the initial group elected Roy E. Larsen, president of *Time, Life* and *Fortune,* as chairman of the commission, and James F. Brownlee as vice-chairman and later as acting treasurer. The choices could not have been more fortunate. Mr. Larsen, at first somewhat embarrassed to find himself in a field of endeavor in which he and many other members of the commission were not at home, proceeded to study with ardor and thoroughness the problems that faced him. By the time the commission was incorporated on December 29, 1947, for a period of six years, he was in command of his task. With the able backing of Mr. Brownlee he put our case before the Carnegie Corporation, the General Education Board, and other foundations with such persuasive arguments that the commission was assured of adequate funds for two years and of additional contributions if we achieved satisfactory results. Our grants have been generously continued on the merit of the popular response which the commission has achieved.

What cheered us and made us realize the appeal of our public schools, was the immediate acceptance of all the new members who were invited to join the commission. The total membership is now thirty-four. The other officials, in addition to Mr. Larsen and Mr. Brownlee, are Leo Perlis, Director of Welfare for the C.I.O, secretary; and an executive committee, elected by the full membership, who manage the affairs of the commission between the three annual meetings. The members of this executive committee in addition to the officers are Lester B. Granger, Mrs. Samuel L. Lewisohn, Robert Littell, Harry Scherman, Louis B. Seltzer, Richard Joyce Smith, and myself.

The commission's initial pronouncement defines its purposes:

> The problem of its children's schools lies at the heart of a free society. None of man's public institutions has a deeper effect upon his conduct as a citizen, whether of the community, of the nation, or of the world.
>
> The goal of our public schools should be to make the best in education available to every American child on completely equal terms.
>
> Public school education should be constantly reappraised and kept responsive both to our educational traditions and to the changing times.
>
> With these basic beliefs in mind, the National Citizens Commission for the Public Schools has set for itself two immediate goals:
>
> To help Americans realize how important our public schools are to our expanding democracy.
>
> To arouse in each community the intelligence and will to improve our public schools.

These objectives summarized everything I had been trying to say about public education since the end of the war. The whole relationship of the school to the community must become closer and more realistic. Let's admit that we still have isolated schools whose walls must be broken down. The understanding between the school and the home cannot be left even to the best P.T.A. because it depends on the individual relationship of the teacher to the parent which should begin before the children go to school and continue until they graduate. We talk much about the importance of public relations, but the best salesman for public education is the happy child who understands what is happening at school and explains the excitement and interest of these activities at home. In order to be a good teacher, in order to help the child grow in its community consciousness, the teachers themselves must be encouraged to become active members of the community. Only when this close democratic school-community relationship is neglected, do fears, hostility and unjust criticisms of the schools come about. To encourage in each community this close relationship has been and still is the commission's chief objective.

It is a heavy assignment as anyone knows who has worked on a nation-wide scale. We had to think out ways and means of reaching the people in every community, explain our purpose, and arouse their enthusiasm for their schools without arousing their suspicion of our motives. The schools have so often been used by people with ulterior and selfish aims that they have to be on their guard. It took almost a year before the local educators, the P.T.A.'s and the school boards were really convinced that this commission of laymen wanted nothing but a chance to be of service to them.

The commission has sponsored workshops in hundreds of communities at which local groups could discuss and iron out their chief difficulties and arrive at active programs for their solution. The Junior Chamber of Commerce, the P.T.A.'s, the Kiwanis and Lions Clubs are sponsoring similar workshops in their local affiliates throughout the country. A booklet has been printed embodying the results of the first few workshops which is entitled: "What Do We Know About Our Schools?" It lists the questions most frequently asked by a community concerning its schools and the answers that were considered the best by the workshop participants.

After three years of such activity, the commission is in active correspondence with some 2000 new local citizens'

committees. The total number of such committees is about
8000, and more are coming into existence every day. These
numbers may not be very impressive when one considers the
vast extent of our country. But the impetus they have given
to the interest in education has been tremendous. For these
groups of leading local citizens feel that they are not isolated but a part of a broad nation-wide movement. Thus
the enthusiasm for public service becomes infectious and
spreads an aura over what used to be a humdrum, unre-
warding chore. It is no exaggeration to say that the commission deserves much credit for the fact that there now exists
throughout the nation an active, growing interest in public
education such as has not been felt in our country since
Horace Mann and Henry Barnard created a similar bur-
geoning of support for the public-school system one hundred
years ago.

The commission members realize that their hardest work
still lies ahead. Their efforts will be redoubled during the
next two years after which the life of the commission will
end. Twenty-one states already have established state-wide
laymen's committees for the support of the public schools,
appointed by the governors or established with the co-
operation of the state boards of education. The commission
anticipates that every state will have such a committee before its activities cease, and that they will in turn elect a
national council as a permanent framework of local citizen
participation in the advancement of the public-school system. Then the National Citizens Commission for the Public
Schools can safely terminate its work and hand over its activities to this new group of lay leaders.

In spite of the large sums devoted to the expansion and
improvement of the public-school system in recent years,

it is conservatively estimated that ten billion dollars are needed over the next three years just to house the flood of war babies who will be reaching high-school age during that period and the equally large numbers of new elementary pupils. Additional sums will be needed for the trained personnel to staff them. Can we afford these gigantic outlays for education? It is far more realistic to ask ourselves: "Can we afford to do without them?" Whoever has seen the effects of inadequate educational opportunity upon the children, their parents, and upon our society as a whole can only wonder why the American people should hesitate over this momentous question.

Yet I can understand the reluctance of people who live in prosperous suburban areas or in big cities that have first-rate schools, to shoulder the bill for assisting other states to improve their educational facilities. When I worked only in Westchester County, I was as blind as many another person from similar happy environments. There were always more greatly needed improvements that I wanted for my own county and when I first heard of Federal aid to education, I was indignant. "Leave me alone," I said in those days to people who wanted me to advocate this measure. "We have so many problems to solve in Westchester that we need all of our tax resources right here." But when I got around the highways and byways of our country during the war and saw the frightful poverty that still haunts many areas, my point of view changed completely. Furthermore, I began to realize that the impoverished Southern Negroes who were streaming into New York City and into my own county would be an increasing problem to our schools unless we helped them to get a chance to live a decent life in their home communities.

I consider that my work for the public schools is the

cornerstone of my endeavors to help reorganize the community so that its existing public and private health and welfare agencies can be made as effective as possible.

My experience in cities like Orange, Texas, which had to cope with an influx of unbelievably primitive folk from adjacent rural areas, taught me that the public school is the only institution existing in every American community which can serve as a clearinghouse for our plethora of local welfare services, both public and private, and bring to bear their whole salutary influence upon every family. J. W. Edgar, then head of the Orange schools and now State Superintendent of Education in Texas, used all the facilities of the Junior Chamber of Commerce, all the service clubs, the P.T.A.'s, the churches, the health services, the defense council, et cetera to guide and actually to housebreak the crude, neglected families that surged into the little city from their hidden lairs in the thicket of Deep East Texas. Had he not been successful in doing this, pandemonium would have reigned in Orange. For many of these people had lived a violent undisciplined existence and were strangers to the most elementary decencies of life. The schools opened at 6 A.M., when the mothers working on the first shift dropped their children at the nursery, and remained in session until 6 P.M., when parents returning from the second shift picked up their youngsters with instructions as to what they had had to eat and what they ought to have for supper. Not only were these children educated in the broadest sense of the word but the parents left Orange when war work ceased, with a wholly new concept of decent living and family responsibilities. The social problems in Orange were extreme. But precisely because these conditions were a severe challenge to the school authorities, they proved all the more clearly how far reaching the influence of the pub-

lic school can be when it draws the whole community into
its orbit and radiates its influence outward into every home.

It sounds cold when educators speak in the current jargon of community-centered schools. What they mean is that
the learning process absorbs old and young alike, and that
the children are brought up not in an isolated building to
which they drag their feet unwillingly, but that the school
is a second home where they learn gladly, where they absorb knowledge not by rote but from thought and deed, because the parents share their interests and all of their
meaningful experiences.

Community Service Centers, such as the admirable one I
described at Bridgeport, Connecticut, are desirable as an
additional source of community solidarity. But they take
time to organize, and a rare type of leadership. Therefore the
public school is undoubtedly the most generally available
focus for a total community program for the protection of the
child and the family and for the total enrichment of our
national culture.

The postwar migrations, during which more than a third
of our people changed their residences, made the whole
problem of community life and of decent orderly living just
as acute as it was during the war. The sudden shift of great
masses of people who have had no time or opportunity to
become acclimated in their new environment, makes for
deep social and emotional unrest throughout our nation.
Even in old established communities, the settled population
with traditional mores is often completely snowed under by
the multitude of unadjusted newcomers. Each group re-
sents the other, which makes it difficult to achieve a new social equilibrium. Those who have lived in these communities only a few years resent those who came later. Those

who moved in last month resent those who moved in last week. If we add the race problem to such a situation, the antagonisms in our country are easily understood. The children get the brunt of the discontent. Caught in a chaotic situation between unsettled homes in vast new housing projects and overcrowded schools, it is no wonder that we have ever rising figures for crime and delinquency, and that even the strongest youngsters are in danger of serious moral deterioration.

In order that the reader may not suspect that I am exaggerating the destructive effects of the environment with which our schools are contending, I shall repeat here verbatim part of a sociological study I made in one county which was overrun by thousands of new housing projects. Its accuracy has never been challenged and is further substantiated by the fact that it won the 1951 Award of the Education Writers Association. I omit the name of the county only because it should not be stigmatized for conditions that can be found throughout the country under similar circumstances.

I had the sensation as I studied conditions in this county that a great fire is raging in our social foundations which threatens the whole structure and that it is high time we stop pretending it will burn itself out without doing irreparable damage.

In every school area, I found that about half the mothers were working at a regular job. Even in this well-to-do county many of them are obliged to eke out the family income; the others prefer to work because it is "more stimulating." Some have the desire and the ability to look after their children in spite of the job. Many have neither the one nor the other. The poor children whose mothers are obliged to work derive a sense of security from the knowledge that their mothers are making a sacrifice for their well-being. The upper-bracket child who knows that his mother does not have to work, that she prefers a job to him, often hates his mother with a pent-up fury.

At the bottom of the urge that leads both parents to earn more and more money is the American rat race to "get on in the world." And getting on is too often seen purely in economic terms with a complete disregard of the spiritual, emotional and cultural values. "Our American civilization educates people to material desires," said one principal. "They sacrifice the profoundest joys of life to get cars, radios, television sets, good food, furniture and a bicycle for Johnny."

This can be most clearly seen in the expensive housing developments, inhabited by professional people, where the parents are mostly college graduates and the father's income sufficient to support the family. The mothers are often executives with high salaries. Others earn only the equivalent of what it costs them to hire a housemaid.

"These women have no real love or understanding of children," said this principal. "They praise them lavishly one moment and box their ears the next. But that is the gamut of their affection and their attention to the child's education. These educated women who make big salaries are far more dangerous to their children than the poor mother who works, and their children are far more dangerous to the community."

When the school authorities try to discipline these unfortunate youngsters, nine tenths of them reply, "Mother cannot be reached until 7 o'clock." In the past, the American family was a great institution, even when it was tragic. Today vast numbers of families lack the dignity to be tragic. They are merely sordid.

"What we have to contend with," said teacher after teacher, "is the breakup of the home through absent mothers. That the children all have fine possibilities is certain. They actually welcome the discipline of the school as an escape from their disorderly lives the rest of the day.

"It would be unjust and even absurd to condemn all parents. But there are too many irresponsible ones in these new communities that haven't settled down. These parents are more upset than they were during the war. Then they were working toward an important goal. Now they are just living from day to day and teaching the children to do the same."

"This terrible neglect of childhood is now so often taken for granted by mothers and by our society as a whole," continued this principal, "that we don't even realize what we are doing to the children and to the future of the country. This is going to be more serious as time goes on. More women will work, more children will be neglected, and since the school can never do the whole job and cannot replace mother love, we are headed for trouble."

But in the meantime the school has to try. It is assuming more and more of the home responsibilities. The all-day school is just around the corner. But that means magnificent modern equipment. It means recreational facilities, gymnasiums, auditoriums, playgrounds. It means nursery schools and kindergartens on one end, and junior colleges at the other end of our educational systems.

It means more and better teachers, guidance teachers, psychologists and visiting teachers who will link the school with the home and draw the parents into the orbit of the school and its educational influences. That is why our overcrowded schools, our lack in some communities of the most elementary facilities, and our shortage of trained personnel constitute a social disaster.

"If things go on like this," concluded the principal, "we can't possibly have good, stable citizens in the next generation. In spite of the fact that the fathers are now at home, children on the whole are even more insecure than they were during the war. If we don't move quickly on this school problem, we shall have twice as much youthful delinquency and crime in a few years as we have now."

It is through factual studies such as this that my passion for improving our public-school system is kept at a high pitch. It is knowledge of conditions such as I have here but faintly outlined that makes my heart ache and my mind apprehensive of the nation's future when Federal aid to education is defeated by selfish interests.

I realize as keenly as anyone that the prime need of the nation today is military security. We are all of us willing to pay the stupendous cost of military defense because it is necessary for survival. We shall discover that we can pay the cost of first-rate public schools as soon as we realize that they, too, are necessary for survival. The mental, moral, and physical development of America's future citizens is in fact our first line of defense. If we neglect our children even the future of our military might will be undermined. For a time we shall still be strong enough to ward off attacks from without. But we shall ultimately be defeated by the enemy within — the cancerous growths that even now are sapping the vitality of the body politic.

With such convictions haunting my imagination I shall continue my battle for more and better public schools as long as I live. Victory will not come easy, now that certain reactionary Senators and Congressmen have joined the conspiracy to hound our educational institutions under the pretense of ferreting out Communist professors, teachers and textbooks. The highest values of life, sovereignty of mind, reason and conscience are at stake in this issue. It is, therefore, essential that we realize that the relationship of government to education has never been thoroughly explored in our country. As a result, the universities and the public-school system are now in a precarious position, lacking clearly defined safeguards, and exposed to the demands of any pressure group with economic interests to protect or with ideological nostrums to preach. In other words, our tradition of academic freedom is not firmly grounded and our whole educational system may be brought under Federal government control unless we at once proceed to clarify the role of our public and private universities in the national scene, of the public schools in the community, and hold aloft the profound human reasons why academic freedom is the very foundation of civil freedom itself.

CHAPTER XV
Health for All Americans

WHEN I THOUGHT ABOUT MY PLANS for the protection of American children, the obvious fact that my own active life and that of my husband and children depended on the blessing of rugged health came constantly to mind. I love the old dictum *mens sana in corpore sano.* I wanted to reach out protective wings that would guard other American children as I had guarded my own against illness, malnutrition, and other unnecessary suffering. Aside from my efforts to improve our public-school system, nothing involved me in more arduous labors; for I soon discovered that modern health clinics connected with the public-school system could not function in an organizational vacuum. As a result I was drawn into the complex problem of achieving better medical and hospital services for the nation as a whole.

I saved myself much wasted effort by seeking the best expert advice available in Washington, that of Dr. Thomas Parran, the Surgeon General. I had a deep respect for his judgment as I had come in contact during the war with the work of the United States Public Health Service throughout the country and found the field men to be a group of Federal agents who knew exactly what they were to do and how to do it.

Dr. Parran captured my imagination with the plans he published in 1945 for a co-ordinated, decentralized system of hospital care, which would touch every section of the country and reach our school children with precisely the kind of local clinics that I had visualized.

The haphazard distribution of hospital facilities was one of the serious weaknesses in the medical situation, and Dr. Parran's plan projected a large central hospital with its medical school making available its specialized facilities to the subsidiary area hospital, to the smaller community hospital, and to the local health center. All the benefits that modern medicine has to offer would be channeled from the large medical centers to the remotest rural hamlet. From the top down would flow an educational program, both in-service and pre-service, for all types of health personnel — physicians, dentists, nurses, technicians and others. On the other hand, there would be a referral system for patients from the local community health center, to the area or community hospital, to the large medical center.

This clear-cut method of reaching the community with the most recent medical knowledge would protect the years of early childhood. The co-ordinated protection of the child between two and six is still relatively untouched by the medical profession, the schools, the welfare agencies and the churches. Yet that is the age when behavior disturbances begin, and when the fortunate child develops the sense of competency which we all recognize as vital to successful living.

A shocking article by Colonel Anthony Standish in the *U.S. Army Combat Journal* (April 1952) reveals the effects of our indifference to the protection of the home and the preschool child far better than anything I could say.

Careful research carried on by army psychologists during World War Two and during the fighting in Korea, has brought out the startling revelation that ". . . we have 75% [of all soldiers] with mental stability limits too low for great mental stress."

With typical oversimplification, these military experts put the blame for this lack of stamina upon the "soft" up-bringing given their sons by American mothers. They fail to take into account that working mothers, constant migration, broken families, and a society disorganized by the technological revolution also have a disastrous impact on American children in their tenderest, most impressionable years. If we really want to attack the problem of producing stable, healthy and mature adults, if we are ever to become less superficial in our attempts to cope with mental aberrations, alcoholism, delinquency and crime, we must rally every resource of scientific insight to protect our future citizens during earliest childhood.

To further my knowledge of the understanding and care of the preschool child, I went to Rochester, Minnesota, in 1945 to report on a community-wide child-health project under the leadership of the late Dr. C. Anderson Aldrich and to Yale University to describe the reports on child growth of Dr. Arnold Gesell. The latter material has now been widely accepted, but the broad therapeutic and educational objectives of the Rochester Child Health Project are still too little known. It is an attempt to organize the resources of an entire community behind a plan to bring up the whole child, physically, mentally and emotionally, from infancy through high school. Sponsored by the Mayo Foundation and the University of Minnesota, it is one of the most carefully thought out, scientific, and humane attempts to enrich our national culture by stabilizing family life through a deeper understanding of the parent-child relationship.

The program begins in the hospital with the newborn child. Routine schedules for feeding are eliminated, and the mothers are encouraged to treat their infants as individuals with individual needs, especially for mother love and attention. Breast feeding is emphasized in the mother's education as Dr. Aldrich considered it emotionally as well as physically important. Factual material is gathered to determine why, in spite of all our care, the highest human mortality occurs within the first two weeks of life. The public health nurse continues the philosophy of the program in the home until the children enter nursery school, where they first learn the arts of living and the lessons of co-operative citizenship. These schools are used as demonstration centers for all mothers not only those whose children are among the pupils. The teaching of parents goes hand in hand with that of all kinds of professional people concerned with child care and education.

The Rochester elementary schools became deeply interested in the program and the teachers were invited to take part in the conferences, on diagnosis, corrective services and medical attention. Professors of education from the University of Minnesota in touch with the program helped the public-school authorities with teacher-training courses. The schools were also doing research on present social conditions in order to measure accurately, in fifteen years or more, the progress made through this application of scientific knowledge of human growth to the upbringing of a whole generation. "It is not impossible," said Dr. Aldrich, "that human nature, when it is given a chance to mature under favorable circumstances, may have deeper and broader co-operative possibilities than we have hitherto believed."

The program constitutes a revaluation of all our values; it points the way to more sensitive human relationships, and thus to higher ethical standards.

When Dr. Aldrich died two years ago, the various local officials carried on as best they could without his inspiring leadership. Fortunately, Dr. Henry F. Helmholtz, famous pediatrician emeritus of the Mayo Clinic, who helped originate the program, has now organized and is chairman of a local community council which will carry on this important experiment in child guidance. Even in the early stages the program was beginning to introduce at Rochester an atmosphere of stability and self-reliance, which our loose-jointed social structure needs if we are going to combat the shocking health and nervous conditions of our people that were revealed by the army authorities.

As thorough efforts to co-ordinate our health and educational agencies are costly and presuppose not only good schools but adequate medical centers, I returned to Washington to help make Dr. Parran's plan a reality as member of an advisory council which he appointed. Perhaps the menace of the propaganda for compulsory health insurance accelerated the thinking of Congress. At any rate, Dr. Parran's ideas were translated into legislation called the Hospital Survey and Construction Act, which was enacted by Congress as the Hill-Burton Bill in August, with an appropriation of $75,000,000 for the fiscal year of 1947-1948. The same sum was voted in 1949 and the life of the bill extended four years. The law was also amended so that areas with insufficient tax resources, instead of providing two thirds of the cost of construction, contributed a proportion varying between one third and two thirds, according to population and per capita income. In the intervening years the appropriations were increased to 150 million in 1950, 85 million in 1951, and 82.5 million in 1952. Every state in the Union has taken advantage of the program to its full allotment. Thus far, 81,662 beds have been added to the nation's hospital facilities, largely in rural areas. But more than half of these beds are replacements of outmoded facilities. Construction in large urban areas and in state institutions has increased to a point where the additions provided under the Hill-Burton Act represent only 40 per cent of the national total. Priorities under the Act were established according to existing facilities. I was especially happy that 265 local health centers were built mostly as community projects, a major proportion of them in the South where they are urgently needed.

We are far from realizing Dr. Parran's balanced, integrated nation-wide hospital system. We are still, conservatively estimated, about 800,000 hospital beds short of the nation's actual need in all categories, and 230,000 short in beds for general use. But the progress made under the Hospital Survey and Construction Act is so heartening that Congress should feel encouraged to augment the grants. In case of atomic warfare this nation can no longer ignore the inadequacies of our hospital facilities, and the need for a unified nationwide hospital system, with local control.

In speeches and articles I pointed out that we cannot in the long run support two public hospital construction programs. The merging of the Veterans' Administration hospitals with those being built with Hill-Burton funds and with the existing civilian hospitals, both public and private, is a necessary step toward an integrated national health program. This cannot be done at one fell swoop. It will have to come gradually. But President Truman established a valuable precedent when he ordered that the Indian Service hospitals be opened to other citizens.

The veterans' organizations have opposed integration of their hospitals with a national system on the mistaken theory that they are giving something away if their facilities become a part of the nation's total medical resources. No humane person would favor integration of the veterans' hospitals with a national system, if it meant curtailment of services to any veteran, least of all to those veterans with serious disabilities. But the veterans actually get far better care in community hospitals not because the Veterans' Administration hospitals are inferior, but because in illness immediate care is often the decisive factor. In the treatment of tuberculosis, for example, the Veterans' Administration can never hope to give as effective service in widely scattered tuberculosis hospitals as the men can get in their own local institutions because the VA cannot duplicate our state and local T.B. case finding, control, and treatment services. Local hospitalization would also save veterans the serious consequences of isolation from their families and the exasperation of red tape which is especially hard on a sick person.

The veterans' organizations should bear in mind that General Bradley and General Hawley lifted the VA hospital service to its present efficiency by using community health resources. What is more obvious than to carry this procedure to its logical conclusion by turning the VA hospitals over to the communities and opening them to everybody? The veteran commanders are now begging the medical profession to help them staff their many hospitals. Yet wasteful staffing in VA hospitals is one reason for the present shortage of medical personnel. The tragic fact is that many VA doctors and nurses are losing their professional enthusiasm and efficiency in the VA hospitals because they have to spend their energies upon many patients who stay two or three times as long as they would in a community hospital. The comparative figures of the Hoover Commission on this point are revealing.

	Non-VA Hospitals	VA Hospitals
Appendectomy	7.8	14.3 days
Tonsillectomy	1.4	15.1 days
Hemorrhoidectomy	6.9	34.3 days
Herniotomy (Inguinal)	10.3	27.0 days

But we shall make no impression on certain Legion commanders by pointing out the wastefulness, extravagance, and inefficiency of Federal Hospital Administration. We must bring it home to them that the veterans themselves, their families, their neighbors and friends will suffer, if they persist in their isolationist policy. This policy now obliges the states to ignore VA hospitals when reporting to the Surgeon General, under Public Law 725, how many beds they need for their total population. For the present this does not create serious duplication as the need for hospitals is so great. But eventually it would lead to the establishment of two separate systems for which we have neither the money nor the medical personnel. Furthermore in case of another world war, the heaviest casualties will occur among the civilian population, a possibility for which we can prepare only by organizing a single, co-ordinated system of hospitals.

We must persuade the veteran leaders that only by using the VA hospitals for veterans and civilians alike can we effectively supplement the present total facilities with those to be built under the Hospital Construction Act. If the veterans cannot be persuaded that they are primarily members of the community, the people should organize in powerful civic groups to demand their rights in the community and the state.

Precisely this step was one of the chief recommendations of the National Health Assembly in which I took part as a member of the executive committee. It convened in May 1948 at the request of President Truman to establish a ten-year health program for the nation. "A health program," said our report, "is everybody's business. Its development depends upon local initiative and a knowledge of local needs and therefore on the preservation of local autonomy." Health was defined by this assembly "as a state of complete physical, mental and social well-being, not merely the absence of disease or infirmity." Since health is a function of the community's total way of life, the furtherance of health is dependent in our democratic nation upon local initiative, support and participation of the entire community. It is also dependent upon such closely related factors as education, housing, nutrition, and a basic standard of living. Therefore the first step toward dynamic planning for health is the formation of state and local citizens' councils wherever they do not already exist, to serve as the conscience of the community on all matters of the general welfare.

These councils should bring together lay and professional groups and individuals for the study and solution of their health problems, and for the correlation of all services affecting health. These councils should be appointed by the governor or mayor if their reports are to carry weight with officialdom and with the people. But the citizens themselves may often have to take the initiative to nudge their officials into action. These citizens' councils should join forces with local health departments and with the state hospital authorities appointed by the governors under Public Law 725. This would be the quickest way to achieve co-operation between public and private endeavor and the surest method of eliminating the hostility between the expert and the lay leader that is now one of our chief handicaps to medical progress. These councils should gather factual data to establish existing health needs, and develop methods for the effective implementation of planning.

Only by the encouragement of this grass-roots movement can we get the necessary impetus behind a sound national health program. If our citizens learn by direct participation in planning for their own health that the problem is closely enmeshed with the availability of local facilities, they will be sure to reject authoritarian overcentralized plans that might destroy the very aims they seek.

A nation-wide study of health councils estimated that there are 37 state and 1300 local councils. Local councils, the report showed, are now in operation in one out of four counties in the United States. In each one of the 91 predominantly urban counties — those with 50,000 inhabitants or more — there is at least one health council functioning. The activities of these groups are aimed at problems in such fields as social hygiene, safety, nutrition, industrial health, rehabilitation, maternal and child health, mental care, alcoholism, public health nursing, health education and sanitation. The National Health Council, an association of forty-two voluntary health and welfare organizations, has stimulated the formation of these councils on a state and local basis for the past thirty-two years. Its program is not unlike that of the National Citizens Commission for the Public Schools in the field of education, which I described in the former chapter. Eventually the health councils and the committees seeking to further public education should learn to co-operate in the many objectives that they have in common. One of the important by-products of all these citizens' committees is the experience derived by the thousands of members in community planning, executive capacity and democratic leadership.

This democratic approach to a national health program is a slow process. But our people must face the fact that if they want truly civilized, humane, and serviceable institutions, if they want health in its widest aspects, mental, physical, and even political, then they must achieve them in their own good way. They must make their own institutions, or their institutions will make them. The battle over the organization of a nation-wide health program has been violent, because its solution on democratic or totalitarian lines goes to the roots of our existence as a nation of free men.

In fact, the health problem illustrates better than any other the immense difficulties which confront democracy in its battle with totalitarian ideas. Those of us who are fighting the onward march of the Socialist state with democratic means have two strikes against us.

First — true democracy is hard work. It means tolerance and unremitting effort to reconcile opposing views. It implies a passionate devotion to truth, morality and justice. It means the use of our intelligence, reason and foresight. It demands patience, more patience, and yet more patience in a period of history when the temptation to resort to totalitarian short cuts is very great.

The second strike against democracy — especially in a grass-roots problem such as health — is the lethargy of our people and our ineptness in mobilizing them through effective publicity. It is far more difficult to sell the unending struggle for democratic progress to our people than to inflame their passions with utopian promises. The smooth propaganda of the advocates of a nationalized health program have led many people to think that all we need is Federal legislation to implement it and, presto, every medical need will be met. These people should not lose sight of the hard truth that a compulsory national plan supplies only organization and money but does not supply hospitals and clinics, nor doctors, nurses, dentists, technicians and other essential personnel.

Nevertheless, we shall be forced to accept compulsory health insurance, if the American Medical Association continues to impede the gradual progress toward adequate health protection. The sabotage by this group of S. 445 providing Federal assistance to state communities for the establishment of local public health units is a case in point. Two thirds of the country still lacks health departments meeting minimum standards. Dr. Haven Emerson asserts that "not more than 4 or 5 per cent of our people are today receiving a local public health service that measures up to the simplest demands of science and to an art of preventive medicine which our state of general culture has a right to expect."

"Full-time local health departments in every city and county or combination of counties are essential to a sound health program," said the report of the National Health Assembly. "Until these local health units are established throughout the nation, there will be failure in every other area of endeavor."

Does this impress the A.M.A.? Certainly not. The Senate passed S. 445 last year but it is held up in the House because the A.M.A. is quibbling as to what constitutes public health and is trying to define it so narrowly that the communities would be limited to a program that is self-defeating.

In the same spirit of blind reaction the A.M.A. defeated the Medical Education bill which would have increased the number of doctors, nurses, dentists and other technicians which the nation sorely needs.

Here is the way the National Health Assembly, in which the A.M.A. was amply represented, defined the various services that should be obtainable in every local health center:

1. Mechanism for tabulating vital statistics and interpreting their significance.
2. Control of communicable diseases.
3. Sanitation.
4. Diagnostic and laboratory procedures.
5. Hygiene of human reproduction.
6. Information on health education and laws of living.

The recommendations of the Medical Care Section of the National Health Assembly are of sufficient importance to be repeated here in full:

1. Adequate medical service for the prevention of illness, the care and relief of sickness and the promotion of a high level of physical, mental and social health should be available to all without regard to race, color, creed, residence or economic status.

2. The principle of contributory health insurance should be the basic method of financing medical care for the large majority of the American people in order to remove the burden of unpredictable sickness costs, abolish the economic barrier to adequate medical services and avoid the indignities of a "means test."

3. Health insurance should be accompanied by such use of tax resources as may be necessary to provide additional: (a) services to persons or groups for whom special public responsibility is acknowledged, and (b) services not available under prepayment or insurance.

4. Voluntary prepayment group health plans, embodying group practice and providing comprehensive service, offer to their members the best of modern medical care. Such plans furthermore are the best available means at this time of bringing about improved distribution of medical care, particularly in rural areas. Hence such plans should be encouraged by every means.

5. The people have the right to establish voluntary insurance plans on a co-operative basis, and legal restrictions upon such right (other than those necessary to assure proper standards and qualification) now existing in a number of states should be removed.

These findings have weight because both the A.M.A. and the labor-union representatives agreed to them as well as farm organizations, co-operative health federations, and numerous voluntary health and welfare groups. Although the A.M.A. did agree to all the recommendations, it is still fighting a rear-guard action against voluntary health insurance and the expansion of group practice. The A.M.A. insists that the patient-doctor relation must be maintained; yet it fails to realize that it is chiefly through the practice of group medicine that this intimate relationship can be maintained, now that modern medicine has become too complex for one man to handle.

Such arguments were constantly breaking out during the meetings of the Health Council. It often took diplomatic intercession to keep the labor-union representatives in the same room with the A.M.A. The union men actually started to walk out of the meeting when Oscar Ewing, Federal Security Administrator, and Chairman of the National Health Assembly, announced that he had invited Dr. Morris Fishbein, former editor of the *American Medical Association Journal,* whom the labor unions detest, to make the chief address at the banquet meeting. The able A.F. of L. repre-

sentative Nelson Cruikshank was so indignant over this high-
handed procedure that he bawled out Ewing in the committee meeting and prepared to leave. I held on to Cruikshank's
coattails to calm his wrath. Because he knew I disapproved of
the notorious Dr. Fishbein as much as any labor leader, I
finally persuaded him to stick it out. For the whole object of
the Health Assembly was to arrive at a maximum area of
agreement between the A.M.A. and the labor unions which
favor compulsory health insurance, and find a middle road
toward the solution of the nation's health and medical problems.

As the banquet meeting was now in danger of violent
disruption if Dr. Fishbein made one of his usual tactless
speeches, Oscar Ewing, who should have presided, drafted
me to undertake his job and keep the peace. I put on my
most becoming Queen of Sheba dress, a feminine advantage
I have never scorned, and only just managed to keep
tempers from flaring into the open. I almost lost control of
the situation when Dr. Fishbein called compulsory health
insurance "peasant medicine," but quelled an incipient riot
by holding this term up to such ridicule that the audience
laughed itself back into good temper.

I mention the incident in such detail because the function of catalyst in these democratic conferences is often
salutary. It takes infinite patience, self-control, and fast foot-
work to keep some of these supposedly friendly national
gatherings from flying to pieces. When I get into these face-
to-face, touch-and-go situations, I am grateful to my old
Westchester boss, William L. Ward, whose tactics in political conventions trained me in the art of moving around
among hostile factions. Only long experience gives one the
insight to realize instantly when to be conciliatory and
when to stand like a rock on principles that cannot be

sacrificed. When I get discouraged about the good I have failed to accomplish, I indulge in cheerful reminiscences, now and then, by thinking about the evil that I have prevented.

After I have milled around the country studying various problems and have picked the brains of the experts in half a dozen different fields, practice and theory begin to jell in my mind. When I was invited to speak at the annual meeting of the American Public Health Association at Boston in November 1948, I felt ready to take a carefully documented stand against Compulsory National Health Insurance. I knew it had been rather generally taken for granted among my administration friends that, as a liberal, I would naturally be in favor of the Murray-Wagner-Dingell bill. Several times Senator Murray's staff had pressed me to testify in favor of the bill. I refused to speak for or against the bill as I did not as yet see the problem in all its intricate ramifications. But when I spoke in Boston, the reception of my carefully argued attack on compulsory health insurance came like a bombshell and revealed to me the intensity with which the battle was being waged pro and con. The medical men, the hospital administrators, and the public health officials at the meeting and long thereafter showered me with expressions of gratitude. But some of my "Fair Deal" friends talked as if I had stabbed them in the back.

One reason why so many of our people advocate a revolutionary, overcentralized, Federally dominated organization for health protection is that they see no alternative. They know very little of the sound, decentralized, and truly democratic experiments that are being carried on in various parts of our country.

Realizing that we must give greater publicity and exact information on some of the constructive efforts for the better distribution of medical care on a state-wide basis, I spent a month studying and describing the Maryland Health Plan. There I learned to what extent the problem of a national health program is a problem of the organization of state and community services and efficient administrative methods.

What are the main facets of the Maryland Health program? After three years of painstaking research into the health conditions of Maryland, the Medical Care section of the State Planning Commission decided that a state program should begin by serving the most helpless segment of the population, the indigent and the medically indigent, and that the program throughout the twenty-three counties should be financed by state funds.

In the creation of its administration, two major objectives were kept in mind. First, since the treatment of disease involves not only physical but powerful emotional disturbances, no system of health protection can be effective which imposes a rigid, universal pattern of procedure and ignores the individualities and the varying needs of the people. And, secondly, an administrative system that fails to provide for the professional development of the practicing physician, for freedom of research and ready access to the latest achievements of research, will defeat its own ends because it would freeze our medical progress at its present level of development. With these objectives in mind the Maryland State Department of Health was asked to formulate and administer the program for the counties, as this department seemed the logical organization to integrate the state's whole facilities for health protection. The Department of Welfare was given the responsibility of certifying its relief clients. The more difficult certification of the medically indigent was assigned to the Department of Health. Services include not only free medical and dental care but essential supplies, drugs and biologicals.

To administer the program, a bureau of medical care was established under the State Department of Health whose chief executive must be a doctor, experienced in the organization and distribution of medical care on a full-time basis.

Flexibility is attained by decentralization and placing authority in the hands of the county health officers, all of whom in Maryland are physicians and full-time employees, intimately acquainted with the local population and its medical problems. The county health officer also has an advisory council composed of private practitioners, dentists, and leaders of voluntary health organizations. The doctors feel the program is *their* program, since they are represented on this local advisory council, which guides the development of all new policies.

These local advisory councils have developed into highly significant groups which concern themselves not only with the curative program but with such problems as the causes of illness, poverty, ignorance of proper diet, bad housing, and bad sanitary conditions. The advisory councils bring to bear upon these problems many public and private agencies which had previously functioned without knowledge of each other's activities.

The quality of medical care given under the program is necessarily uneven, if only because the doctors vary in ability and hospital or clinical facilities are inadequate in several counties. But the significant thing is that the quality of medical care is rising, as the local practitioners take more and more advantage of the local diagnostic clinics that have been established by the State Department of Health in many counties which lack hospitals. Here and in the local hospitals they can consult the leading specialists of Baltimore's medical schools and hear them lecture on recent discoveries. The two great medical schools in Baltimore have become the hub of a wheel whose spokes radiate into the remotest rural areas and hold the program together.

It remains for the statistical medical experts to decide in specific areas where the insurance dollar and the tax dollar should meet. Whether we have voluntary or compulsory health insurance, the health bill for the indigent and medically indigent will have to be met by the taxpayer.

Careful local controls by the medical profession have kept the per capita costs of the Maryland program remarkably low in the twenty-three counties. It now reaches 24,837 people at the average per capita cost of twenty-eight dollars per annum. This is an indication of what the annual cost should be for medical care per person in a system of voluntary insurance. Nobody is in favor of dropping the program. Various county medical societies and the Medical and Chirurgical Faculty at its last meeting on September 12, 1952, passed resolutions supporting the program and requesting the legislature to continue the appropriation of sufficient funds to provide for its proper administration.

The Baltimore City Plan differs somewhat from the State Plan, largely because of the presence in the city of two great medical schools, those of Johns Hopkins and the University of Maryland, and their well-known institutions.

Under terms of a legal contract with the City Health Department, each of these hospitals agreed to organize and maintain a medical care clinic for the specific benefit of the indigent. The clinic is the administrative center for all clients and all participating local physicians. Two such clinics have now been in operation four years, one under the supervision of the Hospital of the University of Maryland, the other under Johns Hopkins Hospital. Since then four more clinics have been established.

The main functions of the clinic are the following:

1. It accepts enrollments, does a complete health examination of each client and keeps the records.
2. It arranges for the assignment of the client to a local participating practitioner. Both the client and the doctor are free to accept or reject the assignment. Payment to the doctor is on a per capita basis, $7 per year per client.

The new plan is a vast improvement on the ambulatory care given solely through the established hospital clinics, as the clients often failed to return after costly examinations. Now they are under constant observation of a private physician who keeps them under continuous treatment. It is an improvement also on the specialized clinic which examined patients only for its specialty whereas here the examination is comprehensive.

What the Baltimore Plan does is to reach out the protective wings of the hospital over the whole indigent population of the city, whether the individual is in immediate need of medical care or not, without disrupting the complex medical structure already achieved or destroying the independence of the local practitioners.

As both hospitals are situated in the slums of Baltimore, what the plan in general accomplishes is the social extension of the hospitals' functions into the neediest sections of the city, and the establishment of contacts with the neighboring physicians who heretofore were as isolated from its influence as any doctor practicing in the remotest corner of the state.

This redefinition of the hospital's role in modern society can be readily extended to the medically indigent. Since the control is in local hands, the delicate problem as to what constitutes medical indigency can be adjusted, as it should be, to local economic conditions. At the same time all voluntary insurance systems can experiment to determine how far down they can reach in the economic scale with varied rates of insurance.

"Thus a state or national health program is not a problem in medical economics," says Dr. Lowell J. Reed, former Vice-President of Johns Hopkins University, "but a problem in organization of services. Once the services and the administrative methods are clarified by a plan such as this, the economic aspects can be figured as definitely as in actuarial life insurance. *That is why we cannot answer the problems posed by a national health program quickly but most go at them in an evolutionary manner.*"

The Maryland Health Plan is worthy of study not merely because it has mobilized a whole state behind the care of the indigent and to some extent of the medically indigent. It is above all a warning to exponents of compulsory health insurance to stop, look and listen before they plunge our country into chaos. The strength of our situation is that we still have an opportunity to make local experiments such as that of Maryland under widely different conditions. It is far safer for us to prolong this experimental stage than to take any dramatic step toward a nation-wide solution of our health problems on insufficient evidence of its permanent value.

On the other hand, a practical program of medical care for the vast number of families whose budget cannot be stretched to include health insurance and for those who are actually on relief, including the growing number of recipients of old-age assistance, is the crux of the whole problem of nation-wide health protection. Once this basic need is solved, the methods can be modified and expanded to give the same fundamental care to the whole population.

That is why I am opposed to the plan suggested by the Magnuson Commission for a nation-wide mechanism of Federal-state insurance for assistance recipients and for the medically indigent without a means test. Insurance benefits are meaningless unless a community organization exists which makes hospital and medical care readily accessible to the indigent. Even those rural inhabitants who can afford to pay for medical treatment frequently neglect their health rather than travel miles to the nearest hospital. This proves how useless insurance for the people on relief would be if help in times of sickness or accidents is not readily obtainable. And if an organization for local medical service has been created, for the care of those not able to pay, then the Maryland or related plans are more economical because of local supervision and because they avoid the building up of another vast and costly Federal-state bureaucracy. As for the means test, I found the medically indigent in Maryland had no more objection to it than have the well-to-do clients of the Mayo or other clinics who go through the same process. After all if a prolonged, serious illness strikes, all but a few Americans become medically indigent. If we would stop using the words "means test" which got a black eye during the political wrangling in Britain over their National Health Service, we would think more realistically concerning the necessary controls for the financing of nation-wide medical care.

I have been accused of giving too much importance to the Maryland and Baltimore Health Plans, on the theory that they are practical only in states that have two such excellent teaching hospitals and such outstanding medical leaders who can sell an organized effort of this kind to their fellow practitioners. But in less populous areas two or more states could adapt these plans to their use by integrating them with a teaching hospital adjacent to all of them. Health plans developed by the states in co-operation with their counties would always call for adjustments to local conditions, local needs and local facilities. And the less prosperous states would undoubtedly need Federal assistance both for adequate medical care and for hospitalization. But local plans of this kind locally controlled would permit of elasticity in determining the point of medical indigency, which differs not only from state to state but from county to county. An adjustable local tax-supported program could also be used to protect the health of marginal income groups, thus preserving their independence and productivity and keeping them from sinking into indigency and total dependence on relief funds.

Another major objection to a Federal insurance program for the medically indigent is that it would be a first step to comprehensive compulsory national health insurance. In fact it has the support primarily of the leaders of our large labor unions who have always been in favor of a compulsory national insurance program. The unions have secured high wages, the highest old age security benefits and the most comprehensive medical protection for their own membership. They wish now to forestall the inevitable resentment of the vast majority of nonunion workers by advocating insurance of the medically indigent as a quick cure of indefensible advantages.

Since I wrote my articles on the Maryland Health Plan, the state of Washington and Hawaii have organized similar programs. The Tennessee legislature has introduced legislation for a state-county plan in which the state agrees to reimburse hospitals for the care of the indigent on a matching basis with counties that agree to co-operate. The State County Medical Association has announced its support of the measure and agreed to give medical and surgical care free of charge. Local voluntary committees of laymen in each participating county will determine who is medically indigent, and the patient's doctor will decide whether hospital care is needed.

This is a generous decision on the part of the Tennessee medical profession, but it seems only just that the doctors should receive some reimbursement for the care of relief cases and the medically indigent as in the Maryland Health Plan.

My faith in the merit of the Maryland Health Plan has been strengthened by the report made December 1, 1952, by a committee of medical and laymen appointed by the Governor of Maryland to review and assess the value of the program:

> If the Program were abandoned or seriously curtailed, it would create a chaotic state of affairs in many parts of the State and would throw a heavy economic burden on the doctors who would take care of some charity patients while others would go untreated and uncared for. . . . There is no reason why poverty should be an obstacle to medical care. . . . The aged and the chronically ill have a sense of security given them by possession of their medical care card. Many persons on relief, because of illness in the family, may now become well enough to earn a livelihood. Children who might become chronically ill and in later life become permanent public charges are given early treatment under the program. The good results from the preventive point of view are incalculable. They represent a great saving to the State.

As the Maryland Plan makes it clear that the hospital, especially the teaching hospital, is the basis of a state-wide plan for medical care, it is only common sense to rescue our voluntary hospitals from the bankruptcy that threatens most of them. To do this, the expanding cost of free hospital care must be taken off their backs.

In many big cities, the municipal governments have already increased their contributions for the free hospital care of relief clients. It is now absolutely essential that every local government should assume the total cost for hospital treatment of the indigent and the medically indigent. In some cases, the states will have to supplement the payments of municipalities in proportion to the local tax resources. This is but justice to the voluntary hospitals, now that their sources of income are drying up while their costs are skyrocketing. If the hospitals are relieved of the heavy cost of free care, they could use their endowment funds and other financial resources to reduce charges considerably for the lower and middle income groups. By this redistribution of hospital costs and by the expansion of group practice and of local medical centers financed by the Blue Cross, the Blue Shield and other voluntary insurance systems, such as H.I.P. in New York City, better care can be secured for the average person at a price he can pay than by a revolutionary upheaval in the financing and distribution of medical services.

Research of the Committee of the American Hospital Association for the Study of Hospital Costs, of which I am a member, reveals that there are some five to six hundred different methods used in our country for meeting the costs of free care in our voluntary hospitals. This confused situation, plus the fact that these costs vary from hospital to hospital in the same community, as a result of good or poor business management, and of differences in services rendered, impedes progress toward total payment for such care by the municipalities, counties or other governmental units. It is not for me to anticipate the answers which the Committee of the A.H.A. will find to these complex questions, but the members are well aware that they must suggest methods by which the voluntary hospital can meet its budget and the average man can pay his hospital bills, if the public is not to lose patience.

The ferment in our country, the hard thinking being done by many groups and individuals, on the problem of health for all Americans and the creative vision shown by the most progressive members of the medical profession is bound to lead to new experiments of a revolutionary kind. One of these that has made the widest appeal though still in the blueprint stage is the American Federation of Medical Centers. This is an ingenious plan for community health centers, organized on modern concepts of preventive and curative medicine, and supported by graduated rates of insurance covering the total community. In all of these endeavors we can take courage from the conspicuous progress in health, medical science and the control of communicable diseases our nation has made in the past fifty years, epitomized in the single statement that since 1900 the average life-span of Americans has increased from 19 years to its present high level of 68.3 years. We are undoubtedly on the verge of a new era that may well mark a turning point in the course of American health protection and medical care. If the A.M.A. would only stop behaving like an Inquisition, I have every confidence that the American people would soon begin to deal effectively with what is unquestionably one of the most serious problems of the day.

My most recent assignment in the health field is appointment by the Secretary of Defense, C. E. Wilson, to the Citizens Advisory Commission on Medical Care of Dependents of Military Personnel. This is a delicate task, fraught with political and social repercussions, which would be unnecessary if the nation now had an orderly and comprehensive system of medical care.

CHAPTER XVI

Women Aren't Men

As I LOOK BACK to my childhood one of the greatest revolutions in my time is the transformation in the lives of American women. My mother's activities, her influence upon her children and the general atmosphere of our home were closer to the descriptions in Homer's *Iliad* than to the conditions which now prevail in family life.

What is the salient point about American women today? It is the rise of a greatly augmented middle class and the growing awareness of these economically secure, intelligent wives and mothers that they are the chief arbiters of morals, manners and cultural values as a whole. "What is civilization?" asks Emerson and replies: "The power of good women." When women first gained this sense of power at the turn of the century, it brought some of their weaknesses to light, especially among the extreme feminists, but the gradual expansion of power now reveals their strength, especially among the younger matrons.

It is a significant fact, as yet too little appreciated, that the average American income which in 1939 amounted to $1325 had risen in 1952 to $4300. It is the young married women of this augmented middle class that are "the index of the coming hour." Regardless of income they do their own housework. They have larger families than similar income groups of the previous generation, an intelligent understanding of husband and children, and an amazing ability to conduct a well-rounded life in which individual interests are balanced by social responsibilities. They use household machinery with a matter-of-fact dexterity wholly foreign to women of my era and they accomplish the inevitable chores of family life without letting them absorb too much time and without sacrificing their personal development as wives, mothers and citizens.

Many influences are responsible for this new type of young womanhood. Chief among them is their improved education in the public schools which is frequently continued through college. The exercise of the franchise has also expanded the civic thinking and experience of American women. The right to vote has not brought about the millennium which the feminists prophesied; its chief influence thus far is its educational influence upon women the full impact of which will only be fully realized over the years. Birth control has also been an important factor in freeing women from the debilitating effects of excessive childbearing and has given them greater control over their own destinies.

Mentally, morally, and physically the young women of America have become a potent element in our national life; their influence on the future of our country it is as yet difficult to estimate but their force for good can already be discerned. We can glimpse the immense possibilities of woman's new influence if we consider only this one phenomenon — the effects upon civilization of a rising birth rate among the middle classes. Past civilizations have always been retarded by the heavy birth rate among the neglected, unhealthy and ignorant populations. This is already being offset in our country by the higher ratio per family among the middle classes whose children start out with a good heritage and receive proper nurture, protection and guidance. A more vigorous democratic culture is bound to be the result.

Why then has there been so much criticism of the American woman from our own pundits and from Europeans? Primarily, I think, because the effect of the social revolution on women's lives was not understood quickly enough, and secondly, because the feminist movement with its emphasis upon competition with men for place and power was a false lead.

Historians and feminists dwell upon the various legal disabilities from which women suffered in antiquity. They seem to minimize the woman's role as priestess, ruler and moral arbiter; they ignore the salient fact that as creator of domestic conditions woman formed the child and thus the future of her race or nation.

This feeling of the family as the fountain of life was still intact when I was a child. As an educator, for example, my mother, whose formal schooling was elementary, was far more sure of herself than I who was well versed in the latest educational theories, because she was repeating instinctively well-established principles culled from the wisdom of generations. Her own inner security became the chief source of her children's confidence in themselves and in life. Only thirty years later when I began to educate my own children this world of accepted traditions had crashed about our ears. What was best in my own teachings was a conscious application of the unconscious influences of my own happy childhood. I did not need to go to Tahiti or the Easter Islands to know that childhood security depends on the preservation of instinctive responses to the immediate environment, especially to the parents. But like our anthropologists I had a hard time applying this knowledge in a scientific era. Above all, these childhood experiences made clear to me that the feminist preoccupation with legal disabilities and the whole gamut of equal rights put an undue emphasis on the exterior form of life rather than its content, and upon woman as an isolated phenomenon rather than a social being who derives her greatest influence through wide and creative human relationships.

The influence of the feminists upon American women has been especially disastrous because they encouraged women to compete with men at a period when free enterprise and a laissez-faire economy had begun to develop in our people a philosophy of everybody for himself and the devil take the hindmost. Instead of using woman's instinctive gift for co-operation to assuage the fierce struggle among men for ever greater material success, the American wives and mothers measured their esteem for the men of the family by their ability to bring home the bacon. With the expansion of the factory system and other avenues of productive endeavor, women entered the labor market and professional fields to outdo the males in this frenzied rat race for economic, social and political prestige. It has now come to the point where many married women work and neglect their children because the duties of the homemaker became so depreciated that women feel impelled to take a job in order to hold the respect of the community. It is one thing if women work, as many of them must, to help support the family. It is quite another thing — it is destructive of woman's freedom — if society forces her out of the home and into the labor market in order that she may respect herself and gain the respect of others.

When I first published this statement, I received numerous letters of which this one is typical: "I am a Phi Beta Kappa. I had decided to give up my remunerative editorial job and devote myself to becoming an intelligent wife and mother. It was a hard decision made easier now that you helped me to understand the false pressures driving me to keep my job." These younger women now realize that there is no task more exacting, more rewarding, and more necessary than that of housewife and mother with all the community responsibilities which these tasks imply for good schools, health provisions, and general community stability. They are devoting themselves to becoming a moral force in society through the stabilization of the home and of the whole social structure. The influence which women like my own mother exerted instinctively and unconsciously, has become far more potent among these modern matrons, because they go about their broader responsibilities with a conscious awareness of their wide ramifications. With all the social, scientific and cultural insight which these educated women possess, they can and will be the standard bearers of a civilization higher in every respect than any we have ever known before. They have recaptured the wisdom of the ancients that just being a woman in the fullest sense of the word is their central task and their greatest opportunity. They understand what it means to be responsible for the continuity of life, not merely in the physical but in the historical sense. It is a task that challenges their whole being — their characters, talents and imagination.

As a result there are probably more ideal marital partnerships in our country today than ever before in the nation's history. But there are still many women who have not escaped from the feminist dissatisfaction with being women

and therefore with being wives and mothers. I am not trying
to drive such women back into the home. The married
woman who is rebellious about family life does her children
more harm by staying home in such a frame of mind than
by leaving them to some kindly relative or sending them to
boarding school. It is the frame of mind of such women
that is wrong, that must be understood and changed. For
these women are equally disastrous as an influence in their
working environment. God protect us from the efficient, go-
getter businesswoman whose feminine instincts have been
completely sterilized. Wherever women are functioning,
whether in the home or in a job, they must remember
that their chief function as women is a capacity for warm,
understanding and charitable human relationships. Women
are throwing their greatest natural gift out of the window
when they cease to function as experts in co-operative living.

Another fallacy about women which is receiving far too
much currency is the accusation that they have lost the
adventurous spirit of "their older sisters" who battled
successfully against "male domination." The magazines publish a plethora of articles deploring the fact that women
are only too often content with minor positions in the
business world. "Their willingness to accept the status of
useful but humble cog in an enterprise directed by men is
baffling to me," says one author. She wants them to conquer
their "humility and lack of confidence."

Now I fail to see any exaggerated humility in this
modern feminist type of woman. On the contrary, I find
too much of the exaggerated American emphasis on success
and too little upon service. These feminists should bear in
mind that women become far more cruel than men when they
hurl themselves into ruthless competition with the opposite

sex. History has proven this since time immemorial.* Even in our own era, the women who successfully fought their way to power in Communist Russia and Nazi Germany became far more brutalized than many of the male leaders. We need only remember such hard, pitiless characters as Ana Pauker, "Red Hilde" Benjamin, and Ilse Koch, the "beast of Buchenwald," all of whom revealed what happens to the female when she forgets her role as the guardian of life, morality, and human compassion.

In my opinion, humility is the greatest possible asset in any human being, particularly in women. True humility is the understatement of a powerful personality. It is innocence triumphant which Emerson has described as "the most powerful critic of all that passes through its alembic." It is the ability to understand reality as it confronts us. This ability, so characteristic of woman's inherent personality, to adjust herself to outward circumstances, to the husband in marriage, to the employer and fellow workers in business and industry, is not a sign of weakness but of strength. The woman who tries to control situations by force and by aggressively overplaying her hand in every human relation is the weak woman trying to overcompensate for her weakness.

These are the worried, restless, immature females who complain bitterly that there are not enough women in high executive positions in the business world and in government. Last year I attended a gathering of brilliant women, all college graduates, who were especially indignant that women were ignored in the State Department and the world of diplomacy. I asked them to name the women whose talents for determining our foreign policy had been overlooked. After much debate the group could agree upon only three

*See *Woman as Force in History*, Mary R. Beard, Macmillan Co., 1946, pps. 278-286.

women whom they considered eligible. My realistic approach to the discussion made me very unpopular at the time.

These aggressive, frustrated women actually make the role of woman in business and public life more difficult because more suspect. They are precisely the female types under whom neither women nor men want to work. The balanced, mature woman who knows her inner worth does not run around the world complaining of the injustice of men. She is quietly expanding her area of influence. This wise, subtle, and effective type of woman meets with appreciation wherever she is active, not because she is *demanding* recognition, but because her gifts are recognized as extremely rare and invaluable. If I were asked to define the principal quality of such exceptional women, I should say that it is the capacity to accept the triumphs of life without pride and the sufferings of life without despair. The wisdom of these truly feminine and humane personalities is summed up in the words of Saint Paul to the Philippians: "I have learned in whatsoever state I am, therewith to be content. I know both how to be abased, and I know how to abound."

The Chinese poet Tu Fu expressed sublimely the natural aspirations of womanhood in a warring world when he wished for huge wings that could be stretched out over all sensitive, suffering humanity. What the world needs today is not more competition but woman's native genius for sympathetic co-operation. Competition is so acute because society has crumbled and left the individual atomized and unprotected. Unless we women succeed in modifying this competitive spirit through more effective co-operation between public and private endeavor, between management and labor, between the contending religious groups, between the family and the community, between one individual and another, then there is little hope for our democratic civilization. This is women's great opportunity — to ease the acute and dangerous tensions of American life.

I am not asking women to overdo self-sacrifice to a point of self-abasement. We all know extreme feminine types who use this masochistic weapon not out of a desire to serve, but to conquer and subdue their victims. Women must learn to keep self-respect and self-sacrifice, the social and the biological functions, in balance. Such women have the most friends because they defend their own personalities while giving free play to the expansion of other personalities. Those are the women who are called blessed because they constitute the happiness of their families and of the whole community.

Such women, moreover, are not concerned with the modern cry for equal rights and public positions because they are too sure of themselves and of what they have to give to the world. They seek to develop their personalities as whole human beings, that is as women and as individuals. They know that woman confronting the world has no greater resources than those she finds within herself. Are women people? Only to the extent that they fuse their inherited and acquired characteristics into a dynamic, functioning unity which alone is worthy of being called personality.

The feminist cry for equal rights has been especially pernicious in two areas, those of sex and of marriage.

The freedom of women has brought the whole problem of sex into a new focus. The sexual morality of our nation has never been lower, because in seeking for equal rights women have dragged their standards downward. This sex freedom which so many women are practicing is a delusion. It is a pseudo freedom which ruins the lives of many young women before their mature life has begun, because they have no scientific understanding of the ramifications of sex in the female organism. For woman cannot get away from the fact that her biological, emotional, and psychic faculties are closely intertwined. Women's sexuality, if it is not to be destructive to her and to society, has to be sublimated through a spiritual relationship to her mate whether in or out of marriage.

Thus woman runs the risk of warping her whole personality unless she uses the postadolescent years to develop her individual human traits, her character, her mind, and her Platonic idealism as contrasted with her physiological equipment. If this period of sublimation is curtailed by premature sexual experimentation, it not only leads to disappointment but it will endanger what I have emphasized as woman's greatest need, the harmony of the sensual and the supersensual aspects of woman's character. By seeking change as in itself of value in her sex life, she also endangers her capacity for permanent human relationships and therefore her interest in a lasting marriage and lasting friendships. The woman who guards her sex life as intimately related to her development as a whole human being is the one who is likely to make few mistakes in her emotional relationships, the one who achieves the highest type of sex life, and the one who is apt to attract, to choose, and to hold the devotion of the right husband.

The adult world is wholly responsible for the fact that youth lacks competent guidance today in the conduct of life in general and sex in particular. Too little attention has been paid to the sexual experimentation now occurring even among the very young, because the adult world is uncertain of its attitude toward the problem. What is youth to think when an anthropologist, with all the prestige of science and a university professorship, declares that we shall accept premarital sexual promiscuity as a commonplace in another generation or two?

The churches, on the other hand, have lost much of their authority over youth because they have refused to re-examine their religious sanctions and their dogmatic preaching in the light of modern physiology, psychology and sociology. And parents, for lack of generally accepted sexual moral principles, have surrendered so much of their influence over the behavior of their children that they now blame the schools for not handling the problem more effectively. The poor schoolteachers! In our modern society they are supposed to be clergymen, doctors, nurses, psychiatrists, sociologists and educators all rolled into one — one fallible, underpaid public servant. Obviously sex films, with which the schools are experimenting, cannot make an important contribution to this most difficult of all problems. Sex is not a thing by itself and should not be emphasized as such. If sex as a physical manifestation is going to be taught in the schools it must be brought in naturally during the study of biology, and its higher aspects must be a by-product of the whole academic program.

In the meantime the unhealthy overemphasis of sex in literature, advertising, and the films make sexual self-expression a matter of competition like everything else. Young women are afraid of being unpopular if they do not accept the low sex standards of today and refuse to run with the crowd. What matters is how many "dates" they have — the quantity, in other words, rather than the quality of their friendships. Sex has been vulgarized and reduced to a competitive pattern because individuals are too isolated to use their sex as the basis for all human relationships. Sex is not something we can take or leave. Sex permeates and illumines the whole personality. And despite the crude, unscientific Mr. Kinsey, it is not the physical aspect of sex, but the ability to translate it into higher manifestations of permanent value, that determines the quality of a civilization.

What we need today is not a negative, puritanical asceticism but a positive enthusiasm for right conduct. The best answer to the present disorientation of sex life lies in the early development of our children. If the education of mind, emotions and character is fitted to children's needs in our complex technological civilization, the maturing boy and girl, the young man and woman, will have such vital interests that sex will find outlets in achievement and growth of personality. Too early and too great an interest in sex by adolescents is largely the result of poverty in other areas such as the love of learning, of adventure, and the development of creative imagination. Women should be the first to realize that to remain healthy the human spirit needs daily exercise just as much as the human body. Without spirituality, without the intuitive love of the moral, the mental, and the mysterious elements of life, woman loses her whole unique influence upon the course of civilization. And nobody suffers more than woman herself if she endangers the home and the stability of an orderly society upon which her whole security depends by renouncing her rightful position as the guardian of moral values.

Because woman, if only for self-protection, must preserve monogamy and keep the home intact, it is woman who should make herself responsible for the success of marriage. Never will we be able to decrease the divorce rate until modern woman faces and accepts this responsibility as her obvious duty. Making divorce more difficult will do no good. On the contrary, our divorce laws should be uniform and a divorce accessible by common consent in those cases where gross abuses make divorce unavoidable. But in most cases it would not be necessary if young women could lead lives that permit them to mature toward the balanced womanhood I have described as characteristic of our younger matrons, and chose their husbands not as a consequence of some infantile repressions or mere sex appeal but with a view to permanent partnership. If marriages are made purely on a basis of sex, they will be dissolved for the same reason, and that is a game which women cannot win. It is a threat to their whole status in society because it implies a disrespect for the importance of the marital bonds and of monogamy. Thus the mounting divorce rate is a sign that women as a whole do not realize that they are committing what can only be described as social suicide.

The egoistic desires of women have been so accentuated by the indiscriminate struggle for equal rights that the discipline of marriage, the subordination of self that it entails, and the adjustment of personality upon which it depends have become increasingly difficult if not repugnant to them. Far too many women have not only lost their instinct for self-protection; they have lost their sense of joyousness and their sense of humor. What do these self-centered, egoistic women expect in the man they marry — a paragon of all the virtues and a wealthy one to boot? Even though he be a genius or a millionaire, the husband of the neurotic, introverted female is doomed to failure. If she has the one, she will begin to yearn for the other. Her pathetic search for personal happiness never lets her decide whether marriage should be a feather in her cap or a feather in her nest.

As I go about my social research today, especially among uprooted families living in the vast new housing developments, I am almost forced to the conclusion that there are more good fathers today than good mothers. The infantilism of selfishness, the desire for a false self-expression, and a consequent desiccation of instinct lead all too many women to despise the role of housewife, to reject their children and resent the father. I fear it is too late to change many of these women. When they seek a divorce they rationalize this supreme act of selfishness by telling themselves that their children will only suffer if they grow up in a divided household. Of course they will. It does not occur to such women that theirs is the prime duty to see that the household is not divided. And though occasionally divorce may be the only way out of a deadly impasse, nine times out of ten the wife who lets her marital relationship get into such an impasse has only herself to blame.

To be sure, there are external conditions today which seriously threaten the family and make the life of women extremely difficult — constant migration, inadequate housing, poor educational, health and welfare facilities. Furthermore our society has been shamefully dilatory in providing for the needs of married women who are obliged to work to support the family. We groan about rising rates of delinquency while the economic structure forces more and more women to work outside the home and to contend singlehanded with the protection of their children. We need not only more nursery schools but other provisions for the care of infants of working mothers and the management of their households. Here is a great opportunity for the growing numbers of able-bodied older women with "nothing to do" because their own growth was arrested through faulty education. They could readily be trained to become useful as paid full-time or part-time assistants in the homes of the working mothers.

At the same time we must guard against attempts to solve the problems of the family with meretricious answers. There is growing agitation in our country for the Socialistic device of family allowances instituted in Great Britain, France and Canada where they were considered necessary largely because these countries lack many of the community services, family assistance programs and the high wages which exist in the United States. Nothing would be more disastrous to democracy than to put every family on a Federal dole. Politicians would vie with each other to increase it. It would corrupt the government which administers these allowances as well as the parents who accept them. Above all, it would penalize the taxpaying middle classes that should be encouraged to have more children, by the imposition of heavier taxes. This would undoubtedly force them to restrict the size of their families whereas the lowest income groups who pay little or no taxes and who have not been educated to the use of contraceptives would breed more recklessly than ever.

It is not more people that are needed in the world but better people, physically, morally and mentally. This question of raising the quality of our American population must also be taken into account in the question of immigration. The slum problem in New York was almost solved before we allowed the Puerto Ricans to roll into the city like a plague of locusts. If we now open our ports to European refugees with no selectivity, the uneducated who are the biggest breeders will flood the country, because they are the hardest

hit in their homelands, having already created the problem
of overpopulation in their own nations. These ignorant,
highly reproductive masses, would not only create an overpopulation problem in our country but they would put an
intolerable burden on our health, welfare, housing and
educational facilities as the invasion of the Puerto Ricans
has demonstrated.

The basic world problem is overpopulation. We must
help solve it by improving food production abroad. We
cannot solve it by letting the overpopulated nations dump
their excess people upon our shores. We must make our
contribution to the refugee problem created by the exodus
from Russian-dominated lands, but the times are gone when
we can say that the United States is morally obliged to
accept all the homeless, the impoverished, and the oppressed
who wish to come to our shores. We would merely weaken
our own country to a point where it could no longer carry
its world-wide responsibilities to the have-not nations.
Romanticism must now be supplanted by scientific state-
craft. We must make it perfectly clear that any country
which encourages irresponsible breeding will henceforth
have to face the economic results. On the other hand, we
can admit more immigrants if we exercise the right to
determine their qualifications. We should insist upon a
thorough health examination and basic intelligence tests for
every person who seeks entry to the United States. For the
educated middle-class mothers of America who want large
families of their own and who can thereby raise the quality
of our citizenship, would be the first to restrict their births
if overpopulation becomes a danger here. Nothing would
be more unjust to American womanhood. Nothing would be
more harmful to the future of our democracy.

To clarify these fundamental problems of our society and to remedy its many existing defects is the duty of women whose children have grown up or who for other reasons are free to devote themselves to public service. The wide gaps which still exist between our social ideals and the sordid realities need not be discouraging if we see our shortcomings as a spur to greater effort. Democracy is, first and foremost, the perpetual revelation of greater capacities in the human mind and soul. It is the only form of government that sets no bounds to the possibilities of man. Its doors all open toward the future. It converts every end into new means. And it will not get the reverence it deserves until America makes manifest throughout the world that democracy is not earthbound, but a divine quest for humanity's perfection. Since perfection is not an attainable goal, its pursuit is both tragic and heroic. And it is precisely this heroism consciously sustained in the face of every defeat that constitutes the glory of democracy. Upon woman, who is biologically close to nature and to whom the tragic idealism of democracy is a natural instinct, rests the chief task of reminding the country that our republic is not restricted to the desire for creature comforts but strives with intelligent and unfaltering zeal toward an ever expanding concept of man's destiny.

Is this call to the moral rejuvenation and the heroic defense of our society too exacting a role for American womanhood? No, and again, no. As I said at the outset, there are already numerous indications of the reorientation of woman's thinking as evidenced, among other things, by an idealism among the young as passionate as it is practical and well directed, by many successful young marriages of the finest type, and by an abundance of children in our educated middle-class families. If it is difficult to carry out the high role of woman in our modern society, it is also a great honor to be a woman in this critical historical period. Now that destruction threatens us from within and without, woman's role in society is again recognized as the fundamental, conservative and vital one that it always has been. For as mother, woman represents the focal point of time and eternity and the perpetual triumph of life over death.

CHAPTER XVII

Out of These Roots

THE SUMMER of 1952 at the farm had been a happy one, the house filled with our children, grandchildren and friends. When we returned to Washington, we found the atmosphere in the nation's capital full of the lamentations of outgoing Democrats, most of whom are convinced that the country will go to the dogs without their leadership. Since I remember that the Republicans felt the same way when President Hoover was defeated in 1932, I am amused to see how all things repeat themselves. Power held too long by either party is apt to distort an official's concept of his own importance.

Yet the bitterness of the outgoing rulers of the country made me realize that I have lost all the passionate partisan involvement I, too, used to feel when I was politically active. Today I do not so much care whether the people with whom I have to deal in my efforts to achieve social progress are Democrats or Republicans; I want to know what kind of human beings they are and what their attitude is toward our major problems. At a time when our nation is so hard pressed from without and within all men of good will must transcend party lines and work in unison to keep the world on an even keel.

This nonpartisanship, or rather bipartisanship, was for me

a purely fortuitous development. The last Presidential campaign in which I was active was the abortive one of 1936 when I helped nominate Landon and conducted the Republican women's radio program during the campaign. Thereafter Eugene's ownership of the *Washington Post,* which he ran as an independent paper, prompted me to sever my connections with the Republican organization, though I am still enrolled as a member of that party.

But I must not give the impression that I think women should keep out of politics and refuse to hold public office. I hope I have made it clear that my training in Westchester County under Boss Ward in straight party organization work was the basis of all my public activities, the best possible school for understanding politics, community organization, and the relationship between Federal, state and local government. Since most women are tied to the home, local political activity is the only outlet for public service available to them. But it is also the most important field in our democracy.

If all of our counties, cities and villages were efficiently and honestly governed, the Federal and state governments would not be obliged to take upon themselves so many functions which do not properly belong to them and which make for overcentralization of political power. The tax situation with its overemphasis on Federal taxes, makes Washington a center of enormous latent power. Unless we correct this situation, states' rights will become more and more of a fiction. For lack of financial resources our local communities suffer from an inferiority complex concerning their ability to deal with their own problems. If local leadership continues to abdicate its responsibilities, it is only natural that Federal leadership will try to fill the void.

Local voluntary leadership must continue to assert itself. The grass roots have always been the training ground of

national leadership. The evolution of our American statesmen, of whom Lincoln is the supreme example, through
local and state governments to Federal office, is the best
guarantee that a man who achieves high place in national
affairs has gone through a long educational apprenticeship.
The future of our democracy depends upon bringing to the
top this experienced and responsible type of leader who
combines administrative capacity with sympathy for his
fellow man.

Until the tax situation is modified, the best answer to
social rigidity lies in decentralization of administration.
This will only be successful if the local citizens, especially
the women who usually have more leisure than their men,
take an active interest in local politics, local schools, local
health and welfare problems and all the other functions
that make for good community housekeeping. For the
average American citizen must learn to control the ever
increasing government agencies, and the professional experts
in charge of them, or the professional government officials
will control them.

Some Americans are so pessimistic about the whole situation that they claim people do not really want to be free,
that they are ready to barter their freedom for security
handed them on a platter by the Federal government. I know
that is not true. Many of our citizens are baffled, inhibited
and discouraged by the social confusion which has resulted
from two world wars, the depression and the cold war; in each
of these emergencies the power of Federal government has
been steadily augmented. If this trend is allowed to continue
the United States will inevitably become a Socialist state.
That is why the intelligent, enthusiastic efforts being made by
milions of American women to preserve local autonomy is

now more important than ever. They demonstrated their will power in the last Presidential election. As I look back upon my own various activities, I can assure them that local politics are more rewarding, more immediately satisfying, and more fun than any other avenue of public service.

As for holding public office, every woman must make the choice for herself. But if she decides to run for office, the best way to command the respect of the men who still control the nominations, is by proving that she has not been above ringing doorbells and that she has the ability to get out the vote. The glamour girls who want to start at the top never last very long, even if feminine charm gives them a head start. Continuous, successful political action rests on power derived from service to our fellow beings, and from human integrity. The best proof to women that this is so can be found in the career of our only woman Senator, Margaret Chase Smith, who has earned the enormous prestige she now possesses in the Senate and throughout the country by these two basic qualities. But the women whose family responsibilities make it impossible for them to contemplate a political career should not refrain from political activity on that account. For the character of our public officials, the preservation of our liberties and the ultimate world role of our nation depend more on the disinterested service of millions of local citizens than upon any other factor.

At present, for example, we are shocked by the revelations of dishonesty among some of our Federal, state and local officials. But quite apart from these extreme examples of immorality in the political world, the perpetual compromises which are forced upon our public officials from the Presidency down to the minor positions, are a severe indictment of our democracy. Even Lincoln had to make serious compromises which may in part explain his melancholy and his mordant wit. A story about Lincoln that is little known, illustrates his bitter realization of human frailty and its effect upon officeholders. While the newly elected President was besieged by office seekers in the White House, a doctor forced his way through the milling crowd to enter Lincoln's private study. After examining the President he informed him that he had a mild case of smallpox. "At last," said Lincoln with weary humor, "I have something that I can give to everybody."

The best solution for a higher morality among our officials lies in an alert and educated electorate that will refuse to exert tyrannical pressures, to say nothing of bribery, upon its public servants. Our officials will never be any better than we want them to be. And since women in every civilization have shaped its morality, theirs is the chief responsibility to exercise the franchise and to clean house politically by selecting candidates of a high order. If, as in my own case, family responsibilities keep them from holding office themselves, let them remember the admonition of my Westchester Boss, that it is more satisfactory in the long run, especially for women, to wield the power behind the throne than to occupy it.

The poet Goethe said that those people are the most fortunate who in their maturity return consciously to the unconscious wisdom of their youth. That is precisely what, by the grace of God, has happened to me. Like most of my contemporaries, I absorbed throughout childhood, the great gifts of a young, strong, hopeful democracy, faith in humanity and the spiritual fortitude, the love of liberty and the confidence in the triumph of good over evil that are inherent in this noble heritage. After deep inner schisms which tore me away from these roots and even made me hostile to the values they represent, my life has swung a full circle and brought me back to my native beliefs. I traversed the path which Paul Claudel calls *"ce chemin épouvantable vers moi-même."* I was at home again with my innermost self; I was grafted once more upon the powerful roots from which I had sprung. To be reconciled with oneself in this fashion makes for a deep serenity that proves the power of childhood influences and constitutes the greatest blessing of old age.

The sound American culture in which we older people grew up has been shaken, not only by our own moral confusion but because we allow ourselves to become defensive under the barrage of ridicule which the Communists have leveled at our "bourgeois" civilization. It takes courage to defend the simple virtues of the middle-class life that is now threatened, of the family as the cradle of goodness, of an orderly society as the source of morality, and of individual freedom as the basis of human happiness and of constructive human relationships. I think I value these qualities the more because I, too, went through a trying period of being a confused, self-centered intellectual largely because of my reaction against my father who embodied all these bourgeois virtues in my childhood, and because a purely academic training separated me still more from the influences of my democratic youth.

What saved me from straying into futility was the ineradicable power of this meaningful upbringing. My own fortunate marriage, a husband who demanded much and always gave more than he demanded, and constant family responsibilities awakened the memories of blissful confidence in my own early family setting. Service to the community in which we lived brought about a total recall of the importance to me of an integrated democratic world of school, society and nature. Fortified by a new sense of emotional security, I could at last face my father complex and overcome it as a lesson in the dangers of overindulgence in abstract ideals — *Schwärmerei,* as the Germans call it — which my father symbolized first to an enchanting and later to a painful degree. In the conquest of this haunting dilemma John Dewey's philosophy, the wisdom of the Chinese sages, and Thomas Mann's biographical novels which alike teach distrust of the abstract and the absolute, of utopias whether created by romanticism, Communism or religionism, were another source of my ultimate reconciliation with my father and all the agonies he had caused me.

Only after I had escaped from this psychological prison-house, did I realize how unjust all children are toward their parents when either one fails to measure up to the dream concept the child forms during the impressionable years of infancy.

As a result of my democratic, active, experimental approach to life, I now have the faith and the quiet confidence to resist authoritarianism in any and all forms, whether in our own country or abroad. The Marxist "planners" pretend that they can foresee the future in their ideological crystal balls. As they also pretend to be very scientific, they should know that the best we humans can do is to take the most intelligent advantage of all circumstances; to do this we must be free to choose alternatives and decide the next step in human affairs with what I have called the divine prerogative of discrimination. To be sure, the free peoples make tragic mistakes; but the authoritarians make more. The Communist planners cannot make the best of things as they present themselves, because their ideological blinders restrict too severely the choices they are willing to make. But they are dangerous for two reasons: when they reach the end of their blind alley, they may have no alternative left except the resort to force; in the meantime, their promises of utopia have a strong appeal for the destitute masses and for the rootless intellectuals who are always entranced by abstract ideas.

The vitality of American democracy as opposed to European societies is reflected in the history of the Socialist party. We, too, used to have a strong Socialist party which has withered away because with rational discrimination we took over the constructive parts of the Socialist program — social security, unemployment insurance and aid to dependent children — while rejecting extreme measures, such as nationalization of industry, as unsuitable to our free-enterprise system and to freedom in general. On the European continent, especially in France and Italy, the Socialists largely became Communists out of despair of obtaining greater freedom and justice by democratic means. And Great Britain, though it warded off Communism, did so because it went Socialist and forced a recalcitrant conservatism to accept an overcentralization of power in the hands of the government. Though fingers of scorn are constantly pointed at our democracy because of our injustice to the Negro, nowhere in the whole wide world has the Negro made more and steadier progress toward equality than in our country, a progress that has become accelerated within the past twenty years.

Our social progress has been sounder, and more continuous, because we feel free to experiment and emphasize methods rather than goals, whereas the abstract planners, whether Communist or Socialist, subordinate method to their rigid purposes. Thus I feel through actual experience of this experimental process that democratic civilization is indestructible, the most comforting knowledge one can possess in an era of deep and constant social transformation. Communism, even the Russian perversion of it, inspires me with interest rather than fear. I see the Russian revolution as a necessary but temporary upheaval in a society that had remained feudal while Western European civilization developed a strong middle class which, as Goethe pointed out, was the source of all its magnificent cultural achievements. In short, I am incurably bourgeois and not in the least apologetic about it.

The genius, the virtues, the stability of the middle class of European society from the Reformation to the present day are the greatest achievement of the Western world. In America the middle class has steadily expanded largely as the result of applied intelligence, hard work and public education. In the less mobile society of Europe they have been ground to pieces temporarily by the upper and the nether millstones. But every human being, whether European or American, lives on the hope for self-development and social recognition of his worth as an individual. This hope must be encouraged in the rigid European class structures rather than mere improvement of economic conditions important as that may be. With our moral as well as material support, the Communist and even the Socialist trend in Europe will eventually come to a halt. A new invigorated middle class will rise again in Europe as human capacities are liberated and constitute the bulwark upon which Communism will eventually founder.

Thus the idea of a classless society is to me a disastrous mirage which cannot be maintained without tyranny of the few over the many. It is even more pernicious culturally than politically, not because the monolithic state forces the party line upon its intellectuals and artists, but because it has no social patterns to reflect. Society like a house stands firm when its opposing stresses are carefully balanced. The Russians have built a house of cards, artificially held erect, because all of its stresses pull in one direction. It is doomed to failure, because society like every other great manifestation of human achievement must have form in order to endure. Henry James was speaking for a wider realm than the aesthetic when he said: "Form is content to that extent that there is absolutely no content without it." And form implies balancing stresses and strains that establish an equilibrium.

It is not surprising that Henry James has become so popular today and that eighteenth-century artists like Pope, Boswell, Walpole, Mozart, and political scientists like Jefferson and Madison are coming back into fashion. For the works of these men reflect an orderly world, which had the harmony, balance and the definite structure that we have lost and yearn to restore. Probably the next manifestation of this return to the last classical period — and classicism is merely the triumph of form over extreme individualism — will be a revolt against abstract painting, atonal music, modern domestic architecture and other manifestations of the formless. In the long run humanity will not and cannot endure monotony, nihilism, the amorphous, for they are all the equivalent of death.

The equilibrium of society is unfruitful if it becomes static as it often did in ancient China when Confucianism became too powerful and curbed the individualistic Taoists. It can be utterly destroyed when one element becomes all powerful as in Russia today.

Our American democracy is a government that promises to be indestructible as long as it keeps open its many avenues for the development of the individual. For this gives it an elasticity which creates an ever new equilibrium. Because democracy allows all opposing forces to exist, its equilibrium is constantly challenged and preserved from rigidity. Its balance is always threatened by strong pressures from above and below. The upper millstone that now bears down on the American middle class is no longer the rich individual as in the past, but the powerful industries, the powerful labor unions and a powerful government. The nether millstone is represented by the poor whites of the South, the Negro population which still has to battle for equal rights, and the millions of American workers, especially the self-employed, the white-collar class and the agricultural laborers, who belong to none of the large unions.

Fortunately the middle class, which acts as a buffer between the groups in our country that have too much power and those who have too little, has been greatly strengthened of late. It has been augmented by seepage from above due to the decrease of big fortunes and by accretions from below due to the rise in wages, the improvement of educational opportunities and technological progress. There is great ferment in our society but most of it has been so constructive that a new and stronger equilibrium is in the making, if the Russians do not destroy the world's peace and we remain free to continue our social readjustments.

Tension is, in short, a prerequisite for creative living. But class tensions must be tempered by social justice — the *sine qua non* of a free society. If justice is too long impeded, class warfare breaks out and the struggle for power displaces the sense of justice. Democracy is based ultimately on tension kept within bounds by justice, whereas all forms of Socialism are based on absolute power which destroys the creative tensions. Just as the middle class in any country is the most creative because it is kept alert by the fact that its existence is challenged from above and below, so also our American nation will become more creative now that our country is challenged by other ideologies of the right and the left.

Our American democracy is the middle region between the governmental extremes of the right and left which Goethe's Faust visualizes at the end of the second part, a modest community of men, never absolutely secure, constantly surrounded with new dangers, forced to redeem their freedom and their lives, each day anew.

Democracy is the strongest and at the same time the most adventurous kind of government, calling for perpetual change while preserving its continuity. The fluidity of this form of government is its greatest source of strength. That is why equal opportunity for education, health, housing and social security are fundamental to its permanent expansion. Democracy was never more challenged than at present, for it is now obliged to cope with an accelerated tempo of change from within and a powerful, rigid, unchanging and unchangeable Communist society from without. Life is threatened by death, freedom by tyranny, social flexibility by a monolithic society that keeps the masses immature and helpless.

There can be no reconciliation between the democratic forces of light and the totalitarian eclipse of mankind's struggle toward an ever brighter future. Yet the military defenses that we are building can never constitute more than a holding operation. We can be victorious over a rigid society only by introducing greater flexibility into our foreign relations to create a new equilibrium among the free nations. To do this abroad with confidence we must first re-establish a new, more stable equilibrium here at home. That is why I have been content to refuse all recent invitations to work abroad except in one case — a study of the refugee problem and of labor-relations in postwar Germany

— and confined my efforts to the amelioration of living conditions here at home. Only when Americans feel once more the unconquerable sense of security that we older people gained in a democracy still sure of itself, can we be successful in helping the formless masses of the improverished nations build a social structure that has meaning because it has form.

These hopes for a brilliant future depend upon our ability to control inflation and avoid another depression which would assuredly be as great a threat to democracy as another war. But depressions are not acts of God. They are made by man's ignorance and therefore they can be avoided by man's knowledge and foresight. I count upon the pooled intelligence of our industrial, business and labor leaders, their growing sense of responsibility for the general welfare and the hard lessons learned from the past, to steer our economy through the turbulent years that lie ahead of us. The consciousness that the future of civilization depends largely upon our solvency, is already forcing our best minds to devote themselves to this problem and Americans have never failed their country in periods of utmost peril.

In developing a program for a more orderly American society, I do not imply that a change for the better in our environment will in itself usher in the more perfect democracy we seek. But I am convinced that lifting the feeling of oppression from millions of individuals and families will give them a sense of belonging which they now lack, and arouse their ambitions to make the most of their natural capacities and of the ever growing leisure afforded our people through technological progress. It will also lift an enervating sense of guilt from the minds of those who are aware that our uneven democracy has favored some of us to the disadvantage of others. Moreover, by working together with our fellow citizens to create external improvements, we shall recapture through actual service to humanity the moral values of democracy, the love of freedom, the respect for the individual and the spiritual significance of brotherhood. His own freedom can mean nothing to the just man as long as his fellow men are oppressed. Our own freedoms are not even secure unless they are shared by our fellow citizens. They can only be preserved by their constant extension to more and more people in our own country and throughout the world.

My life has thus become a rational, yet inspired pursuit of the promised land, a journey of which this book is all too pedestrian a record. But the end is not yet. This is no valedictory. For the past year as one friend delicately put it, I have been eligible for old-age insurance. But I hope I may be granted many more years to continue waging the many battles that have not yet been won and to begin a few new ones for which I have never heretofore found the time. These precarious adventures find me young, despite my age, and will keep me so.

I feel as if I were poised on the brink of a vast, unknown ocean with strong currents and crosscurrents in which I must learn to swim. But come what may, the love of life and living will sustain me; the love of family and friends, of nature and the arts, of solitude and silence. These are the elements that nourish the spirit and keep it valiant. They give impetus and a sense of consecration to all that we do. And what we accomplish matters less than the arduous labor to make a better world. Our achievements are often written upon sand which the next tide obliterates, as those who are too cowardly, too confused or too tired to believe in human progress are constantly reminding us. But what endures even through periods of frustration, failure and defeat, is the continuity of the struggle and the faith it engenders that we are all brothers of one another marching side by side toward a future whose splendor it is impossible to foresee. American men and American women giving themselves wholeheartedly to their country — what can they not achieve for the good of their own nation and for the whole wide world!

What are the main features of the program I have outlined for the spread of justice and freedom and human happiness:

1. A public-school system worthy of the new democracy we hope to create that begins with nursery schools, through elementary and grammar grades, to junior or community colleges. These schools to be so equipped that they can function as a center for young and old alike and a focus of community solidarity.

2. Federal aid to public schools and public schools only, in all states with inadequate tax resources.

3. Local health units, in every county or group of counties, co-ordinated with the public and private school systems, which will act as referral centers to the community hospital, and when necessary to the large medical centers.

4. Elimination of slums and steady expansion of the public housing program through local-state-Federal co-operation.

5. An integrated, nation-wide system of hospitals with sufficient beds and personnel to meet the requirements of our population. Expansion of voluntary medical and hospitalization insurance programs, and of state-wide programs of free medical care for the indigent and the medically indigent.

6. Thorough study of Federal security programs, unem-

ployment insurance and Federal grants to the states to achieve soundness as to financing and administration.

7. A review of all voluntary welfare programs to achieve integration with the public-welfare systems and to prevent duplication or omission of services.

8. Equal opportunities for the Negro in our political, economic and social structure. Above all, that the Negro be considered a citizen and an American rather than a person whose skin is of different hue.

To this evolution I have tried to contribute through all my commitments and endeavors. The layman I have found has special advantages over the expert in the battle for social progress and the extension of human freedom. He is not afraid of being wrong as he has no professional status and ambitions to protect. His imagination is not impeded by overspecialization in techniques. He is not inhibited by the sodden weight of statistics and the theoretical prognostications of the trained sociologists; nor does he need to wait for certainty in order to act but arrives at practical solutions through intelligent experimentation. Above all, his language can remain simple in an era when most professions are developing a complicated jargon which my brother Frederic Ernst has aptly called "desperanto."

This is, in fact, an era calling for the voluntary worker, equipped with the broadest culture, who will devote himself to the national welfare in a spirit of selfless devotion to the good of humanity. At no time has the world beckoned more alluringly, especially to young men and women to lead a life of austerity, hard work and sacrifice as the road to the greatest self-fulfillment and happiness.

I well know how hard countless Americans in every city, village and hamlet are working to remake their communities so that privilege may yield to equal opportunity for all. If this spiritual-sociological biography has value it is because I am one of these devoted millions who wishes to encourage her fellow citizens by reminding them why our cause is sacred and why we cannot be defeated by authoritarian ideological forces within or without our nation. The conflict will be long, but not as long as we now anticipate if we make it possible for the uprooted, whether in our own or other countries, to send new roots into a fertile democratic soil. And the victory will be assured as soon as we win the essential battle within our own minds and hearts. For democracy is not only service, action, brotherhood — it is spirit — spirit free, indefinable, all-pervasive, that holds us to its revelations even when we seek to escape them.

INDEX

Index